THE COMPLETE BOOK OF ROLLER SKATING

THE COMPLETE BOOK OF ROLLER SKATING

BY ANN-VICTORIA PHILLIPS
FEATURING PHOTOGRAPHS BY THE AUTHOR

WORKMAN PUBLISHING, NEW YORK

Library of Congress Cataloging in Publication Data

Phillips, Ann-Victoria.
  The complete book of roller skating.

  1. Roller-skating. I. Title.
GV859.P47   796.2'1   78-73722

ISBN: 0-89480-067-1

Art Director: Paul Hanson
Book Design: Robert Fitzpatrick

Cover Design: Paul Hanson
Cover Photograph: Ray Solowinski
Make-up and Hair Stylist: Steve Lowe

Illustrator: Fredric Winkowski
Research Coordinator: Mablen Jones

Workman Publishing Company, Inc.
1 West 39 Street
New York, New York 10018

Manufactured in the United States of America
First printing June 1979
10 9 8 7 6 5 4 3 2 1

For Ray

ACKNOWLEDGMENTS

Being a part of roller skating's current growth as a recreation and as a sport has been my most thrilling personal and professional experience. I appreciate the trust and generosity of all the skaters, coaches, and parents who have shared their experiences with me.

Especially prominent in my memory is the friendliness of the first skater contacted on the project, Fred Morante, and his mother, Cathy Morante, a skating coach who provided me with invaluable assistance and information.

To all members of the Levittown Skating Club, East Meadow, New York, to their coaches, John and Barbara Dayney, and Jack and Honey Burton, to George Petrone, the manager of the Levittown Arena, and especially skate mechanic, Mike Schneider, thank you for introducing me to the world of competitive skating.

Other coaches and skaters who have provided expert assistance are: Tim Abell, Charlie Aybar, Kevin Baker, Bill Butler, Maurice Cooke, Mike Dorso, Jr., Butch Ford, Victor Hernandez, Randy Higginson, Ron Jellse, Bill Lee, Kenny Means, Jerry Nista, Jim Pringle, Jane Puracchio, Wilma Ryan, Mary Schluter, Dick Sisson, Chris Snyder, Maren Talbot and Charles Wahlig.

To the man who has set out to unravel roller skating's rich, historic past, Dick Young, and to those Skating Vanities and Roller Derby skaters who lived every minute of it, especially superstars Gloria Nord and Gerry Murray, thank you for sharing your experiences and memorabilia with me.

Further, I deeply appreciate the kindness of Joe Shevelson and Gordon, Bob, and Jack Ware of Chicago Roller Skate Company who entrusted me with their valuable, historic photo collection, and the warmth of their staff, who extended every courtesy to me.

Best wishes and thanks to Judy Lynn of The Goodskates and Jeff Rosenberg of Cheapskates for your interest and your help.

Thank you to the owners and staff of Blueberry Hill, the Airport Marina Hotel, Texas International Airlines, Del Mar Skateboard Ranch, Lakewood Center Skatepark, The Runway and Super Bowl I, who graciously cooperated in helping me set up photographic shootings.

Also thanks to Garold Whitlock and Jack Montag of Omaha, Nebraska, who shared extraordinary tales of the good old days and directed me to my favorite skating family, Les, Joan, Kevin, and Lynn Wittmer of Estherville, Iowa, operators of one of the last portable rinks in America.

Thank you to Michael Christopher, Barbara and Colleen Daly, and Walter Rohan, Bob De Voogd, Linda Erf and Gus Swift, Kathy and Baylis Glascock, Pat MacPherson, Jerry and Elayne Nista, and Kirk Vanyan and Glenn Terrell, all of whom provided a warm reception for me while I was on the road. And love to Emma Herrera of New York City who supplies me with care and support here at home.

Manufacturers and distributors who have provided equipment are Chicago Roller Skate Company, Classic Sales, Harlick, Mattel, Riedell, Smoothill Skates, Sure-Grip International, and Western Skate Sales. Harry Ball and John Poe of Sure-Grip International were always available to provide technical information and their interest in my project was especially valuable.

Thank you to the models and amateur and professional skaters who participated in the following special shootings: Linda List

(Lessons), Saundra Pearson, Ray Martucci, and Jenifer Smith (Fitness), and Bill Butler, Butch Ford, Anthony Forde, Rebecca James, Karen Katz, Cathy Lipinski, Jackie Myers, and Doug Turner (Roller Disco).

Thank you to Berenice Hoffman for her enthusiastic presentation of me and my talents to my publisher; to Mablen Jones, research coordinator, for her clarity and refined creative assistance; and to Judy Fireman for being wildly enthusiastic about roller skating and initiating the project.

My heartfelt gratitude and respect goes to my publisher, Peter Workman for his constant encouragement and support; to my editor, Suzanne Rafer, for her dedication and tasteful editorial direction which is realized in the spirited treatment of the book; to Bob Fitzpatrick, who exquisitely styled the book and whose sensitivity helped me achieve the creative potential of the project; to Paul Hanson, who designed the dynamic cover; to Gail MacColl, editorial assistant, who invested so much of her positive energy throughout; to Fred Winkowski, who captured the freedom and joy of roller skating through his illustrations; to Bobbie Crosby, photo researcher, whose warmth and style secured the cooperation of hundreds of people in this project; and to the highly professional and talented staff at Workman, especially Sallie Jackson, whose effervescent spirit proved to be a daily inspiration. Al Chernewski, Ruby Katayama and Rolisa Schrade contributed their expert technical skills in the final preparation of the book.

Thank you to Jim Galate, Gene Merinov, Helga Schening, and Kathelene Davridge of Kemtek Photographic, and Rick Rankin of Professional Camera Repair for providing expert photographic advice and service, and for their continuing interest in my work. Thanks also to journalists, Mary Horowitz, editor of *RollerSkating* magazine and Jack Monahan, editor of *Skater* magazine, who graciously shared information and resources with me, and George Pickard, Executive Director of RSROA, who generously supplied historic skating research materials.

There is one woman, Suzi Theis, Publications Director of the RSROA and Executive Editor of *Skate* magazine, without whose sensitivity, generosity, support, consideration and personal involvement, this project would not have been possible. Thank you, Suzi!

Two women who shared important creative and personal insights with me are Alma Daniel and Joan Poelvoorde.

Lastly, I extend deep personal thanks to my closest friends: Ray Martucci, Joyce Snyder, Isabel Herrera, Sue Conrad and Ed Kindermann who have assisted, advised, loved, supported, and endured.

Ann-Victoria Phillips

Ann-Victoria Phillips
June 1979

CONTENTS

INTRODUCTION

READY TO ROLL

Remember the delight you felt as a kid wearing your first pair of clamp skates; the out-of-doors freedom and flight on driveways and sidewalks? For many, it's an unforgettable sensation. More than just a fond recollection, it's a nostalgic dream fantasy. What happened then? Why did so many of us stop skating when we grew up?

As surprising as it may seem, millions of Americans never stopped skating at all. While many city rinks had to close during the '50s to make way for modern office buildings, the suburban rinks and those in small, outlying towns con-

Library of Congress

Outdoor skating has been an American institution since the 1930s.

The fashionable scene at an open air skating rink in Berlin, Germany, is the subject of this 1881 Max Klinger drawing.

tinued to flourish. In short, roller skating didn't die, it held it's own, although it never attracted the attention of the mass media.

HERE IT COMES AGAIN

In fact, roller skating in America *never* dies. Since its birth in 1860, crazes for the sport emerge regularly. The first roller skating phase lasted for a few years during the 1860s, the second craze began about 1880 and continued until about 1910; the third time the sport had a heyday, it went from the 1930s through the '40s and mid-'50s. Now it has emerged again.

Each roller revival is related to technological

One, two, three, four, five, six, seven, eight,
Standing in a row and ready for a skate.

"Rinking" in days gone by was a formal affair.

Arena Gardens Skating Club
of Detroit
Opening of 1937-1938 Season

The image of the roller rink as a well-regulated family entertainment was established in the 1930s.

developments—improvements in the skates. This time, in the late '70s, skating is so different it barely resembles the old style at all. The new skating has taken technique developed in other sports and combined it with dance and music to create an exciting new roller sport that offers something for everyone. But perhaps the most basic change is that roller skating no longer tries to imitate ice skating—it has developed its own distinctive style. The conservatives may cry, "It will never be the same," but we say "Thank Heavens!"

ROLLING WITH THE RICH

In the early years of development, back in the 1860s, rinks were private clubs and roller skating was considered a pastime for the rich. Membership was limited to wealthy socialites who had to supply references as well as money to be accepted into the elite circle of skaters. Rinking, as it was called, was a slow, round-and-round routine done in small spaces on awkward, hard-to-maneuver,

clamp-on skates. You didn't *glide* on those early wheels for they had no ball bearings; instead you pushed yourself along. It was a lot of work compared to the ease of skating today. Since the pleasure of gliding wasn't known to early skaters, it was the novelty of the activity and the social contact that were the prime attractions. Not only was it a proper way for boy to meet girl, it was the right thing to do in the right place. Rinks provided a socially correct setting for young romance.

Later on, when decorum was the keynote factor of the Victorian era, it was too embarrassing for any gentleman of social standing to risk looking undignified or for a young lady to appear athletic. Vigorous skating was out for them. Only the professional speed and show skaters had acquired the skill and coordination needed to be truly graceful. As roller skating became acceptable to members of all social classes, the glamour of exclusivity disappeared, and the roller skating fad soon followed.

Bill Butler, Anthony Forde, Mickey Idlett, and Maurice Gatewood at a modern disco rink.

After the turn of the century, a new craze erupted when ball bearings were invented. Hundreds of new rinks were built—all open to the general public. Roller skating, this time around, was something to enjoy for its own sake rather than for its social side-benefits. One could dance, play games, and do things on skates with more ease than was possible during the earlier period. But, again, roller skating lost its public appeal—in the '20s baseball, football, tennis, cars, radios, movies, and the Charleston proved to be too much competition for what was, by then, considered a tame form of recreation.

ROLLING THE BLUES AWAY

The third great roller revival came during the Depression of the 1930s. Inexpensive skate rentals made it one of the few forms of recreation people could still afford. Most of all, it satisfied a longing for romance in the terrible times of mass unemployment and economic hardship. Movies featuring Sonja Henie, ice skating star of the 1932 Olympics, helped to stimulate interest in the beauty of both ice and roller skating. More importantly, during this period came the first attempt to organize roller skating as a serious competitive sport.

By the '40s, roller skating was transformed from being primarily a recreational sport into an occasion for mass spectacles. Of these, there were two distinct varieties, each featuring a skating style diametrically opposed to the other—the Skating Vanities, a variety show on wheels, was as glamorous and lovely as its counterpart, the Roller Derby, was aggressive and violent. They both had mass followings, demonstrating the two kinds of appeal inherent in the one activity. Since the Derby preceded the Vanities by several years and was mass televised in the early '50s, it tends to be recalled, in public memory, as the dominant image of roller skating spectacles.

At the same time that people were enjoying

these roller entertainments, the manufacturing of skates and use of rinks were being adversely affected by the war effort. From the beginning, and through to the end, of World War II, some rinks were appropriated for military purposes. And also during this time, metals were rationed in the national interest so skates ceased to be manufactured for public use. By 1945, the Chicago Roller Skate Company had a backlog of over one million unfilled orders. By the late '40s rinks had become hangouts for local toughs and returning military men; the romantic image of skating disappeared.

Superstar Gerry Murray (right) battles it out in a 1945 Roller Derby game.

Gloria Nord, the star of Skating Vanities, in "Flirtation Walk," a production number from the 1947 show.

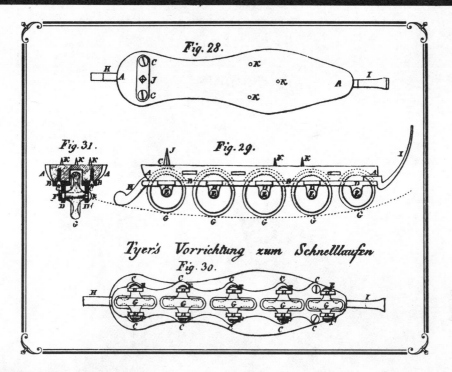

Fig. 28.

Fig. 31.   Fig. 29.

Tyer's Vorrichtung zum Schnelllaufen
Fig. 30.

THE EARLY SKATE

From their anonymous beginning in eighteenth century Holland when some unknown ice skater nailed wooden spools to strips of wood, to our contemporary, space age, urethane-wheeled, disco-dancing specials, roller skates have been constantly evolving.

Joseph Merlin, a Belgian inventor and musical instrument maker, is credited with the first patented roller skate in 1760. Merlin , however, shattered any public interest in his wheeled invention by crashing into an expensive plate glass mirror during his first roller skating demonstration.

Next, in 1790, a Parisian medal-cutter, Monsieur Vanlede, invented a version he called "Patin-a-terre," or ground skate. This was soon followed by models designed to imitate the ice skate blade. In France in 1819, a Monsieur Petitbled patented a roller skate calling for either three or four copper, wood, or ivory wheels of the same size lined up in a row. Unfortunately it could only be used for skating in a straight line. Then in 1823, Robert John Tyers, a London fruit merchant, perfected a skate he called the "Volito." Each skate had a lineup of five wheels, with the center one larger than the rest. You skated on either of the small two-wheeled sets at the front or back and used the center wheel as a pivot in turning. Five years later another Frenchman, J. Garcin, made a

three-wheeled version of the "Volito," (called the "Cingar") with one large center wheel and a smaller wheel to the front and back of it.

The break with the ice skate model finally came in Paris in 1849 when the composer Meyerbeer commissioned Louis Legrange to supply roller skates for the cast of his opera "Le Prophète." The cast was to look as if they were ice skating outdoors. Legrange created two separate designs, one for men and another for women. The men's skate had only two wheels, in a line, with a space between them. The women's skate featured the modern arrangement of the two pairs of wheels, one in front and one in back. Supposedly designed to compensate for a feminine weakness of the ankles, this arrangement at last created the stable supporting surface for roller skating.

The Americans completed the necessary refinement in the skate design. In 1863, J. L. Plimpton of New York finally created a roller skate in which one could turn. He called it the "rocking" skate because the wheels were so geared that they curved to one side or the other when the skater tilted the foot plate while leaning. Levan M. Richardson of Milwaukee, founder of the Richardson Skate company, added ball bearings in 1900 and installed round rubber cushions as shock absorbers. Skating finally became a smooth, almost effortless, form of recreation.

Chicago Roller Skate Company, the oldest manufacturer of roller skating equipment in the US, promoted the sport in the '50s with illustrated booklets emphasizing its social and health benefits.

A NEW IMAGE NEEDED

By the mid-'50s, most sports were competitive and team-oriented. This was the period when roller skating developed its worst image problem. People began to think of it in the same way as bowling and miniature golf—something for the kids to do, if there was nothing better around. Skating seemed old-fashioned. Compared to other high-powered events and activities it was corny.

Very little was done to advance the cause of roller skating as a fun activity or as a sport during the '60s. If you went to a rink you would be faced with unbearably strict regulations—proper dress, then, meant no jeans, or shorts; everyone had to skate at the same rate of speed; no fast or trick

skating; and no backward skating. Your whole evening of skating was pre-planned: "All skate." "Clear the floor." "Couples only." "Trios only." "All skate." People were made to feel like they were still in grammar school. The skating sessions weren't fun; they were mindlessly boring. No matter how pleasant the sensation of rolling along on wheels, it wasn't worth the regimentation.

In the early '70s rink owners still self-consciously overcompensated for skating's bad reputation by trying to exclude undesirable elements. This, they felt, had been the cause of roller skating's decline. Strict dress and rink regulations were imposed at suburban skating arenas in an attempt to disengage public memory from the earlier tough period. Owners aimed their pitch at

the parents of eight to 16 year olds, a group they thought to be their main customers. Rink advertisements stressed, to an absurd degree, how safe, comfortable, clean, well-lit, and supervised the facilities were.

THE VIGOROUS HYBRID

Now, with the '80s fast approaching, owners have taken on a more balanced outlook. Roller skating today offers sensational challenges, and thrills, not only unknown, but also impossible, as little as five years ago. Many elements have combined to produce a vigorous hybrid more appealing than any of its predecessors. Technique developed by skateboarders, for example, has been assimilated into the sport to create something unique: the

new skating offers fresh challenges in self-propulsion, speed, and aerial flight off of banked-walled terrain. For those who prefer grace and skill to thrills, there are new skating steps, maneuvers, and dances. In short, it's a new sports frontier.

Ask anyone who skates and they'll tell you that roller skating is flight on wheels. It is for people who want to fly. The most basic of all fantasies is to glide without effort, to seep, to flow, to speed. Flying is freedom, a victory over gravity and inertia and inhibition. Forgetting roller skating, we forget our dreams, the joy of the sound of spinning wheels like wind and far-off thunder. Remember your roller skating joys of the past and assure yourself of a roller skating future.

ROLL 'EM!

"Hollywood" likes roller skating just as much as everyone else. From Charlie Chaplin in *The Rink* (1916) to Marsha Mason in *Promises in the Dark* (1979) there have been actors and actresses gliding, wobbling, or falling through scenes featuring wheels—whether they're show-stopping production numbers as in Busby Berkeley's *Gold Diggers of 1933* or just comedy routines as in Warner Brothers' *Domestic Troubles* (1928). Even the superstars have been known to give their roller wheels a whirl for the sake of cinema—Barbra Streisand skated *and* sang in *Funny Girl* (1968), while Lucille Ball went roller-shopping in *Mame* (1974).

Nancy Ellison

Domestic Troubles

Promises in the Dark

Funny Girl

Gold Diggers of 1933

Mame

The Rink

Courtesy of John Milazzo

WHO CAN SKATE?

Skating is an ideal sport since it can be done as leisurely or as vigorously as you want, depending on how you feel. The first thing is to find a rink that attracts people with your interests. You're not going to enjoy yourself if you want to disco and the rest of the crowd wants to waltz.

Children: Roller skating is a good way for children to get exercise and meet and play with people of all ages. Children as young as two years old have learned to skate, but you can't push them. They must want to do it themselves. Instruction should be minimized. The most important thing is that they have fun.

If their feet are too small for boot skates, start them out in inexpensive plastic or metal clamp-on skates. If an instructor works with a young child who can fit into boot skates, he or she can adjust the wheels so that they have a slower roll. Children can also get used to skating by starting on a carpet instead of a slippery floor.

Roller skating will help increase a child's general coordination and balance. In addition, roller skating has been known to cure some minor handicaps: it has been prescribed by doctors for many years to correct knock-knees, pigeon-toes or other problems with ankles, knees, and legs.

Teens and Young Adults: The "new" roller skating has enormous appeal for 18- to 35-year-olds in particular. It creates an enjoyable way to be with friends and to meet new people. Roller music is chosen from the latest hits featured on the top-40 charts. Importantly, skating satisfies the group's interest in exercise and it fits into a health-conscious lifestyle. And most of all, the "new" skating has the exciting flavor of being current— it's what's happening right now!

Unless a known medical problem exists or a person is overweight, roller skating is one of the best sports around for people in this age group.

Adults and Senior Citizens: Before starting *any* exercise program, people over the age of 35 should get a complete medical examination from a doctor. If learning to skate for the first time, avoid going to a disco rink where you might feel inhibited, or large public sessions that feature fast skating. Joining a group skating class might be a good idea since there will be far fewer people on the floor during a class than in an open session. In no time at all, you'll be able to roll to the sound of your favorite beat either by yourself or with a special partner.

1. INDOOR SKATING

STEP INTO MY PARLOR

In the early days, people may have been tempted to clamp on skates and head out the door for a whirl, but one thing held them back. If the streets were paved at all, they were laid with cobblestones, instead of concrete or asphalt. This, compounded with the hardness and tiny diameter of the steel or wooden wheels, made outdoor skating a bone rattling and precarious adventure. The answer, of course, was the roller rink, then called a skating parlor.

A turn-of-the-century couple waltzing in a roller palace.

EARLY RINKS

James Leonard Plimpton, the American inventor of the "rocking skate" (a model that turned as a skater shifted weight), built roller rinks in this country in order to promote his skate and assure its success. He began, in 1863, in Manhattan, with a private, socially exclusive rink located in his own furniture warehouse. He continued his success with a fashionable "parlor" which occupied the ballroom of the Atlantic Casino Hotel in Newport, Rhode Island, and to which the society people and press were invited to skate. This was the first public rink in America. Finally Plimpton set off, like a rolling Johnny Appleseed, cultivating plush rinks instead of apple trees throughout the land. He toured the country teaching classes and demonstrating new and dramatic dance, ballet, and ice skating techniques adapted for roller skating.

Plimpton also devised an incentive system and proficiency test in skating. Anyone who passed his highest-level exam could skate free at his "skating parlors." One can only guess how many paid-for lessons and practice sessions might have been required to reach that level of proficiency! One thing's for sure—Plimpton made a lot of money. Initially, he gained by never selling his skates. Instead, he leased them to rinks. In order to rent a pair of skates at his rinks, you had to fill out an application (subject to the approval of Plimpton or his rink operators) and provide written references proving that you were of good enough character to skate there. Despite all the red tape, Plimpton was hailed as the "greatest social innovator of the age" for popularizing the healthiest, most socially proper and graceful sport of the time.

Plimpton was not alone. His early competitors constructed their first rink floors of wood, asphalt,

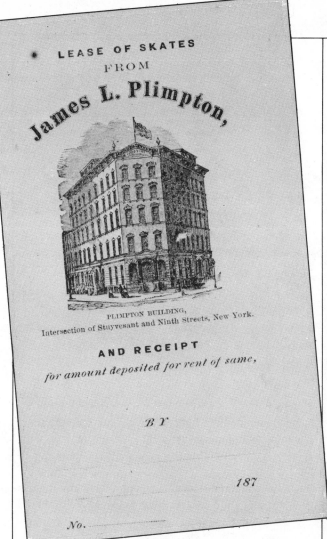

LEASE OF SKATES
FROM
James L. Plimpton,

PLIMPTON BUILDING,
Intersection of Stuyvesant and Ninth Streets, New York.

AND RECEIPT
for amount deposited for rent of same,

BY

187

No.

Grand Hall of London, open from 1890 to 1912, displayed the largest roller floor in skating history—68,000 square feet of space in which to roll. Today's rinks only average about 14,000 square feet and this is found to be ample.

These rinks encouraged roller dancing by hiring professional instructors and exhibition skaters and by publishing booklets describing such popular steps as the "Choctaw Cross," "On to Richmond," "The Philadelphia Twist," "Picket Fence," and "Mercury Three."

In London roller rink skating became the pastime of the nobility. They skated at places like the

The "Choctaw Cross" being demonstrated by a 1910 skating instructor.

or concrete but Plimpton's original maple floor design won out in the end. Asphalt got gooey in hot weather, causing the skaters' wheels to sink, and concrete was considered less than elegant. Plimpton cut narrow maple strips across the grain, reinforced them with a backing material, and fastened the boards together in a tongue-and-groove fashion. However, the small size of these floors, the strictness of rink rules, and the monotony of continually skating round and round in a circle, were some factors that caused the craze to temporarily die out.

IN THE GRAND STYLE

It didn't take long for rink owners in the late 1870s and '80s to wise up and build huge decorative roller palaces. These offered more floor space as well as often featuring 30-piece orchestras which attracted thousands of adults at 25 cents and children at 10 cents apiece. The famous Chicago Casino drew a crowd of 5,000 to its gala opening in 1884. The

Crystal Palace and the Prince's Club. Admission was restricted to a chosen few—preferably only the rich, members of Parliament, former Lord Chancellors, and guardsmen. But rink skating began to catch on with the general populace—soon every town in Victorian England had its own rink. By 1885 it was estimated that over 20 million dollars had been invested in British skating properties.

Nineteenth century rink ritual included a few flirtatious moments with the skateboy.

Roller parlors of that era forbid women to sit with men while they donned their skates—what would happen to proper society if they should reveal their ankles to male companions while raising their long dresses slightly to adjust their skates! How they managed to fasten their clamp-style

Taking an old-fashioned fall in the full-skirted skating costume of the day.

skates without showing some leg to the skate boy (whose job it was to tighten the clamp skates to the shoes with a skate key) we'll never know.

In the early 1900s the appeal of six-day bicycle races caused rink attendance to decline but it reached yet another peak in the '30s and '40s when roller skating became the cheapest form of Depression era recreation. Popular skate dancing as well as figure and artistic skating, all of these stimulated by dance and ice skating films, shared the spotlight with professional and amateur speed skating. In addition, when rinks were not filled with masses of skaters, these arenas then staged Mardi Gras, Halloween, and other holiday carnivals, music concerts, boxing and wrestling matches. Joe Louis, the famous heavyweight boxing champion, started his career at the Arena Gardens skating rink in Detroit, in the late '30s.

Clothing pattern manufacturers such as Vogue and Butterick carried skating dress patterns for home sewers. Rinks sold memorabilia to collectors. Rink stickers and roller skate jewelry were popular. The *New York Journal American* newspaper started a skating column in 1947, recording both the social and athletic aspects of roller skating.

FITNESS IN THE '40S

In 1942, after the outbreak of World War II, the United States government promoted skating as a way of advancing national fitness. The First Lady,

Eleanor Roosevelt, was reported to have taken up the sport. The Civil Defense Department issued a statement declaring that, "Skating is one of the sports sponsored by your government because those who are engaged in this sport are better fitted to prosecute the war. We are organizing a national skating project to build physical fitness."

Nevertheless, the government, because it was rationing metal, prohibited roller skate manufacture for general public sale (servicemen could get skates, however) and also appropriated some rinks for military use.

By the end of the war, although most rinks still rented clamp-ons, boot skates previously used only by professional skaters started gaining in popularity. Fast dancing to records was popular during the late '40s. But many rink operators still featured organ music.

Ironically, while US attendance at rinks dropped again after the mid-'50s, the style of operation became a model for all international skating emporiums from Canada to India, and all points in between. American rinks survived, but barely. Teenagers dropped skating for rock-n-roll music and dancing. These were the years skating gained

its reputation as a kid's sport. This meant lean times for roller rinks.

Finally, by the '70s, our awakened health consciousness combined with recent technical innovations, restored rink skating to its earlier graceful status. Urethane skate wheels, originally designed for skateboards, made roller skating smoother and quieter. In addition, slick-as-ice, plastic-coated floors and sound-absorbing ceilings helped bring a degree of auditory comfort to rink skating that was unknown to earlier generations.

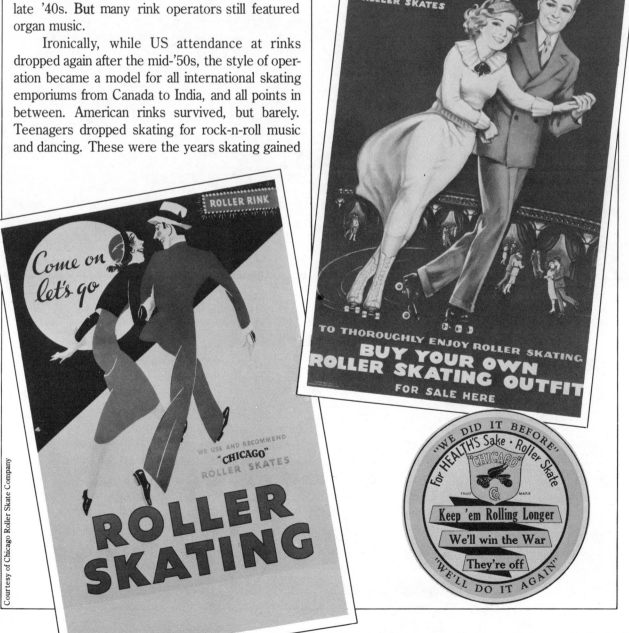

ARENA LIFE

In the old days, roller rinks were show places built to accommodate large crowds with ease and style. The modern era features a more functional design—neon signs have replaced the decorative scrollwork of the past. Gone, for the most part, is the family operated arena. Rinks are now big business and J.T. Strickland, owner of a Florida chain, even had a car in the shape of a skate built to advertise his plush skating centers (facing page, upper right corner). But at the Clearview Rink in Clear Lake, Iowa, Wayne and Marlene Oswood, with son John and daughter Julie, are still making arena life a family affair (facing page, lower right corner).

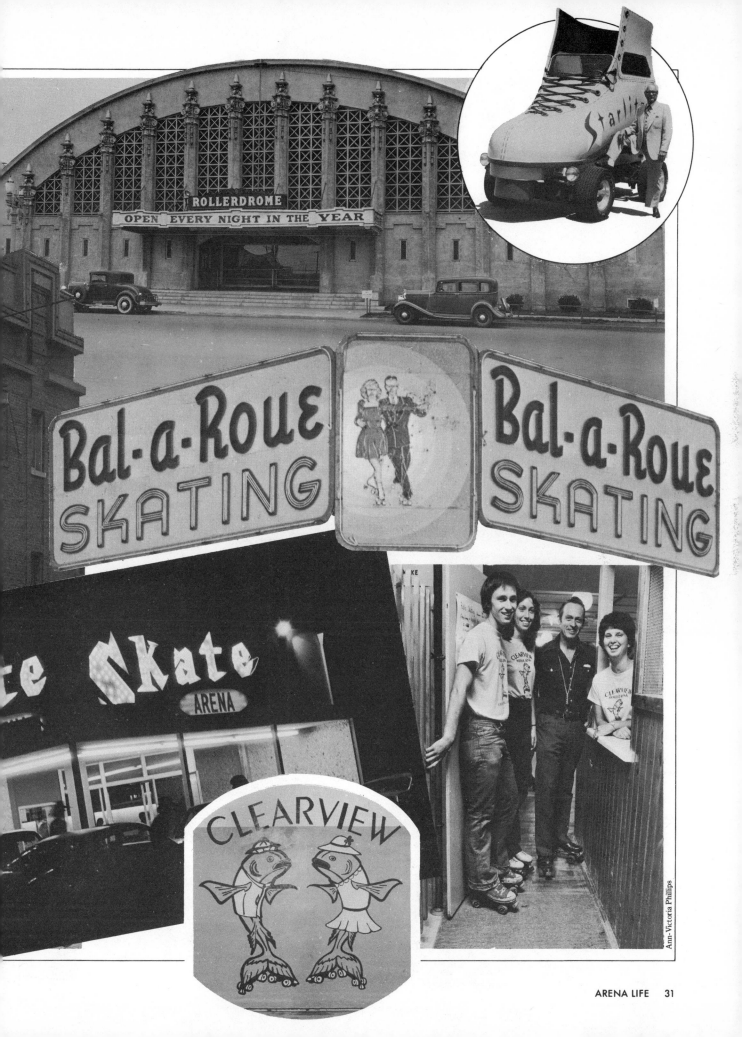

ROLLERDROME
OPEN EVERY NIGHT IN THE YEAR

Bal-a-Roue SKATING

Bal-a-Roue SKATING

Skate ARENA

CLEARVIEW

THE GREAT INDOORS

The owners claim, "You can't call them rinks anymore." They consider "rink" a crude old-fashioned word that is not consistant with their new image. The rinks are now referred to as "skating centers" or "full service recreational facilities."

What you can expect in any of the approximately 4,000 roller rinks? A total range of experience. Some are sophisticated, presenting audiovisual extravaganzas with light shows; some are discotheques with computerized stereo equipment run by professional DJs. Others are small, charming, family-fun businesses with recorded, sometimes live, organ music including waltzes and nostalgic music of the '40s. As a matter of fact, the famous Wurlitzer organ from the old Madison Square Garden, with its waterfall console, can still be heard at the Axel Rink in Chicago.

The Golden Skate in San Ramon, California, recreates an antique Western town with train station ticket window, bank, general store, opera house, party room, saloon snack bar, and water tower marquee. Sportsworld in Greenville, North Carolina, is a multi-purpose sports center which has a roller rink plus a store selling every kind of sports equipment. Its circus-like decor features animal wall fixtures (including a life-sized rhinoceros in the snack bar) while the casino has all the latest electronic games.

EVERYONE'S ON WHEELS

Who skates? Everyone, from tots who've just learned to walk to their grandparents who learned to skate at pre-war roller ballrooms. Rinks now

Fred Arnish of the Axel Roller Rink in Norridge, Illinois has been playing old favorites on rink organs for the past 30 years. The organ's pipe chamber, one of the nation's largest, houses more than 1,000 pipes and sound effects.

Ann-Victoria Phillips

have all kinds of open skating sessions: beginners classes, ladies' days, teen nights, family matinees, dance, speed, hockey, and figure competition training. Dress style ranges from sporty at some rinks to dungaree casual at others, depending on the skaters. The choice is yours. Not all people go to skate. Some prefer to watch or to socialize. The rinks are great places to meet people of all ages.

At the other end of the roller spectrum are the countless high schools, Y's, school gymnasiums, and church annexes where roller physical education classes work out. Roller skating gym classes are popping up in such places as Decatur, Illinois; Ansom, Texas; and Ottumwa, Iowa. Moreover, at some colleges roller skating credit is being awarded. Roller entrepreneurs are even considering the possibility of starting skating summer camps, particularly now that roller skating is to be in the 1979 Pan American games.

GROUP LESSONS

Roller rinks no longer cater exclusively to either older traditionalists or to young children. The majority of the population in this country is now between the ages of 18 and 35, and these young adults are looking for challenging lifetime sports, so many rinks offer a full schedule of group skating lessons for teens and adults. If you're free during the day, sign up for a skate exercise class. Weekday evenings are usually reserved for adult beginner, and dance classes. Many rinks today also offer disco skating classes for all age groups.

Most of the different kinds of lessons for adults cost somewhere around 5 dollars each. The price is

RINK RULES IN 1910

In 1892, the Spaulding Athletic Goods Company, manufacturer of diverse playground sports, locker room, and sporting equipment as well as athletic clothing, sought authorities to write about proper athletic practices and management. The company then compiled these essays on each sport into small paperback booklets. The series was called the Spaulding Athletic Library.

The following summary is excerpted from Spaulding's list of recommended roller rink rules, as published in 1910. What is amazing is that these rules have changed very little over the years.

Spaulding's Rink Rules:

1. Begin skating at the stroke of the gong and stop at two strokes.

2. All skaters will move in a uniform direction around the circuit, taking the utmost care to respect the movements of others.

3. All of the following are strictly prohibited:
a. smoking (except in the smoking room) and tobacco spitting

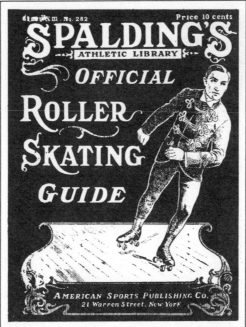

b. crowding, racing, tagging and pushing, or any other rude, noisy, or dangerous behavior
c. stopping (not even for an instant, except to assist a lady)
d. sticks, canes, ropes, or any similar objects
e. skating in a direction contrary to the uniform circuit of all others
f. climbing stairs with skates on
g. skating more than four abreast.

4. Ladies and gentlemen should make every effort to skate in couples for this is most graceful.

5. Remember that most falls occur when the feet are parallel to each other, or nearly so, because in this position one skate cannot check the movement of the other. Therefore, before trying to stand up on skates, place your heels together with your feet at right angles. This is the position you should take when getting up, sitting down, or standing.

6. Only those skaters acceptable to the management will be admitted.

SKATE SAFE: INDOOR RINK SKATING

1. Before skating, make sure that your shoes are properly laced and tied securely. Loose laces will get caught in your wheels and trip you.

2. When entering the skating floor, it is customary to always give the right-of-way to skaters already on the floor and to move with the flow of traffic in a counter-clockwise direction. Backward skating is sometimes allowed on the inner oval.

3. Keep moving on the floor or else those behind you may roll into you. If you fall, get up as quickly as possible while facing the oncoming traffic.

Remain sensitive to, and aware of, those skating around you. Fast skating and playing tag can be injurious to yourself and others. If you want to skate fast, join a speed club.

4. When leaving the floor, move slowly to your right, well in advance of the exit, so that you will not cut across the paths of others and cause an accident.

an extraordinary bargain because, usually, it includes admission to the rink, skate rental, a one-hour lesson, and free practice time during the next public session.

WHAT TO WEAR

When you're starting out in skating, it is best to wear old and comfortable clothes that allow you complete freedom of movement. Skin-tight pants may look great but they can be a nuisance when you're trying to learn the long stroking and gliding movements of roller skating. T-shirts and jeans, the basic roller uniform worn all over America, are a good choice. You can fall down and slide around on the floor without having to worry about ruining good clothes. And if you're comfortable, you'll learn to skate much more quickly.

RENTAL SKATE FIT AND COMFORT

Foot comfort is important at all times, but especially when you are first learning how to skate. If

your skate boot fits well, you'll feel more relaxed and learn to skate more quickly. If you're a beginner, or if you only skate once in a while, putting on a rental skate is similar to wearing a new pair of shoes. Protect your tender feet—remember to bring along a pair of heavy socks.

When you get to the skate room window to pick up your pair, ask the attendant for the same size as your shoe. Most rinks don't carry half-sizes; if you take a 7½, for example, ask for an 8 instead.

If any part of your skate is not working properly—the wheels don't roll freely or if you find it unusually hard to skate corners—return to the skate room and ask for the skate mechanic. He or she will make the necessary adjustments without your having to remove the skates.

All photos: Ann-Victoria Phillips

RINK SCHEDULES FOR PUBLIC SESSIONS

Public rink sessions usually last from three to four hours. Be sure to phone ahead first to check on the schedule. Most have a Tuesday-through-Sunday, open-session program similar to this:

Monday evenings . . . . rink closed/
	available for private parties
Tuesday through Thursday evenings	.7:30-11:00
Friday and Saturday evenings	. . . . . . .7:30-12:00
Sunday evening	. . . . .7:30-11:00
Saturday and Sunday matinee	. . . . . . .2:00- 5:00

PRICE OF ADMISSION AND SKATE RENTAL

Although the price of a skating session can vary widely, depending on where your rink is located, admission may be as low as 50 cents for a Saturday matinee or as high as 4 dollars for a Friday night disco session. The average price of an evening of skating will run about 3 dollars.

The price of skate rental may or may not be included in the price of admission. If not, skate rental is usually 50 cents to 75 cents extra. Rental at disco rinks is usually 1 dollar higher. At some rinks, you can expect to pay one price for admission, regardless of whether or not you bring your own skates.

LEARNING THE ROPES

Rinking provides the skater with a festive atmosphere and freedom from unpredictable weather. But one of the best reasons to skate in a rink is that you are learning to skate under controlled condi-

Session skaters cutting loose at the famous Axel Roller Rink in Norridge, Illinois.

tions. Not only does the smooth floor eliminate any rough spots, cracks, and obstacles that can trip you, but wood is a much more resiliant (and therefore more comfortable) surface on which to fall. It's often difficult to find a clear, smooth, untrafficked area outdoors on which you can practice perfecting your steps and turns.

Relaxation is essential in order to achieve balance and smooth skating. The rhythm of rink music (any variety) helps one to loosen up. In addition to all this, the other skaters at the rink are bound to give you helpful hints, if you seem open to suggestions. You can also learn just by imitating the maneuvers of more polished skaters.

RINK STICKERS

These stickers have become a popular item for collectors of roller memorabilia.

Courtesy of Dick Young

ADULT SKATING CLASS AT THE ROLL-A-PALACE

What's the easiest part of learning to skate? "That's an easy one," says Winston, a 37-year-old construction worker from Brooklyn, New York. "It's falling down! And we sure do a lot of that." Winston, a tall, good-looking man, has huge, bulging arm and shoulder muscles that, he claims, come from his working as a welder. "Besides skating, I also jog and lift weights. If I can't make it to the gym, I'll come to the rink. I like skating and want to get the exercise."

Winston is one of 20 to 25 men and women who once a week take the beginner roller skating class for adults from Charlie Aybar, skating pro-in-residence at the Roll-A-Palace, Brooklyn, New York.

"My students range in age from 16 to 55 years old," says Charlie. "They come into the class with different degrees of skating experience. Some are true beginners—they can barely stand up on the skates. Others have skated session here or at other places in Brooklyn and Queens. They can usually skate forward but don't know much more beyond that.

"Occasionally, I'll get someone who has more experience and can even do some of the dances. They may have learned the dances when they were kids and now want to polish their style."

Betty, a 48-old-year fabric saleswoman from Brooklyn, fits into this last category of student. "This is one of the best deals in town," she says. "We come here every Wednesday night from 7 to 8 PM and pay 5 dollars for each lesson. Many people in the class have their own skates but if they don't, skate rental is included in the price. Also, you can stay over into the public session (that starts at 8 o'clock) and practice dances you've learned in class. "When we talk about dances now, we're talking about the old-fashioned style of waltzes, tangos and fox trots—all done on roller skates," mentions Betty, who has taken lessons from Charlie for six months.

"During the '50s, I skated at the old Empire Rink, (which was then called the Brooklyn Roller Skating Rink), with my husband. He was my dance partner," says Betty, smiling nostalgically. "The old Empire was the most magnificent rink on the East coast. All the skaters there were dance skaters and they won a lot of competitions." The Empire today is still a famous rink, but now it focuses exclusively on roller disco.

"I laid off skating for 25 years to raise a family," Betty continues, "but here I am, back again. This time I want to learn the dances the right way and start taking my proficiency tests." (These examinations are part of a dance program that is offered in most rinks in the United States.)

Ann-Victoria Phillips

Betty Lillis of Brooklyn with her instructor, Charlie Aybar.

All photos: Ann-Victoria Phillips

Safety in numbers–
Aybar's class practices
Shoot the Duck (left) and, a new dance step.

"Like Betty, most of my students want me to teach them dance steps so they can pass the tests," says Charlie as he flips through stacks of records filed near the DJ's booth. "The Roll-A-Palace is not known as a competitive skating rink. People from this community are not interested in that kind of skating. Mostly, they just want to enjoy themselves and learn the steps." Charlie put a record on the turntable and the sound of waltz music fills the huge building with its high ceilings. "Come on, Betty. Let's start." Charlie joins Betty on the floor to begin her Glide Waltz practice. Like Fred Astaire and Ginger Rogers, they glide off around the rink floor, looking like graceful ballroom dancers.

Other students practice simple forward skating and t-stops on the side of the rink floor near the railing. It's a small, quiet, and intimate group practicing here tonight—half the class stayed home because of the heavy snowstorm raging outside. "On a night like this," says Winston who is practicing simple dance steps by himself in a corner, "the rink is the best place to be."

Slava, an 18-year-old Russian who has lived in the United States for only 11 months, is skating here tonight for the first time. He claims that his feet won't do what he tells them to do. "Ice skating is popular in Russia, not roller skating. I don't know anything about this kind of skating, but I'm going to learn it." Slava is trying to skate forward and is stumbling a bit but already he has learned the forward scissors movement. He wants to learn how to stop before the end of the class—quite a high goal for a first-time skater.

The Roll-A-Palace was born two years ago, after a million-dollar renovation of the Sheepshead Bay Century movie theatre. All of Charlie's students agree that this rink is one of the nicest places to learn to skate in the area. The ceilings are so high that the place looks more like a church than a roller rink.

With the exception of Charlie Aybar's special skating classes, the Roll-A-Palace is an all-disco rink—that is, the latest top-40 hits are played during the public skating sessions. You'll never hear a Glenn Miller record or the "Skater's March" after 8 PM here, just Donna Summer, LTD, A Taste of Honey, and Foxy, all popular with the roller disco crowd.

"Do I roller disco? Sure," says 20-year-old Peggy, an office worker from Brooklyn. "But the reason I take classes from Charlie is because, just like everyone else in the group, I want to learn old-fashioned dances, like the waltz."

Kelly, Peggy's 15-year-old sister, is also in the class, and has the same goal. "Both of us learned the basics at another rink. We skated during the session and already knew how to skate forward and backward before we came here. After

I started here, I learned both crossovers and the beginner dance steps—you'd never get that from session skating."

"Both of us got our amateur cards," continues Peggy. That means the skating sisters have registered with the United States Amateur Confederation of Roller Skating (USAC) located in Lincoln, Nebraska. "We can enter competitive meets, if we want. We probably won't. Our mother got us started in this," Peggy says proudly. "She was a show skater in the '50s."

Charlie, who has finished working with Betty, is now watching Slava and some of his other beginner students practice on the floor. "The thing that's funny about some of my new skaters is that they come here the first time and, right away, they want to learn backward skating. They can't even stand up on their skates and they want to learn to skate backward! I guess that's because it's a very popular thing to do for disco music. It's different and they seem to like the novelty of it," Charlie remarks.

The skaters in this class are no different than any other in one regard—they're afraid of falling down. "This is the greatest fear I hear about in the class. People don't realize that everyone, including national champions and professionals, fall down all the time. It's not that big a deal.

"My first-time people are either embarrassed by falling or afraid of getting hurt. What I try to do is get them to adopt a relaxed mental attitude first. Then, I teach them how to fall down painlessly and get up smiling. They practice this by turning their body slightly to the side—this way they don't fall down straight forward or straight backward—letting themselves roll down onto the floor. Believe it or not, learning how to fall can be made into a game. That takes a lot of terror out of the learning process."

Most first-time students, unless they have a lot of previous skating ability, will start out learning the basics. "We line them up straight across the rink floor, near the railing but not touching it," Charlie tells us. "On the first day, they will learn forward skating techniques: the t-start, push-off, and the forward scissors movement. Learning how to stop is another important part of their lesson."

Once a skater has learned this and is comfortable on his or her skates, they can learn to skate backward and to do the crossover steps. Students practice during the class. Additional time is available at the 8 PM session.

"If one practices, the first-time skater should be able to start learning simple steps within a few weeks," mentions Charlie, himself a former competitive dance skater with 20 years of skating experience.

It's almost 8 o'clock—time for the class to end. The lobby of the Roll-A-Palace is now filling up with a different breed of skater—the roller rocker who skates to a different beat, namely disco. This Brooklyn-based rink is only a mile from the famous discotheque where *Saturday Night Fever* was filmed. The "John Travolta look," therefore, is prevalent in the hairstyles and dress the skaters wear.

Charlie's class files off the skating floor. Within minutes, 200 disco skaters are skipping and spinning over the floor. The lights have dimmed and thousands of red, blue, green, and yellow lights dance over the surface of the rink floor, perfectly synchronized with the flowing movements of the skaters and the heavy disco beat.

Florie Melanaski and Jim Macaluso enjoy skating in the traditional waltz position.

AN OLD-FASHIONED SKATING RINK

Les, Kevin, Lynn
and Joan Wittmer
claim skating has
kept the family
together.

Les Wittmer, owner of the Skateranch, one of the very last portable roller rinks in the United States, pointed toward what looked like a circus tent pitched in a cow pasture alongside the completely deserted Emmet County Fairgrounds in Estherville, Iowa. He laughed. "Believe it or not, parts of this rink are almost 25 years old. This thing has survived hailstorms and 100 mile-per-hour winds. It's strong. I know because I made it—the rink floor, the railings, benches, skate storage bins, snack counter, and the 12-piece sound system—all on the floor of my Dad's garage. The tent came from someone else. My first one, bought in 1955, cost 3,000 dollars."

Les got hooked on skating when he was 11. "I was raised on a farm in Alden, Minnesota. Carl's Roller Rink in Albert Lea, 12 miles away, was the closest place to skate. I loved that place—sometimes I'd be there five nights a week. Everyone dressed up. Men wore dress slacks and women wore sweaters and skirts. People will laugh hearing this now, but on Sundays I skated in a suit and tie."

Carl's, a popular spot that featured waltzing to organ music for 50 cents a session, sprouted a number of roller romances between young men and women. It was there that Les met Joan, who became his dance partner, business associate, and his wife.

"My dream was to own a rink," remembers Les, "but I was 22, just married, and couldn't come up with the money. So I studied the portable rink. There were a number of different styles."

Neither Les, his father, nor anyone else in his family had any carpentry or engineering skills, but that didn't matter. He figured out how the portables were put together and built his own.

"All the pieces were designed to fit into a truck, ready to be transported from my Dad's farm, where I stored the rink during the winter months, to my summer location," recalls Les.

Les Wittmer's portable rink fully assembled at the Emmet County Fairgrounds, Estherville, Iowa.

Like their predecessors in the '30s and '40s, the Wittmers set up their rink in tiny farming communities.

The first, in May 1955, was Manly, Iowa, located just south of the Minnesota–Iowa border. Next, they moved 20 miles southwest to Garner, Iowa, and stayed there two summers. "Those were our very best years," says Joan. "We had 75 pairs of Chicago clamp-style skates and they were in constant demand. Garner was so small that going to the movies or roller skating were the only things to do."

Since 1961, except for the few years Les took off to run a freight business in Lafayette, Minnesota (where the Wittmers live during the winter with their sons), the summer home of the portable rink has been Estherville. This sleepy, old-fashioned, country village welcomes visitors with "Hogs Are Beautiful" signs nailed to fences on both sides of the road.

As we talked, Les circled the rink, checking to make sure that everything was alright. He explained the step-by-step construction of his portable. "Nobody can believe how much time it takes to put this thing together. It takes six people— me, Joan, the kids, my father and my nephew— two weeks to set it up from start to finish. We start about May 15 by picking up the first of eight truckloads at my Dad's farm in Alden. We haul it 100 miles here to Estherville. What happens next is that hundreds of wooden blocks—they provide the substructure for the skating floor to rest on—have to be moved into place. Once that is finished, 138 4x12-foot sheets of masonite flooring are laid in, each piece numbered and feather-edged to lock with its neighbor to create a perfectly smooth, seamless skating surface. It's a floating floor. Nails are not necessary to hold it together.

"The gold-colored tent is held up by seven 19-foot center poles and stretched taut by 74 anchor chains. Canvas side-curtains, which can be rolled up on a sunny day or rolled down when it rains, make up the 'walls' of the rink.

"I'm very proud of my rink, especially because I made it. You don't see this kind of thing anymore," Les said, smiling.

What Les says is true. His rink is unique. The

Les adjusts a young skater's equipment (below), an older girl handles her own adjustments (top right) and Joan leads the traditional skater's march (below right).

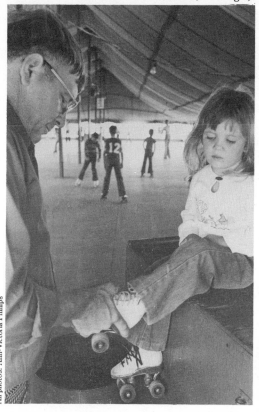

Garold Whitlock's portable rink in Belleview, Nebraska, 1955.

heyday of the portables was in the 1930s and '40s. Depression years brought hard times to many, but the owners of the circus tent rinks never had it so good. Hundreds of portable rinks, the only sources of cheap, summertime entertainment for cowboys, farmers, and other country folk, were set up on the outskirts of small towns. A pair of Chicago or Richardson clamp skates could be rented for 25 cents. Reportedly, the roar of the steel-wheeled skates could be heard for miles. Townsfolk found the noise annoying and some of the rink owners were run out of town.

Later in the '50s, the popularity of the portables declined. Skaters left the rink and headed for the dance halls.

Les continues as he walks toward the rink. "We've survived because we're a family business. I know I'll never be rich, but to me, this is the good life. I'm my own boss and that's important to me. If you

Kevin Wittmer clowns on stilt-skates, a novelty item from the past.

don't mind living in a trailer for the summer, fooling with the tent all the time during stormy weather and never knowing what will happen next, it's not too bad."

All the Wittmers have a job to do, once the session has begun, when the rink is open. Joan collects money and is the floor guard. Les, who opens every session with the "Skater's March" and closes with "God Bless America," flips through his 3,000-strong record collection and plays rock from the '50s as well as all the latest disco music. "I take the time to meet my customers. I entertain them. Nobody knows my last name. Everyone calls me Les."

Kevin, the Wittmers' 18-year-old son, is in charge of maintaining the tent and listening to the weather reports. Lynn, their 10-year-old boy, cleans up the rink floor after each session. Both Kevin and Lynn are popular as dance partners and skate at each session.

"Skating is just about the only thing to do in this town," says Les. "My only competition is the swimming pool. The drive-in blew down during a storm and the bowling alley closed for the summer."

The rink is filled with people, gliding and spinning shapes that cut through the hazy, golden light from the setting sun. Les and Joan two-step around the floor while other skaters watch and clap in time with the music. Their wheels barely touching the ground, they dance much the same as they did 26 years ago when they first met. "I'm proud of my rink," says Les, cheek-to-cheek with Joan. "To me, this is heaven."

2. OUTDOOR SKATING

PAVING THE WAY

Although early European roller skaters periodically took to the streets, Americans, especially in rural areas, had few outside places to skate before the 1900s. Then came the development of smooth pavements and better skates during the 1920s, and America's first major outdoor skating craze spread from coast to coast. Skaters mobbed San Francisco's Golden Gate Park. In New York, Central Park played host to roller contests while recreational skaters took their rolling strolls along the park's many paved walkways.

Besides regular sporting and social events in towns throughout the country, one of the unique

Courtesy of Chicago Roller Skate Company

Flapper era skaters take a break for some minor adjustments.

Yours truly
Arnold Binns
WORLD'S ENDURANCE ROLLER SKATING CHAMPION.

Long distance skating was a popular fad, however John Balazs (below), "The Flying Shoemaker," was a serious rolling marathoner—as his advertising attests.

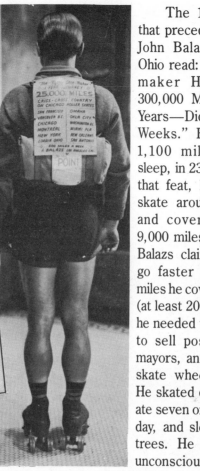

features of outdoor skating, the opportunity for touring and traveling long distances, was seized upon by quite a few enthusiasts. America soon had a new slew of heroes and heroines in the headlines. "Mother and Daughter Team Skate 400 Miles from Kansas City to Peoria" was one of the first of these in 1927. But, according to the *New York Times*, Mrs. Henry Pfetzing and her daughter Anna Catherine skated only 250 of those miles. In some towns they were barred from skating or were forced off their skates by dirty roads and bad weather. By the end of her trip, Mrs. Pfetzing was nursing an injured shoulder and nose (she fell when trying to avoid a truck) but enthusiastically proclaimed, "I wouldn't trade my experience for a million dollars."

Two months later, Arthur Allegretti skated from Buffalo to New York City, subsisting on a diet of hot dogs, and going 58 hours without any sleep. The next year, a 13-year-old Philadelphia boy skated 62 miles from his home to Atlantic City, New Jersey in seven and one-half hours.

The 1928 headline that preceded the tale of John Balazs of Elyria, Ohio read: "Flying Shoemaker Hopes to do 300,000 Miles in Seven Years—Did 9,000 in 12 Weeks." Balazs skated 1,100 miles, without sleep, in 231 hours. After that feat, he decided to skate around the globe and covered the first 9,000 miles in 12 weeks. Balazs claimed he could go faster than the 125 miles he covered each day (at least 200, he said) but he needed the extra time to sell postcards, visit mayors, and replace nine skate wheels each day. He skated day and night, ate seven or eight times a day, and slept under the trees. He was knocked unconscious for a half-hour by a car in Ontario, Canada, but once he revived, he skated on, undaunted.

Another skating pair, Norman Skelley, age 28, and John Shefuga, age 27, skated from Boston to Los Angeles between October 2 and December 4, 1936. They drank nothing but milk and water, ate five full meals a day at 7 and 9 AM, noon, 3 and 6 PM (plus snacks of ice cream, fruits, and vegetables), and had two baths daily followed by alcohol rubs.

What these accomplishments show is that roller skates can be used for day trips, overnight, or even longer vacations (with or without backpacking gear). In this sense, it is much like the current bicycle touring craze—but think how much more convenient it is to board a bus or train to the country with a pair of skates rather than a bicycle. Moreover, if you bring along lightweight sandals, you can carry your skates anywhere without difficulty.

WHERE TO RENT ROLLER SKATES

Roller skate rental shops can be found in many large cities and towns near parks and beaches, from San Francisco and Los Angeles to Denver, Phoenix, Minneapolis, and New York City. Soon, every major town with parks and college campuses will have shops. Roller rental companies are now franchising in suburban areas as well.

Shops are usually open from 10 AM to 7 PM on weekends and from 10 AM to 12 midnight on Friday and Saturday nights. Some shops are open every day of the week, while others are open only on weekends.

HOW MUCH WILL IT COST?

Skate rental prices range from 1 dollar in southern California to 2 dollars for the first hour in New York City. The price of each additional hour, after the first one, will range from 75 cents to one and a half dollars. Usually you can rent skates for the day, and some places rent them overnight. To skate all day is usually 5 dollars and to skate all night is an additional 5 dollars.

RENTAL PROCEDURES

Some rental outfits require a 5-dollar cash deposit plus identification, such as driver's license, credit card, armed service identification, or employment ID. Others ask for identification only. In addition, you must sign a form releasing the skate shop from any liability while you are using their skates. If you are under 18 years old, a parent or guardian must co-sign the release form with you. If you are under 18 and skate frequently, try to get the skate shop to keep your release form on file so that your parents do not have to accompany you each time.

WHAT TO WEAR: YOUR OUTDOOR SKATING COSTUME

Whatever you choose to wear, just make sure it is comfortable and allows you maximum freedom of movement. And if you are just learning the basics, wear old clothes because beginners do take falls. All outdoor skaters, beginner to advanced, should consider wearing knee pads, elbow pads, and leather gloves. A pair of leather, palm-padded gloves (similar to what skateboarders use) is the

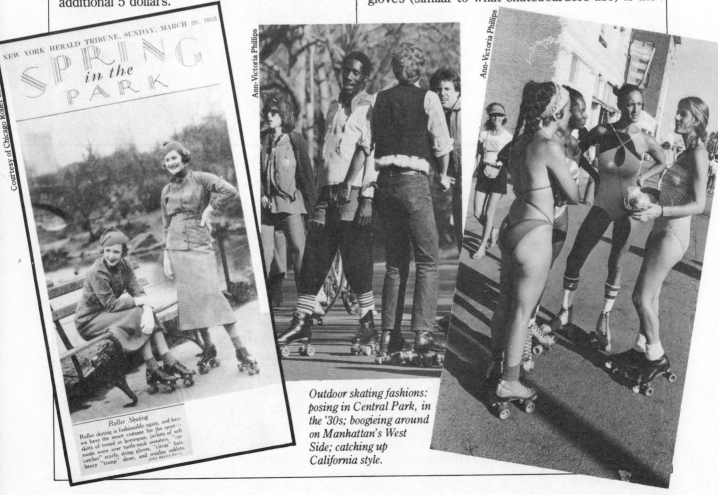

Outdoor skating fashions: posing in Central Park, in the '30s; boogieing around on Manhattan's West Side; catching up California style.

one essential piece of equipment. Buy yourself a pair. Knee and elbow pads can be rented at some shops for 50 cents per pair or they may even be free to borrow.

Your choice of costume depends on what area of the country you skate in. For most places, T-shirts, jeans, and shorts are the most popular choices. Devil-may-care southern Californians, however, consider bathing suits to be the best skating outfit. During winter months, skate in cotton sweat clothes or a ski outfit.

OUTDOOR SKATING AS AN EXERCISE

Assuming you already know the basics, outdoor skating can be more beneficial as an exercise than

More fun than jogging—cutting loose on the open road.

SKATE SAFE OUTDOORS

1. Ask your local rental shop where the best places to skate are and which areas are out-of-bounds. Typically, near a beach, skating is not allowed on the bicycle paths and municipal fishing piers. Although some towns don't like roller skaters on the sidewalks, every place is different.

2. While obeying traffic laws, signals, and signs is expected, stopping at intersections and slowing down when coming out of driveways and alleys is a common sense precaution. Hitching onto moving vehicles is not only extremely dangerous, it may be illegal in most places.

3. When skating outdoors, avoid chipped and rough surfaces. Also, avoid stones, branches, and dirt. Control coasting down hills so that you are able to stop or bypass obstacles. Skating in traffic is obviously risky. However, if you must, skate against the traffic. Never try tricks or stunts in the road; seek protected areas and smooth pavement.

4. Safety Equipment: Use knee and elbow pads when skating on hills, rough pavement or when learning new tricks. When it's dark, wear light-colored clothing or put reflective strips (sold at many sporting goods stores) on your clothing so drivers can see you.

5. Check your skates before setting out. Spin your wheels to see that they are moving freely. Tighten any loose nuts and bolts and replace badly frayed boot laces.

rink skating if you skate fast and for at least 15 minutes at a stretch. You can also skate up hills or for long distances to increase your endurance. Some city areas have great stretches of roads or sidewalks to skate on, such as San Francisco's Golden Gate Park, the six-mile oval road (where the joggers run) in New York City's Central Park, and along beachfront streets and paths of the southern California coast. Most American cities and towns have park roadways suitable for sport skating. If you skate strenuously for at least 15 minutes, rest, and then skate strenuously again for the same amount of time, you'll get a good all around workout, and, in particular contribute to your cardio-vascular health. You might even consider making this part of a regular exercise routine.

WHEELS OF THE WEST

From Golden Gate Park to Venice Beach, Californians show off their free-wheelin' spirit.

Racing in Golden Gate Park.

Skating the Golden Gate Bridge.

Coasting.

Lacing up.

All photos: Ann-Victoria Phillips

Double-rolling trouble.

Relaxing after a good skate.

Making a train, family-style.

Doing the "coffin" down Golden Gate's Conservatory Hill.

Side-surfing.

OUTDOOR EXPECTATIONS

Outdoor skating is for the explorer, the athlete, and the adventurer. Outdoor skaters usually find the pace of rink skating too confining—claustrophobic—and not challenging enough for a vigorous workout. They want to break out of indoor routines and skate as far and as fast as possible at any time of the day or night.

Indoor skating lulls you into a trance-like dream state with its steady, smooth pace and accompanying music; outdoor skating challenges all your senses and wakes you up. You have to be aware of your physical surroundings or you'll fall on your face. Like a motorcyclist, you have to look ahead for patches of dirt, cracks, holes in the road and also pedestrians and traffic. You face the physical challenge of climbing, and coasting down, hills. This kind of skating forces you to develop more muscle strength and endurance skills than you would by ordinary rink skating. You notice details of your surroundings that you may never have noticed before. You can walk along a sidewalk in total self-preoccupation; skating, you become super-alert. You may discover your first butterfly or crocus of the spring season, notice historic public sculptures in your park, and best of all, skate places that you never would have walked.

Now, you set off in new directions, lured on by the sheer pleasure of rolling on skates. Exploring, climbing a hill for the thrill of speeding down the other side, testing the limits of your endurance to see if you can skate farther, faster—all these aspects of skating represent the search for the new and unexpected.

ROLLING WITH THE FLOW

The physical sensations of outdoor roller skating are similar to those of cross-country skiing and,

like skiing, it takes lots of endurance to climb hills, push yourself over bumpy surfaces and negotiate a wide variety of terrain. It's scary to start rolling down hills when you are a beginner because you gain speed so fast that you can easily lose control. To solve this problem, you slalom, just like a downhill skier, back and forth across the walk or path in a serpentine line instead of coasting straight down at full speed. Bend your knees and relax. After you've gotten used to this technique,

Ann-Victoria Phillips

Outdoor skating, cross-country style—a New York skater negotiates Central Park's varied terrain.

you'll find yourself looking forward to the thrill of hurling yourself downhill at speeds of up to 30 miles per hour.

You may feel, at first, that you have a lot in common with joggers and bicyclists but you'll soon notice a few big differences. For one, joggers look grimly serious while counting their laps or miles around the park. In contrast, outdoor skaters smile, talk and laugh with each other as they roll around. You won't feel a strain even though you're getting a good workout, because you're having too much fun. Although you are moving as fast as the bicyclers on downhill grades, you feel different sensations on skates than when on a bike. You'll feel a sense of more immediate maneuverability. There's a connection between you and the ground which you don't feel when perched atop a bicycle. Compare it to the difference between riding in a low, ground-hugging sports car and riding in the cab of a pickup truck.

TO RENT OR BUY

Roller skating, like practically every other sport, is the most fun when you can do it with ease. This ease, of course, comes with regular practice. If you rent your skates, you may find that you spend more time waiting in line for skates than you do skating. Also, some rental places charge 2 dollars or more per hour. This can be expensive if a family decides to skate together regularly or tour the countryside. Try outdoor skating on rental skates first and decide whether you want to make it a regular exercise, then seriously consider buying your own skates. Chapter 14 has valuable information on buying equipment.

The length of the outdoor season varies from place to place with warm, sunny climates attracting the majority of outdoor skaters. California, in particular, has a large number of enthusiasts. However, if you're dressed properly, you can enjoy outdoor skating anytime of year as long as the road is free of ice and snow. In the winter, choose outfits similar to those of joggers, ice skaters, and skiers—lightweight clothing worn in layers, with a warm hat, and gloves.

Skating vigorously during hot weather actually requires more precautions in order to keep your body from overheating. You should drink plenty of liquid along the way to prevent heat exhaustion, and take along a lightweight sunshade

HAVING YOUR OWN RINK OUTDOORS (WITH MUSIC, TOO)

Ann-Victoria Phillips

Colin "Rubberband Man" Courtman of Venice.

You're bound to see outdoor skaters who, wearing radio headphones, dance along in a world of their own. Use your imagination and create your own smooth, outdoor dance floor. Good places to check out are shopping malls after regular store hours, parking lots, plazas in front of office buildings (often paved with marble), civic and cultural centers, in short, any vacant place with a smooth surface. Set down a portable radio or clip on headphones and you're ready to work out.

hat to prevent sun stroke. Heat tolerance is partly dependent on your body size. Heavy people dissipate heat more slowly than thin ones. Remember: it's easy to get carried away skating on a beautiful summer day. Don't be seduced into a bad case of sunburn.

WHAT A WAY TO ROLL!

Gus Swift and Linda Erf on Chicago's Michigan Ave.

Mary Horowitz, editor of RollerSkating Magazine, walking her dog and parrot at Laguna Beach, California.

Bodybuilder Albert Garcia gives Laurie Piepenbrink a lift —San Diego, California.

Hitching a ride in Golden Gate Park, San Francisco.

Taking baby for a stroll, San Francisco.

Rolling to class—UCLA students Jeanie Griffin and Karen Laukka.

"Ring around the Rosie" in Newport Beach, California.

Joe Rice and friend, Julie Lavin, on Hermosa Pier, California

Maurice Cooke dribbles on the roll in Los Angeles.

Impromptu disco-dancing on California's Venice Beach "Skaters' Path."

RENTING YOUR ROLLERS

CHEAPSKATES
VENICE, CALIFORNIA

"The first stunt I pulled on roller skates was in 1975 when I dressed up in black satin shorts and a satin jacket, and skated with my friends to a Halloween party in Venice," recalls Jeff Rosenberg, 24, one of the leaders of the current, nationwide outdoor roller skating craze. "I'll bet a hundred people came up to me and asked me where I got my skates." It was the attention and the interest of other people that gave Jeff the idea of starting his own roller skating business. "On June 5, 1976 I opened the back door of my van along the Venice Beach and rented 25 pairs of Roller Derby skates. I tried to get more durable models but none of the distributors would sell to me because I was an individual and not a roller rink."

Jeff's skates didn't last long under tough, beachfront skating conditions. Water and sand kept getting in the looseball bearings; he spent most of his extra time maintaining the skates. His goal was to buy better equipment and find a permanent home for his rental operation but he didn't have the money. "One night, I went to a movie premiere dressed as Raggedy Andy, in red, white, and blue shorts and matching roller skates. One of the art directors from *Playgirl* was there and decided to shoot me for a magazine centerfold." Reportedly, Jeff was paid very well for wearing nothing more than a gold skate key. It proved to be a lucky key because, says Jeff, "I got my storefront, Cheapskates, in July, 1976. It's the same one I'm working out of now on Oceanfront Drive."

Jeff's business is going strong today. He completely rents out his 300 pairs of skates every weekend. People stand in line, sometimes forty at a time, and wait anywhere from five minutes to an hour for a pair of skates.

Unlike many other roller entrepreneurs, Jeff was not surprised by the great popularity of his roller skate rental shop or the worldwide publicity it generated. "When I started this thing, I was 100 percent sure that the whole roller skating trip was going to happen because it has so much to offer. Skating is a tension releaser. Your mind turns off

All photos: Ann-Victoria Phillips

Jeff Rosenberg, "Mr. Cheapskates," opened the first outdoor skate rental operation in the US.

while your body locks into the rhythm and the flow of the roll. For some, it's almost like meditation.

"I call my customers, most of them between 25 and 45 years old—some are even celebrities like Linda Ronstadt and Cher—the lost generation of skaters. These are people who skated when they were kids and then stopped. Skating was a phase of life they went through—first, they walked; then, they learned to skate, to ride a bike, drive a car, and finally, they became super consumers of luxury items. I feel that people are getting away from that now and are seeking a simpler lifestyle. They are more health-oriented and want to be physically active, instead of just being passive consumers. They're getting away from luxury wheels like cars, and getting back into leisure wheels like skates."

Jeff would like to open Cheapskates operations all over the United States. He has also received a few inquiries from Europe and the Far East. One of the countless projects he has in mind is a serious attempt to design an inter-city transportation system that uses roller skates instead of cars. Says Jeff Rosenberg, "That would be the end of all parking hassles!"

HAMEL'S OF MISSION BEACH SAN DIEGO, CALIFORNIA

Any visitor to San Diego's Mission Beach area is sure to notice the hundreds of men with short haircuts walking up and down the three-mile boardwalk. "They're all servicemen," says Ray Hamel, as he peers out of his skate rental window. "There's a Marine Corps recruiting depot, Camp Pendleton (a Marine Corps base), a US Naval Training Center, and the Miramar Naval Air Station, all within 30 miles. This was, and still is, a Navy town. Where this shop is now used to be a locker club. The guys would come here to get changed for the beach. Now they come to rent roller skates."

Hamel's, a three-year-old skate-and-surf shop that is owned by Ray and his brother Dan, is the main beachfront hangout as well as the center of all sports activities. Besides renting and selling skates, they also rent and repair bikes. Hundreds of T-shirts (some saying "Mission Beach Zoo"), pin-up pictures, plastic sunglasses, rubber sandals, surfboards, and a yellowed photograph of early Mission Beach roller skaters of the '20s adorn the walls. Over 500 brand new roller skates hang from the ceiling by their laces.

The Hamels, sharp businessmen who only look tough, are pushovers—big softies who will rent roller skates in exchange for a bag of jelly beans or a dozen chocolate chip cookies. All the rental skates are painted with big, messy, black

numbers, to prevent them from being stolen, and have strips of black bicycle tire tubing covering the toes, to protect the skates from being scraped on the rough beachfront pavement.

The locals, who affectionately refer to Ray and Dan as "the notorious Hamel boys," include an astonishing variety of people—Vietnam veterans, aircraft and shipyard employees, retired citizens, surfers, as well as members of the San Diego chapter of Hell's Angels (Ray once persuaded them to don skates for a charity roll-a-thon). "You gotta be ready to handle anything around here," says Dan, a former champion bodybuilder.

Mission Beach skaters can roll along the three-mile strip on the ocean side or the four-mile bicycle paths on the Bay side. They can also skate in downtown San Diego, Balboa Park, and near the San Diego Zoo.

Ray and Dan Hamel supply equipment for both skating and cycling enthusiasts.

"Our biggest problem here is rust," says Ray, "the sea air is very moist, especially at night, and we constantly have to re-lubricate the bearings. Also, people have even come back with seaweed wrapped around the wheels; they've gone swimming with skates on!"

One of the biggest attractions of Ray and Dan's skate rental operation is that it stays open late at night. Each day provides the brothers with a never-ending series of theatrical events. "Halloween night is a gas. People come here to rent skates half-dressed and covered with glitter and paint. Every day is new and it's all funny. That's why we call this place the Mission Beach Zoo."

BUFFALO SKATES
SAN FRANCISCO, CALIFORNIA

"Rip-offs are a problem," claims Tom Hartman owner and manager of Buffalo Skates, a successful skate rental van operation. "The last pair of skates I lost was to an ophthalmologist who left his AMA card as security. It adds a little spice to life when I track them down."

Tom started his business in May, 1977, on Fulton Street near Golden Gate Park in San Francisco. He rented out of a little Chevy camper, decorated with his logo, a buffalo with a yellow rose in its mouth.

"We brought the fad to San Francisco," says Hartman, who now operates two large panel trucks, each having 300 skates. Buffalo Skates, once the only rental operation near the park, has a lot of competition. "Now there are seven or eight competitors with names like Fun Skates, Roller Babies, Easy Rider, and one outfit called Harvey's Ball Bearing. It seems as though a new one starts up every week."

Buffalo Skates is open every day of the year, unless it rains. But Sunday, when the car traffic is banned from Golden Gate Park, is the best day for roller antics. In addition to the park skaters, San Francisco has a large population of street performers—actors, mimes, musicians, clowns—who also roller skate. You can find them all performing in the park on Sunday.

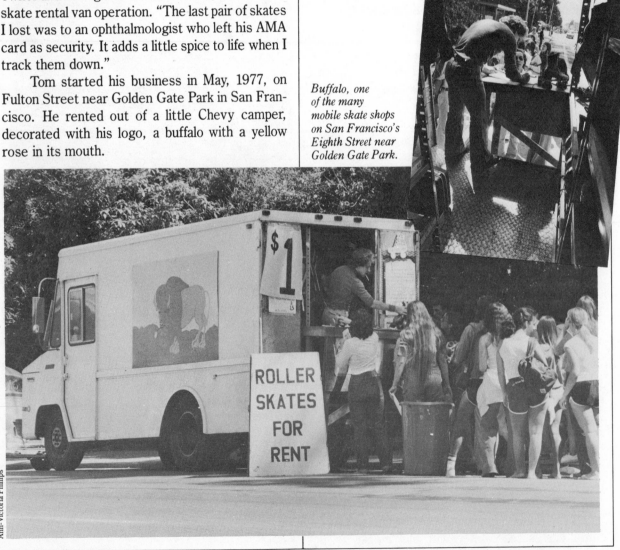

Buffalo, one of the many mobile skate shops on San Francisco's Eighth Street near Golden Gate Park.

Ann-Victoria Phillips

Skating in Golden Gate Park is an unusual sensory experience. Botanical treasures from China, Japan, Burma, and South America enhance the botanical display of more ordinary plant varieties. Depending on the time of year, the fragrance from flowering dahlias, fuchsias, camellias and rhododendrons is fantastically sweet.

There are many sights to see in the park and Tom's skaters have hit every attraction. "Some skaters have come back soaking wet," he said. "We think they must have gone to the Japanese Tea Gardens and fallen in the pond."

ROLLING SOLES
MINNEAPOLIS, MINNESOTA

"I skate up until the day it snows," says Scott Sansby, 27, owner of Rolling Soles, the first outdoor skate rental shop in the state of Minnesota. "The Minneapolis Parks Board wouldn't allow me to rent skates from my van, so I set up shop on a friend's lawn, right across the street from Lake Calhoun."

Scott lives near some of the best roller turf in the United States. The park system in Minneapolis includes 30 miles of bike and pedestrian pathways that connect five beautiful, scenic lakes—Cedar Lake, Lake of the Isles, Lake Calhoun, Lake Harriet, and Lake Nokomis—all located along the west and southwest city limits.

The new shop's first day of operation, June 17, 1978, proved to be an astonishing experience for neighborhood residents. Dumbfounded, they watched Scott drive up in his van, unload his portable skate storage bins, and prepare for his 10 AM opening. "Even though I had only 30 pairs of skates for rent during the summer," recounts the heavily-bearded roller entrepreneur, "my business was tremendous." Scott rented Chicago Skates for one and a half dollars per hour to eager Minneapolis and St. Paul residents.

"I graduated from the University of Minnesota with a degree in Family Sociology and Social Psychology, but never worked in the field. For years, I'd been looking for something positive and healthy. This is the best thing that has ever happened to me. It represents a turning point in my life. Without giving up any of my freedom, I have established a business doing something I love. I haven't made a lot of money, but I'm having the time of my life."

Minneapolis Tribune

Scott Sansby is responsible for bringing outdoor skating to the Midwest.

Scott became an instant local celebrity when he received nationwide press coverage. He was featured in a page one story in the *Wall Street Journal.* "The publicity has completely overwhelmed me," says Scott who, nonetheless, poses for wireservice photographs wearing a T-shirt printed with the Rolling Soles logo, "Why Not Roll Your Own?"

"One of the most amazing things that happened," recalls Scott, "is that my mother and father, inactive for years, have turned into roller fanatics. My dad, who works as a pharmacist during the week, rips around the Lake Calhoun skate paths to tunes from his radio-headset on the weekend. My mom, who got braver by the end of the summer, finally joined him. They both took their roller skates with them on a recent vacation trip to Mexico. Who would ever believe this could all happen?" exclaims Scott Sansby.

THE GOODSKATES
NEW YORK, NEW YORK

Judy Lynn, 33, a free-spirited woman has a dream and won't let it go. She wants to turn the whole world onto roller skating. With the help of Bob White, her business partner, and Bill Butler, her skating director, she has created The Goodskates, a diversified, high-energy roller skate rental operation. It is located in a Parks Department building in the northwest corner of Sheep's Meadow in New York's Central Park. Although other roller entrepreneurs tried for months to persuade the Director of Concessions to let them set up shop in the park, only Judy Lynn succeeded.

Another remarkable feat is that in spite of the fact that there are millions of prospective roller skaters in the city's five boroughs—New Yorkers are, and always have been, skate crazy—The Goodskates still dominates the scene. It has become the "Grand Central Station" of New York's roller scene.

The idea came to Judy in 1977 when a friend complained that there was no place to roller skate in New York City. "We both thought, wouldn't it be great if . . . " remembers Judy. "I thought of dancing on skates."

With Bob White, Judy toured the country's rinks and outdoor skate rental operations. Judy described the trip. "We went to California in November, 1977, to meet Jeff Rosenberg and skate at Venice Beach. With the Santa Ana winds floating around us and the mountains in the background, it was ecstasy," sighed Judy, delighted with the memory. What they saw there convinced them to first try a more modest project, a rental concession in Central Park. Judy said later, "Goodskates was modeled after Cheapskates. It's our brother company."

Back in New York, Judy and Bob faced negotiations that proved to be so tough and complex, it's no wonder almost everyone failed. Judy wanted the prestige and visibility of being located in the park and never gave much thought to an alternate storefront location. She also had her eye on one particular building. "The one I wanted had a courtyard, a lot of grass and was near the athletic center of Central Park, Frisbee Hill, and the bandshell. We asked for the Mineral Springs Building. The Director of Concessions said, 'no, it was out of the question,' and offered us a boathouse.

He told us we'd need 1 million dollars in insurance, the building would be vandalized, all our skates would be stolen and that we'd lose all our money."

Judy was not easily discouraged; she wanted the Mineral Springs Building. Months passed, but the Director could not be moved.

One day Judy skated directly to his office and tried to convince him of the merits of roller skating and why it would be good for Central Park and New York. She told him that "skating is a universal sport (perfect for the space age generation), skating is the most efficient means of transportation, walking is too slow, and simply speaking, skating is ecstasy." Reportedly, at that point, the director gave in and admitted that he had skated as a kid.

That day, after five months of negotiations, they got the Mineral Springs Building, but only for a short trial period. "The director did it thinking we'd back out of the deal," remembers Judy. "After all, who in their right mind would order 20,000 dollars worth of skates on the basis of a four-week temporary permit?" Judy and Bob jumped at the chance. "Three weeks later, we had skates, a letterhead, business cards, a rainbow and a star over the door and there we were!"

Although Judy had good ideas and enthusiasm, she still lacked experience in running a roller skating business. To strike a balance, she recruited New York's resident super-skater, Bill Butler, and named him manager of the Central Park shop and director of their skating group, to be known as Bill Butler and The Goodskates. Most rental shops today have a resident skating team to publicize their business, but few can boast of having a skater of Butler's prestige and experience. (Read more about Butler in the Disco chapter.)

The Goodskates has become a widely diversified company. Special events, such as an outdoor roller disco contest and a long-distance road race, the first since the late '30's, were held in Central Park in November, 1978. The Goodskates van unit transports skates to fashionable New York discotheques such as Xenon and Studio 54 for benefits and private parties. During the Christmas holiday, shoppers were startled to see skate-clad mannequins "rolling" through Macy's 34th Street windows, all of it a visual invitation to get the public into the store and up to their fourth floor roller disco boutique. The shop, which features Goodskates' skates as well as the latest disco duds is so successful that it has found a permanent home in the store.

Also, The Goodskates rental operation has franchised and Audubon Park, New Orleans, Louisiana, is the site of the second rental shop.

The Goodskates owners, Judy Lynn and Bob White, brought roller skating to New York City's Central Park, housing their operation in the tiny Mineral Springs Building.

The latest development in the story is that work has begun on Judy's most ambitious project, the Rollerballroom. Located on New York's East Side in a space that once housed a health and tennis club, the roller environment, described as a "Disneyland for adults," will include a free-form skating rink with a dance floor nestled into the center and a health food restaurant and snack bar.

"Judy never quits on an idea," says Bob White. "She has high ideals and high standards. Judy wins people over with her vision and her dream. She gets a lot of respect. We want a quality roller skating operation."

BIG CITY
ROLLERS

This article, which appeared in the New York American on April 20, 1933, points out the important difference between uptown and downtown skaters.

Outdoor skating has always been popular in the Big Apple—during the summer months in the 1950s, roller skaters took over Central Park's ice skating rink.

Roller Skates Now Nightly Craze of Greenwich Village

Greenwich Village has taken to roller skating, a fad that took a lot of society folks off Park ave. and sent them whirling about in the Central Park Mall.

But the Villagers skate differently than do their uptown neighbors. Society skates daytimes—but the Villagers skate at night. It was chilly last night, but it didn't matter. Washington Square was filled with men and women, boys and girls, all on wheels. Skating in front of buses, behind motor cars, doing fancy stuff.

The 3.2 Skating Club, organized by Eleanor Hackley, of 491 Irving pl., expects to meet nightly on rollers in Washington Square.

National Archives

In the '70s, socializing on wheels became one of New York City's hottest weekend sports.

A DAY IN THE SUN

Sharlote Hillman and her friend, Lucy Sparkman, women in their mid-fifties, who regularly skate the two-mile beachfront strip from Venice to the Santa Monica Pier, meet every Thursday morning at the Sidewalk Cafe, a popular eating spot for the roller regulars.

Sharlote, who lives in a mobile home ("my gypsy tent by the road") with her musician-husband, says that she and Lucy have known each other for years. "We couldn't live without each other and we both know it. We're both college grads, both mothers, and both creative. And, both of us are weirdos. True, we used to be normal, voting members of the PTA but now our kids are grown up and we're cutting loose—the chains that bound us at one time are no longer around."

Lucy, who lives in Sylmar, California with her husband, says, "We love the beach. It's got a free-wheeling style all its own. When we get here, we jump out of the car and cry, 'Yippee!' "

"Our husbands love us doing this," Sharlote reveals, holding up one of her white Roller Derby skates. "This gets us out of the house. We spend less money here than if we went shopping. When we first started skating, it was a parking meter to parking meter roll, but now we're good at it."

"I carry my skates in the trunk of my car," notes Lucy, "along with my bathing suit, racquet ball paddles, fishing tackle, tennis racket, and skin diving equipment."

Sharlote and Lucy pay their bill and get ready to start their long skate to Santa Monica. "Other people sit back and watch the world go by," shouts Sharlote as she skates away. "We jump right in. We don't want to be left behind."

All photos: Ann-Victoria Phillips

Lucy Sparkman, Jack Fletcher, and Sharlote Hillman strut their stuff at Venice Beach.

"I started skating about two months ago," says Jack Fletcher, a 57-year-old actor who is originally from New York. Jack skates wearing cutoffs and a straw hat and carries a small, portable radio. "Skates have changed since I was a youngster. At first, I was apprehensive and scared of the curves, but now I practice every day.

"The kids all yell, 'Hey Pop!' at me. Once a drunk screamed at me, 'Get off those things, old man,' but I whizzed by. I feel I'm healthier because of skating."

Michael Casey, who is employed as a drug rehabilitation counselor, has an unusual talent that

Frisbee master Michael Casey excels at twirling and tossing on the roll.

he developed on the Venice Beach—he plays Frisbee and roller skates at the same time. Accompanied by Tasha, his dog, Michael spends hours coordinating complicated skating footwork with sophisticated Frisbee-spinning handwork, and puts on an incredible show for the sidewalk skaters.

"I'm going to be on a Pepsi billboard and I'm getting a manager and an agent just to promote me as a roller star." Already looking like a star, Smokey wears jingle-bells on her skate shoelaces. "Roller skaters are welcome here at Venice more than any other place in the world," concludes Smokey.

Actress Smokey Grey stretching out before her skate.

All photos: Ann-Victoria Phillips

Beginning skater Danielle Alesia McClure wins friends with her roller antics.

Danielle, seven years old and the younger sister of two hot skateboard park enthusiasts, lives in Venice all year round. "I started skating when I was four years old," she said, "and have been skating at the beach every day since. This is where I meet all my friends."

"I'm trying to become a hot roller skating commodity." says Sharon "Smokey" Grey, a tall and fair-haired Venice Beach resident. "I just finished a skating scene in Cloris Leachman's new movie, *A Long Journey Back*. My producer told me I'm the hottest talent on the beach. Things are going to start happening for me."

June Kanter and Jim Marino relax with a weekend skate to Santa Monica Pier.

June Kanter, who works for a clothing designer in Marina del Rey, and Jim Marino, who works for a recreational vehicle manufacturer, have been friends for years. "I love the beach area," says Jim, who skates with June every Saturday and Sunday during the summer. "It's never dull. People let you be you."

June Kanter is in her fifties and the mother of two. She says, "Our friends sit home and watch the tube and get old. We're out here to enjoy ourselves and have fun. We like to be on the move. It's much better than lying around the pool like a blob."

"Roller skating is my greatest conditioner for skiing," says Gail Remington, a tall, 22-year-old student from Santa Monica, California. "The muscles you use and the movements are the same. When I skate, I get all kinds of ideas about what I can do on skis. When I ski, I think of roller skating and can't wait to get back here to the beach," she mused.

Gail has been skating since she was five years old. She also does jazz dancing, show-style skating, plus downhill and cross-country skiing. "Being a roller skater has affected every aspect of my life. If I buy any new clothes these days," says Gail, "I only get outfits that are suitable for skating: leotards, swim suits, and dance-style skirts."

Skater/athlete Gail Remington is a Venice Beach regular.

"A lot of people come to Venice to get away from the commercialization in L.A. Skating is a pastoral thing," says Dave DeLuca, a 27-year-old singer and guitarist who grew up in New York City. Sports involvement is nothing new to Dave. He has five years experience in karate, as well as skiing and scuba diving.

"Skating," he says, "allows you to shut off the rest of the world in a pleasant way." Dave has only been skating for three months. Typically, he has learned quickly and is already handing out tips to new skaters during the regular 4–7 PM jam sessions held on the "Skaters' Path."

"A lot of people here skate while wearing headphones," says Dave. "It loosens you up. You stop thinking about the mechanics of skating. You move with the music and just go for it. People learn very quickly this way.

"Skating is therapeutic for me," stresses Dave. "It gets my creative juices going. After skating I go home, take a shower, and go to work singing at a club. Music is my number one commitment, but sometimes I need to get away from it. After skating I feel good so it's easy to sit down for four hours and sing and feel good about myself."

Outdoor dancers Kathy Crawford and Dave DeLuca rehearse on the "Skaters' Path."

Ann-Victoria Phillips

3. SKATING FITNESS

IN PRAISE OF FITNESS AND EXERCISE

That roller skating happens to be, not only great fun, but also an extraordinarily efficient and highly rated aerobic exercise is one of the most pleasurable discoveries of this decade. Roller skating is *the* ideal exercise for anyone who wants to be fit and have a great time also.

WHAT IS FITNESS?

There is confusion about what fitness actually is. Doctors used to regard health and fitness as freedom from disease. Today, this is an outdated concept. The President's Council on Physical Fitness and Sports concluded, "Fitness is the ability to carry out daily tasks with vigor and alertness, without undue fatigue, and with ample energy to enjoy leisure time and to meet unforeseen emergencies." In other words, to have the full capacity to enjoy life and overcome its obstacles.

Experts have focused their concept of fitness into very specific categories: the first category is "organic fitness." It describes the body you were born with; your build, size, and physical makeup. The second is called "dynamic fitness." It describes what you do with that body. This is the aspect of fitness we can control and improve.

Dynamic fitness is made up of five distinct categories: muscle strength, muscle endurance,

Hector de Sylvia, an accomplished show skater, doing a split in 1916.

Helen Carlos, world famous show skater, limbering up in 1908.

flexibility, body weight distribution, and cardiovascular endurance. Muscle strength is the power to do a movement once while muscle endurance is the ability to do it over and over again without getting tired. Flexibility allows you to move your joints through a wide range of motions.

Cardiovascular fitness is the most important aspect of fitness, and probably the least understood. This is the ability of the lungs to take in oxygen and pass it along to the heart and blood vessels which distribute it throughout the body. If your cardiovascular system is inefficient, you tire easily and become exhausted by any kind of physical activity. Therefore, if you only have time to do one kind of exercise, it should be one that will contribute to your cardiovascular health.

WHAT IS EXERCISE?

Exercise is one of the most important ways to become fit. Surprisingly, national studies have shown that most people think they get exercise when they really don't. Just because you are busy at a routine job that makes you tired doesn't mean you are getting exercise. Exercise is activity that stresses a *specific* part of the body. For example, if you're on your feet and walking around on a job for eight hours a day, that activity doesn't rate as exercise. If you walk vigorously through the park for 20 minutes, it does. Routine everyday tasks are done automatically and unconsciously. Exercise, on the other hand, is never unconscious. It is purposefully focused on activity or movement for its own sake.

WHAT IS AEROBIC EXERCISE?

Dr. Kenneth H. Cooper, called the "Father of Aerobics" says, "aerobic exercises are those that stimulate the heart and lungs for long enough periods of time to cause beneficial changes in the body.'* Aerobics means "with oxygen," and what these exercises do is increase the amount of oxygen your body can process (your aerobic capacity) and so increase the efficiency of your lungs, heart, and the rest of your cardiovascular system. This "training effect" can only be achieved if you exercise strenuously and for a certain minimum period of time as well as on a regular weekly basis.

ROLLER SKATING AND AEROBICS*

Dr. Kenneth Cooper's Institute for Aerobics Research in Dallas, Texas has rated roller skating with the following system:

Roller Skating	Time	Points
Recreational, (continuous activity)	15 minutes	1
	30 minutes	2
	45 minutes	3
	60 minutes	4
Speed (vigorous activity)	15 minutes	3
	30 minutes	6
	45 minutes	9
	60 minutes	12

*Cooper, Kenneth H., "The New Aerobics," New York, Bantam Books, Inc. 1970.

Prominent DOCTORS SAY: ROLLER SKATING BUILDS *Strong Healthy Bodies*

Examples of aerobic exercises are roller skating, running, swimming, and cycling. There are many, many others—disco dancing, for example.

TRUST THE EXPERTS

Roller skating is an exercise which combines the benefits of a good work-out with fun. Dr. Max Novich, a New Jersey Orthopedic specialist who was a medical advisor to the US Olympic boxing team and is a foremost authority on sports medicine comments on roller skating:

> No other sport provides the agility along with the fun element. Most athletics are punishing and draining. In skating, the body is relaxed and the response is to music. . . . One more point—it's a life-time skill and should be utilized for this purpose. Don't lay off and you will be rewarded with a sound heart beat for a lifetime.[1]

Dr. Novich is far from alone in his view. Dr. Paul Dudley White, revered as the "Dean of American Cardiology," well known as the doctor who treated President Eisenhower, has also praised roller skating:

> I would like to put everyone on roller skates . . . not once in a while but as a routine . . . as an exercise good for the heart and arteries.[2]

And, if health weren't reason enough to take up a sport like skating, many doctors recommend it as a way to lose weight. Dr. Grant Gwuniup, Chairman of the Division of Endocrinology and Director of the Metabolic Research Laboratory at the University of California at Irvine, says:

> There is no secret to healthy weight reduction; the only real way to do it is to increase the expenditure of calories while reducing the intake of calories . . . and roller skating is one way to do it.[3]

1. "For Health's Sake," *Rinksider*, Fall, 1976.
2. "Roller Skate—Says Dr. White," *Rinksider*, Spring, 1972.
3. "Weight-Watching Sells Skating to Adults," *Rinksider*, Spring 1970.

Dr. Cooper developed an aerobic point system based on how much oxygen the body consumes while exercising. He concluded that earning a minimum of 30 points a week is most beneficial in order to achieve cardiovascular health. Further, he suggests that the total number of points should be earned during three or four exercise sessions a week on a regular basis.

POPULAR MISCONCEPTIONS ABOUT EXERCISE

People seem to dislike exercise for a variety of reasons, but the most common ones are that they've either had a bad experience with it or they've found it boring. As recently as the early '70s, physical education teachers told us that if exercise didn't hurt, we weren't working hard enough. Principles of flexibility training, including warm-ups and cool-downs, were almost unknown (which made exercising doubly painful because of resulting sore muscles).

Today coaches, doctors, and other fitness experts have changed their views on exercise so suddenly and dramatically that many people don't realize that it can be fun, no longer painful and boring. With more and more people becoming interested in fitness, it's important to clear up some popular misconceptions.

Exercise is tiring. Wrong! Exercise is an energizer, if you do it vigorously and on a regular basis.

I can become fit by exercising a few minutes a week. Wrong! A good fitness program would include choosing one or several aerobic exercises such as rope jumping, roller skating, jogging, racquet ball, downhill or cross-country skiing, and working strenuously at it for a minimum of several 15-minute periods, at least three times a week in order to become cardiovascularly efficient.

Big muscles will make me fit. Wrong! Weight lifters may have muscle strength and muscle endurance but usually no quickness, flexibility, or cardiovascular endurance.

Exercise will make me eat more. Wrong! Regular, vigorous exercise depresses appetite. You will eat less and also burn off more calories.

Exercise is dangerous for older people. Wrong! Even though body contact sports are not recommended there are a variety of other exercises that doctors do recommend such as walking, swimming, dancing and roller skating.

Vigorous exercise will give a woman bulky muscles. Wrong! Women develop long, graceful-looking muscles, similar to those of dancers.

Exercise will cause a heart attack. Wrong! If you ease into a regular program of exercise slowly and under a doctor's supervision, there is little danger of a heart attack.

I get enough exercise at home and on the job. Wrong! The days of hard physical labor are history for most Americans. Day to day activities are not exercises. Remember, for an exercise to be classified as aerobic, it must stimulate heart and lung activity for a long enough time to produce certain beneficial changes in your body and raise your heart beat. In order to benefit from a flexibility-type exercise, you must stretch specific muscles and joints. Exercises to increase strength must be comprehensive enough to stress all the primary muscle groups.

A QUICK SCOREBOARD ON 14 SPORTS AND EXERCISES

The chart below is reprinted from a pamphlet distributed by the President's Council on Physical Fitness, US Department of Health, Education and Welfare, Public Health Service. It summarizes how seven experts rated roller skating as well as other sports and exercises in relation to elements of physical fitness and general well-being. The highest rating per category is 21. Ratings are based on a minimum of four 30-minute sessions per week.

As you can see, the sport of roller skating scored one of the highest point totals.

	JOGGING	BICYCLING	SWIMMING	SKATING (ICE OR ROLLER)	HANDBALL SQUASH	SKIING-NORDIC	SKIING-ALPINE	BASKETBALL	TENNIS	CALISTHENICS	WALKING	GOLF*	SOFTBALL	BOWLING
PHYSICAL FITNESS														
CARDIORESPIRATORY ENDURANCE (STAMINA)	21	19	21	18	19	19	16	19	16	10	13	8	6	5
MUSCULAR ENDURANCE	20	18	20	17	18	19	18	17	16	13	14	8	8	5
MUSCULAR STRENGTH	17	16	14	15	15	15	15	15	14	16	11	9	7	5
FLEXIBILITY	9	9	15	13	16	14	14	13	14	19	7	8	9	7
BALANCE	17	18	12	20	17	16	21	16	16	15	8	8	7	6
GENERAL WELL-BEING														
WEIGHT CONTROL	21	20	15	17	19	17	15	19	16	12	13	6	7	5
MUSCLE DEFINITION	14	15	14	14	11	12	14	13	13	18	11	6	5	5
DIGESTION	13	12	13	11	13	12	9	10	12	11	11	7	8	7
SLEEP	16	15	16	15	12	15	12	12	11	12	14	6	7	6
TOTAL	**148**	**142**	**140**	**140**	**140**	**139**	**134**	**134**	**128**	**126**	**102**	**66***	**64**	**51**

*Ratings for golf are based on the fact that many Americans use a golf cart and/or caddy. If you walk the links, the physical fitness value moves up appreciably.

ROLLING ACES

World-class Nordic skiers Kirk Vanyan
and Glenn Terrell use roller skis to stay
in shape during the off season.

Dave Cotton,
AAU springboard
diver, shows his
winning form.

All photos: Ann-Victoria Phillips

Suzy Chaffee, former US Olympic skier,
shows off her roller skills by
demonstrating a skating cartwheel.

Ed Kindermann,
karate and judo instructor, loosens up.

WARM-UPS

In the skating world there is confusion about what the word "warm-up" means. Our warm-up is a two-part process that will fully prepare an athlete to skate. *Part one* is a series of flexibility warm-up exercises. *Part two* is the skating part of the warm-up. It consists of a minimum of ten minutes of non-strenuous skating before a hard workout.

Warm-up flexibility exercises are good for many reasons. First, they ready your muscles for action by speeding up the flow of warm, oxygenated blood. Second, warm-ups slowly stretch the muscles you will exercise, thereby preventing injuries like muscle strains, pulls, and soreness. Third, warm-ups improve your performance because you are relaxed and your muscles loose and pliable. After warming up, both you and your body are ready to work out.

BEFORE SKATING

Flexibility exercises should be done just before you skate. For the beginner, it is wise that they be done *off skates*. Indoor skaters can do exercises in a corner of the rink, away from busy traffic on the floor. Outdoor skaters, like joggers, can stretch out anywhere.

Reach for the Sun

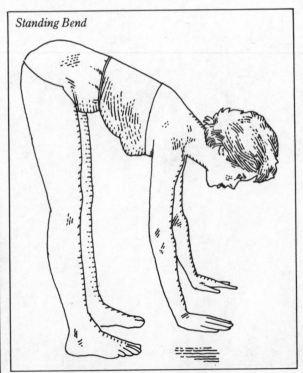

Standing Bend

Everyone's body is different. Some people are loose to begin with and improve their flexibility very quickly through exercise. Others take more time. A person's degree of flexibility is an individual thing, but no matter how stiff or loose your are when you start, stretch the muscles *slowly* and continuously until you feel a strong pull. Don't strain. Never bounce. Try stretching a bit further on each successive day.

FLEXIBILITY WARM-UP EXERCISES

1. Reach for the Sun: Stand with your feet parallel and apart. Raise your hands over your head and stretch upward, first with the right arm and then with the left as if reaching for the sun. Feel your entire torso stretch. Keep your spine straight. Stretch five times with your right arm and five with your left, holding each stretch for a minimum of ten seconds on each side.

2. Standing Bend (like Toe Touching): Stand with your feet parallel and shoulder width.

Bend over as if you were going to touch your toes, letting gravity pull you down. Drop down slowly. Don't strain to touch the floor. If you are flexible enough to touch the floor, don't, just cross your arms and hang loosely. Hold the posture between 10 and 30 seconds. Remember, don't bounce. Breathe deeply into your lower abdomen, exhale, and breathe deeply again. Just hang. You only need to do this once. Come up slowly.

3. Side Bend: Stand upright with your hands resting at your sides and your feet parallel and apart. Without bending your knees or leaning forward, bend to the right. As you bend, let your right hand slide down your leg while your left hand slides up. Stretch and hold five times each side.

4. Upper Body Twist: Stand upright with your feet parallel and apart. Hold your arms

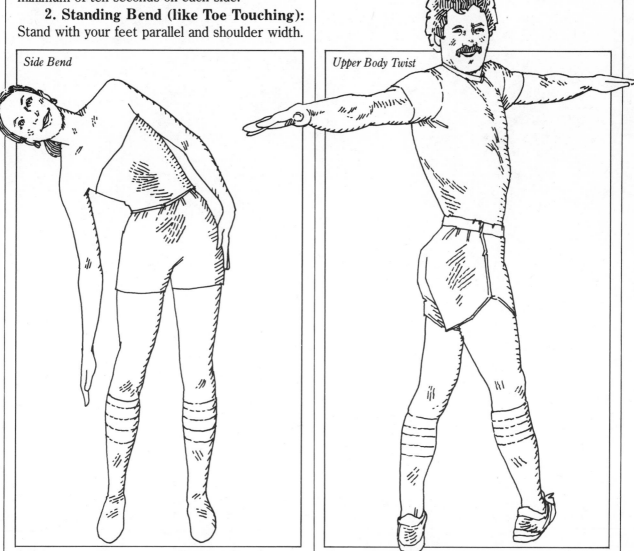

Side Bend

Upper Body Twist

straight out from your sides at shoulder height. Twist your upper torso to the right while keeping your feel parallel. Repeat to the left. Do this exercise slowly, 10 times each side.

5. Calf Stretch (also called the Wall Push-up): Stand about three feet away from a wall (if outdoors you can use a tree). Put your palms on the wall about shoulder height. Bend your elbows and lean forward, keeping your back and legs straight and your heels on the ground. Put pressure on your heels letting them sink into the ground until you feel a strong pull. Hold this posture from 30 seconds to two minutes. You only need to do this exercise once. Variation: place one foot forward bending it at the knee. Keep your rear leg straight. Alternate right and left legs.

6. Ankle Rotation: This exercise can be done either in a sitting or standing position. Extend your right leg forward, bending it comfortably at the knee. Point the toe of your right foot and rotate the entire foot at the ankle, first in a full circle clockwise and then counterclockwise. Do 12 rotations in each direction. Repeat the same exercise with your left ankle.

7. Hamstring Stretch: Standing upright, lift the left leg up to waist height (or higher), resting your heel on a bench, fence, or railing. Keep your supporting leg slightly bent at the knee. Allow your upper torso and head to sink down slowly toward your raised knee. Don't strain. Don't bounce. Let gravity pull you down. Hold this posture at least 20-60 seconds depend-

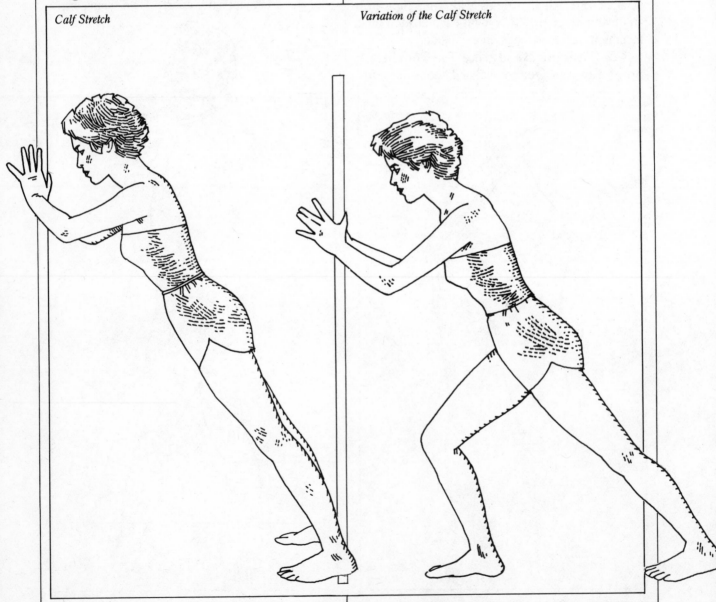

Calf Stretch

Variation of the Calf Stretch

ing on how flexible you are. Repeat the exercise with your other leg.

COOLING-DOWN AFTER SKATING

Cool-down exercises are warm-ups in reverse. After a strenuous skating workout, it is necessary to bring your heart and respiration rate back down slowly to prevent chilling, cramps, and light-headedness. These discomforts are due to an excess of blood collecting in the muscles and veins when you stop doing a vigorous activity too suddenly. Cool-down exercises allow your heart rate to slow down gradually.

Another reason to do cool-down exercises is to retain all the good effects you've accumulated during the warm-up period and while skating.

When you're finished skating, don't stop suddenly. Your cool-down period, like the warm-up, is done in two parts. *First*, gradually change from vigorous skating to non-strenuous skating. This period should last a minimum of ten minutes.

In the second phase of your cool-down, shake out your arms and legs, starting with the extremities. Start with your fingers, and work back to the shoulders. Then shake out your toes and feet and then your entire leg. Next, do warm-up exercises numbers 2 through 5 for the second time.

Ankle Rotation

Hamstring Stretch

MAREN TALBOT: EXERSKATER

With exercise, the name of the game is enjoyment—to get turned on," says Maren Talbot, a Los Angeles-based, YWCA fitness expert and the first person in the United States to teach outdoor roller skating as a means of achieving cardiovascular health. She calls her class "ExerSkating" and defines it as "a combination of traditional fitness exercises and aerobic roller skating."

Although the word "ExerSkating" may have been used before, Maren takes the concept seriously and has developed it into a systematic program. The ExerSkating class, first organized in July 1978, is held at Venice Beach every Tuesday and Thursday morning at 11 AM. The idea for the class evolved from Maren's personal love of sports and fitness, particularly jogging, skating, and weight-training. Her choice of professional career reflects these interests and her philosophy. The theme of the class is that "exercise is one of life's great pleasures. It shouldn't be drudgery. If people find a sport they like, they'll stick with it."

Maren Talbot does a Shoot the Duck as a strength exercise.

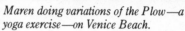

Maren doing variations of the Plow—a yoga exercise—on Venice Beach.

Maren presents roller skating to her students in such a beautifully packaged form, how could anyone resist? First, she appropriately chose Venice Beach as the site of the first ExerSkating class. Venice is the southern Californian community where the most recent revival of the outdoor craze was born. The beach is also one of the most beautiful and fascinating skating environments in the United States. With the snow-capped San Bernadino Mountains on one side and the Pacific Ocean on the other, it's not hard to like exercise. Santa Ana winds, fresh and invigorating, sweep across the beach. Roller skaters can practice and get a suntan at the same time.

Another part of the appeal of the class is the instructor's personal style. Maren, tanned, tall and lean as a bean, is dressed in a white leotard and shorts, white socks woven with glittering silver and gold threads and a white satin cap. Her roller skates, royal blue suede with matching wheels and toe straps, are luminescent. Around her shoulders and across her hip is a blue satin disco bag where she stores her car keys. Maren's presence and appearance is her own best adver-

WHAT IS EXERSKATING?

Roller skating is an ideal exercise—it's one of the few activities that you can do regularly, strenuously, and still have fun. ExerSkating is skating for cardiovascular fitness. While recreational roller skating provides a person with a moderate amount of exercise, it cannot be classified as aerobic unless the skating is vigorous and done in at least several 15 minute periods for a minimum of two to three days a week on a regular basis. Try alternating periods of vigorous skating with those of normal recreational skating. Rest periods are allowed and, in fact, advised.

Disco rinks featuring action twice as fast as those of ordinary session skating are a good place to achieve the ExerSkating effect. Adult dance classes which feature traditional dances, such as tangoes, waltzes, and foxtrots, are also good, provided that the skating is vigorous and continuous.

Speed skating is another obvious choice whether you do it through a club or on your own.

Lastly, outdoor skating provides an excellent opportunity to ExerSkate. To maximize the benefits, plan ahead of time. Like a jogger, set a course for yourself, deciding how many miles you want to cover, as well as your starting and finishing points. At first, skate short distances for short periods of time and gradually increase both. Once rolling, move along at a fast, steady pace, being sure to skate up all hills.

tisement. Maren attended the University of California at Berkeley, getting a BA in education and a Master's degree in painting. After teaching in New York for seven years, she decided to boost her educational credentials in fitness and sports, and returned to California to attend UCLA and Santa Monica City College. Maren has worked as an instructor and Program Director at the West Los Angeles branch of the YWCA since early 1978. In this position, she is able to call upon all her creative and innovative abilities, creating classes, like ExerSkating, that are new and that she personally believes in.

Maren is sure that "a person's appearance is a sign of what's going on inside." As well as serving as a good role model for other people who want to improve their chances of achieving a fulfilling,

happy, and healthy life, Maren nourishes her own physical and spiritual needs: "I'm interested in how I'll look when I'm 80 years old," she says. "Will I stand up straight? I'm quite sure I'll look good and have the body and the spirit of a young person."

At 11 o'clock, Maren rounds up her class and steers them toward the Venice Pavilion. This Parks Department building is near the "Skater's Path," an area away from the quickly moving bicyclists that is specially reserved for skaters. There, she reviews roller basics and flexibility exercises. The beach, usually wall-to-wall on the weekends, is quiet during the week. Solitary skaters and Frisbee players dot the sidewalks near the practice area but don't interfere.

One of Maren's ExerSkating students, Judy, had roller skated, like most, when she was young but felt she wasn't successfully picking it up again as an adult. "I brought my kids here to the beach a few weeks ago, and they were embarrassed to skate with me, so I'm taking the class to surprise them."

Bud, who lives a fifteen-minute skate away in Marina del Rey, teaches music at UCLA and has some free time during the day. "I do yoga, ski, and have tried every other sport. Frankly, I was curious about skating."

Margie, the mother of a nine-year-old skating dynamo named Lisa says, "I got the class as a birthday present from a friend but I'm really here because I want to skate with my daughter. I usually take dance lessons. Now, I want something different."

"Is it time for the palm trees?" asks Kevin, a friend of Maren's who is as fitness-oriented as she. Working out on the palm trees is the part of the class that Maren is famous for. "We stand around the trees like spokes on a wheel, using the trunks for support," describes Maren, who does all the exercises along with her students. She starts out with yoga-style flexibility exercises and moves along through leg lifts, a hand-to-foot stretch, wall push-ups (what joggers do to warm-up) and side bends. Although the ExerSkaters are working out in their skates (usually not recommended for beginners), they are anchored by the grass. That prevents their wheels from sliding out from under them until their balance improves.

One interesting benefit of doing exercises in skates is that the three pound weight of the skate

Maren's ExerSkating class prefers the out-of-doors approach to staying in shape, using a handy Venice palm tree for support.

acts as a leg weight. "When the leg is raised, either forward, or to the side, the resistance from the weight will trim and strengthen calf and thigh muscles," according to Maren.

The strange palm tree scene attracts a lot of attention at the beach. Venice residents, a mixed group of painters, poets, show business people, and other professionals, have seen so many strange happenings throughout the '50s and the '60s that it takes a unique event to stimulate their interest. Maren reports that beach regulars "were astonished by the sight of her class. People thought we were involved in some new counter-culture religion: The Palm Tree Worshippers." Another man had stopped by and watched the group for a few minutes informing them, "You'll never get the tree off the ground that way!"

Exercise around the tree looks both fun and challenging at the same time. "They laugh, they groan, and they fall over, but what we're doing firms the whole body, especially your behind," says Maren.

The ExerSkating class is now warmed up for their mile-long skate up the beachfront sidewalk toward Santa Monica Pier. The class will skate as a group, with Maren's encouragement, and return about 20 minutes later. "Skating is heavy thigh work," says Maren, "and that's good for you. Longer distances are easier on roller skates. A three-mile skate is really nothing, while a three-mile jog is a heavy workout.

"Skating is a good aerobic exercise for people who have trouble with their knees and ankles from jogging, as well as being an alternative for those people who jog to gain cardiovascular health, but don't really enjoy it."

Both a jogger and a skater, Maren has praise for the sports but concludes, "if I had to pick between the two, I'd take skating and have a lot more fun for the hour of exercise."

Ann-Victoria Phillips

Student Smokey Grey and teacher Maren Talbot use the Arabesque as an extension exercise.

4. BASIC SKATING
LESSONS: PART I

TECHNIQUES FOR THE BEGINNER

Most beginners try to learn by continuing their normal walking motion while on skates. Walking on roller skates will cause your rear, push-off leg to slide out behind you and you will lose your balance. Skating is much different from walking. It's a push-off and glide sequence, first on your left foot, and then on your right. The push-off must be done with enough force to obtain the longest possible glide.

Part of learning is falling—this woman has taken precautionary measures.

FOLLOW-THROUGH

Most athletes must train to improve their follow-through. This follow-through motion is also important in skating. Make sure you use your entire leg while pushing off, not just the part from the knee down.

Tips on style when learning how to skate:

● Relax, Relax, Relax! This cannot be overemphasized. A flowing, graceful look—the essence of good skating—can only be achieved when you're loose and relaxed.

- Hold your arms out from your sides in an extended graceful position while skating. This makes you look good and also helps you maintain your balance.

- Keep your knees *slightly* bent, at least while you are learning to skate. This will also help your balance.

WHERE TO PRACTICE YOUR SKATING LESSONS

Indoors: Any very smooth surface is a good place. A school gym (urethane wheels only) or even your house or apartment will do, but your local skating rink is probably your best practice area. The smoother your skating surface, the easier it is to learn.

Outdoors: After you have mastered the basic skills and feel confident, practice cautiously outside. Be prepared to maneuver around the cracked sidewalks, branches, twigs, and stones which you may find in your way. Knowing how to stop is a prerequisite for controlling your speed down hills and avoiding joggers, cyclists, pedestrians, and other skaters.

Practice away from traffic. Wear old clothes and protective gear, such as elbow and knee pads and a pair of heavy leather gloves—the most essential piece of gear for the novice and the veteran alike.

LESSON 1

FORWARD SKATING

First learn the forward scissors sequence. This movement is gliding by transferring pressure from the inside to the outside of your skates. With the scissors sequence, you can learn to skate forward and, at the same time, keep both skates in contact with the floor. This gliding exercise will also increase your skill while strengthening your leg muscles. You should feel a slight pull in your legs while doing this exercise. If you don't, then you're not doing it correctly or not working hard enough.

How to do the forward scissors sequence:

1. Start by standing with your heels together and your toes slightly turned out (A).

2. Put pressure on the inside edges of your skates and push outward until your skates move comfortably apart (B).

3. Next, put pressure on the outside edges of your skates to draw them back together again (C). Don't let your skates come too close together at any point or you'll trip.

4. Repeat this sequence from the beginning. To increase your speed, quicken your in-and-out movements.

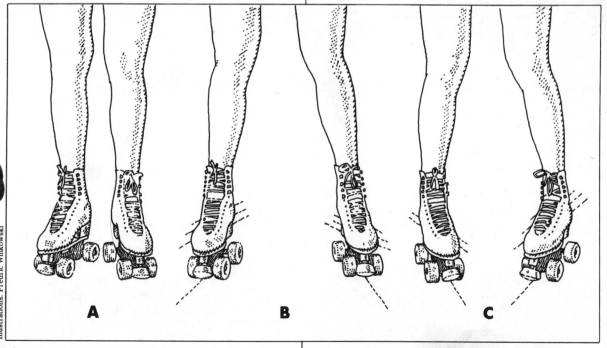

Illustrations: Fredric Winkowski

A   B   C

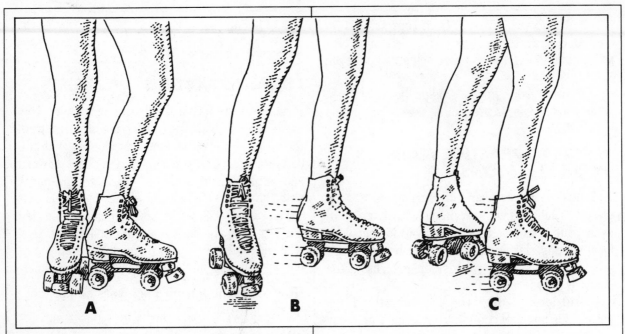

A   B   C

Now that you can skate forward, you're ready to try gliding forward on one foot at a time in a straight line. This is also an exercise to improve your balance.

How to do a one-foot glide in a straight line:

1. To start, place your skates in the "T" position, left skate in front, right behind (A). Push off with your right skate, using your inside front and back wheels.

2. Slowly shift your weight onto your left leg (supporting leg) and lift your right leg (free leg) directly behind you and a few inches off the floor (B). Glide forward as long as possible.

3. Place your free foot back onto the floor and push off (C). Glide on the right leg.

4. Once your balance has improved, increase the length of your glide, first on your left foot, then on your right.

Tips on style:

• Keep your arms extended out from your sides to help you maintain balance.

• As you end each forward glide, you'll automatically straighten your supporting leg. Re-bend your knees slightly before transferring your weight from side to side.

• Even though this is a basic skating movement, you have to have good balance to glide on one foot. It will take time and practice to do this and make it look smooth.

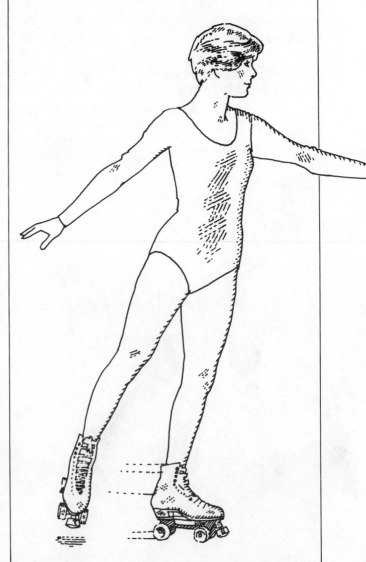

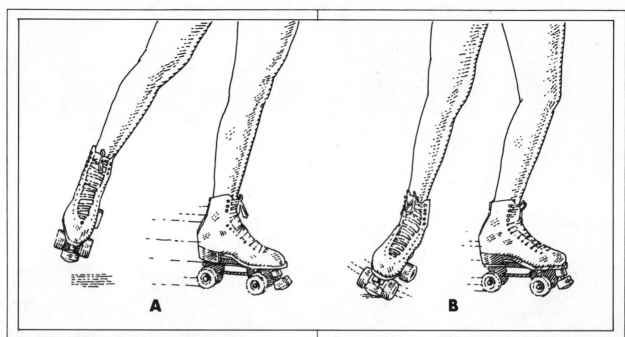

A

B

LESSON 2

HOW TO STOP
(while skating forward)

The T-stop is the only method recommended for the beginner. Although there are several other methods for stopping, the T-stop is the simplest, most effective, and safest. Inexperienced skaters sometimes try to stop by dragging the toe-stop of one skate behind them. This is incorrect technique. Coaches suggest that beginners should learn to skate without using the toe-stops at all because they only become a crutch.

How to stop:

　　1. Glide forward on one foot. Bring your free foot behind the heel of your supporting leg into the "T" position (A).

　　2. Lower your free skate to the floor maintaining the "T" position. (B)

　　3. While keeping your skate wheels perpendicular to the ground, *gently press* your free skate to the floor and brake to a stop (C).

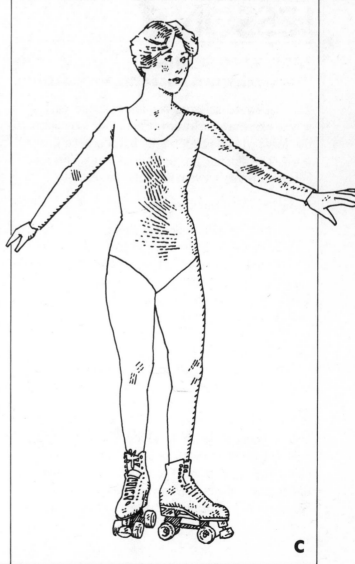

C

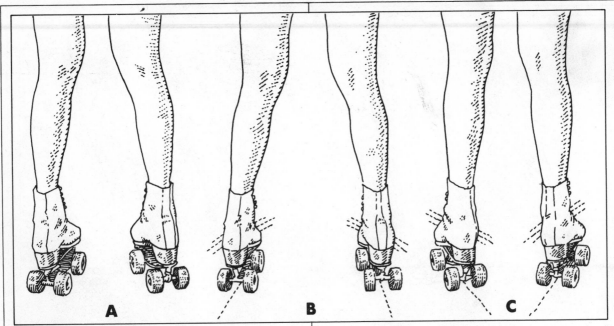

A   B   C

LESSON 3

BACKWARD SKATING
(the backward scissors sequence)

The backward scissors sequence is the easiest way to skate in a backward direction. It's similar to the forward scissors except that it's done backward. The starting position of the feet is different but the scissors movement is the same.

How to skate backward:

    1. Stand with your feet slightly apart, with your skates in a slightly pigeon-toed stance (A).

    2. Push off backward while keeping your knees slightly bent (B). Push outward with both feet.

    3. When you have traveled a short distance, draw your skates back inward (C). Don't bring them too close together or you'll trip.

    4. Without slowing down, begin the sequence again.

Tips on style:

    ● You can learn to skate backward more quickly by working with a friend. Have the person skate forward in front of you with his or her hands under your elbows to help you keep your balance. Skate backward using your friend as a support.

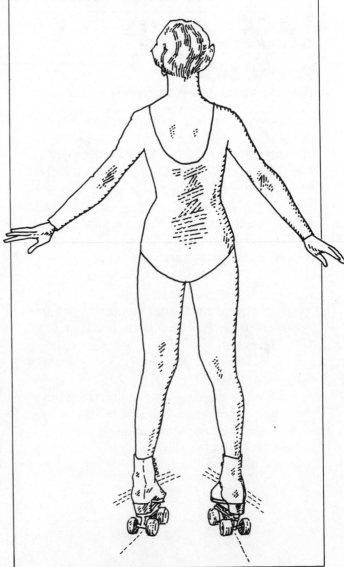

Now that you can skate backward, you're ready to try gliding backward in a straight line. *Important*: practice the backward glide indoors and on a smooth surface.

How to do a one-foot glide while skating backward:

1. To start, stand with your feet comfortably apart, in a slightly pigeon-toed stance (A).

2. Push off by putting pressure on the inside edge of your left skate, and, at the same time, glide backward on your right skate. Straighten your left leg so it's extended forward (B).

3. Bring your left foot (free foot) alongside . . .

4. . . . and start pushing off from your right foot *as* you place your left foot down (C).

5. Straighten your right knee as you finish and push and extend your right foot in front of you as you glide backward on your left skate. Repeat the sequence from the beginning.

Tips on style:

● Keep your arms extended out from your sides to help maintain balance.

● As you end each backward glide, you'll automatically straighten your supporting leg. Re-bend your knees slightly before transferring your weight from side to side.

● The One-Foot Glide is a basic skating movement, but good balance is still a prerequisite. You may find it helpful to practice with a friend.

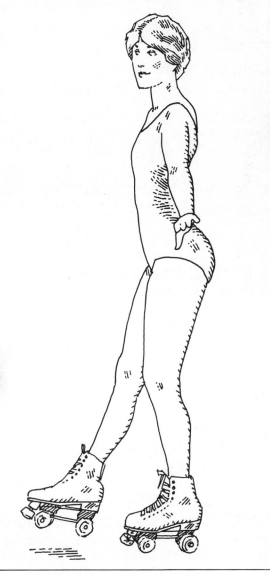

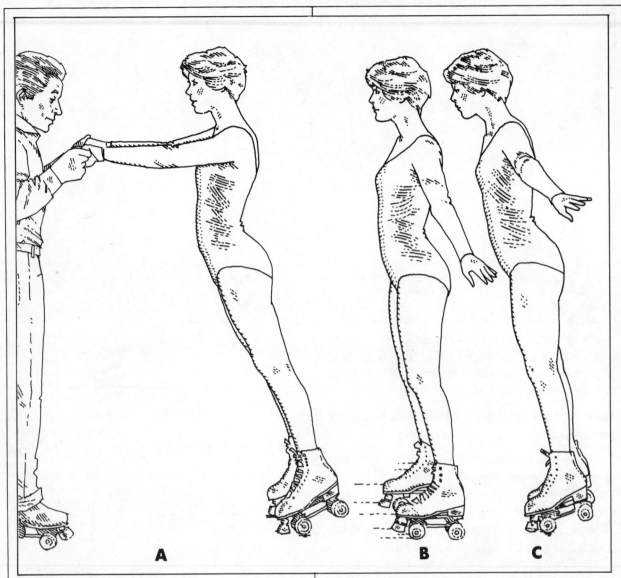

A   B   C

LESSON 4

HOW TO STOP
(while skating backward)

The backward style of stopping is very, very different from the T-stop you learned in Lesson 2. For this stop, while skating backward, you will simultaneously rise up on both skates' toe-stops, much like a ballet dancer "on point," in order to come to an immediate halt. Make sure you lean forward slightly to maintain your balance.

How to do the backward stop:

   1. First, practice at a standstill by having a friend hold your hands and balance you as you rise up on your toe-stops (A).

   2. Practice the stop with the help of a friend, this time while you're rolling. Skate backward while your friend skates forward. Hold hands to help you keep your balance. Bring your skates together in a parallel position and rock up on the toe-stops to come to an immediate halt.

   3. Practice this stop on your own (B and C).

A

B

C

LESSON 5

HOW TO FALL
(and get up laughing)

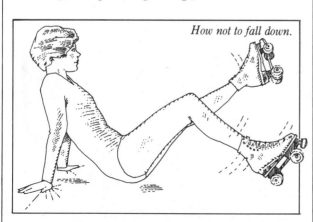

How not to fall down.

Everyone takes a spill once in a while. The thing to remember is to resist using your hands and arms to break your fall. If you feel yourself slipping, never tense up. Try to relax as you fall and your body should easily absorb the impact.

How to fall:

As you fall, let your knees bend. Avoid falling on your limbs (A). It helps to first practice falling off-skates to get used to the feeling.

How to get up after a fall:

1. Roll over onto your hands and knees while facing oncoming traffic (B).
2. Rise from the floor, one skate at a time.
3. Gently stand up (C).

LESSON 6

TWO-FOOT GLIDE ON A CURVE
(understanding body lean)

This two-footed gliding exercise looks similar to a slalom movement used in skiing. This glide is an introduction to learning how to skate on a curve.

How to do the two-foot glide on a curve:

1. Glide forward (A) and while keeping all eight wheels on the floor transfer your body weight, either to the right (B) or left (C), depending on the direction you want to curve.

2. Practice curving to the right and to the left. Your skates will trace a serpentine pattern on the floor. Body lean is the key to mastering this exercise. The more you lean, the sharper you'll curve.

A

B

C

LESSON 7

ONE-FOOT GLIDE ON A CURVE (understanding edges)

An edge is a curve pattern your skate traces on the floor. You learned in Lesson 6 that you can cause your skates to turn by shifting your weight (body lean) from side to side. This shift in weight plus body lean causes your skate wheels to arch out in a curve either to the left or to the right.

Learning to edge is an important skating skill because all basic figure, freestyle, and dance movements depend on knowing on which skate to glide forward or backward, and also which side of the skate to put the pressure on while you are in motion.

Later on, we will use abbreviations when explaining which specific edges are to be used while learning basic skating movements.

The four edges used when skating on the right foot are:

ROF: right foot skating forward on the outside edge

RIF: right foot skating forward on the inside edge

ROB: right foot skating backward on the outside edge

RIB: right foot skating backward on the inside edge

The four edges used while skating on the left foot are:

LOF: left foot skating forward on the outside edge

LIF: left foot skating forward on the inside edge

LOB: left foot skating backward on the outside edge

LIB: left foot skating backward on the inside edge

How to make left and right inner and outer forward edges while skating on one foot:

1. Start by gliding forward on your left leg. While keeping your balance, put pressure onto the

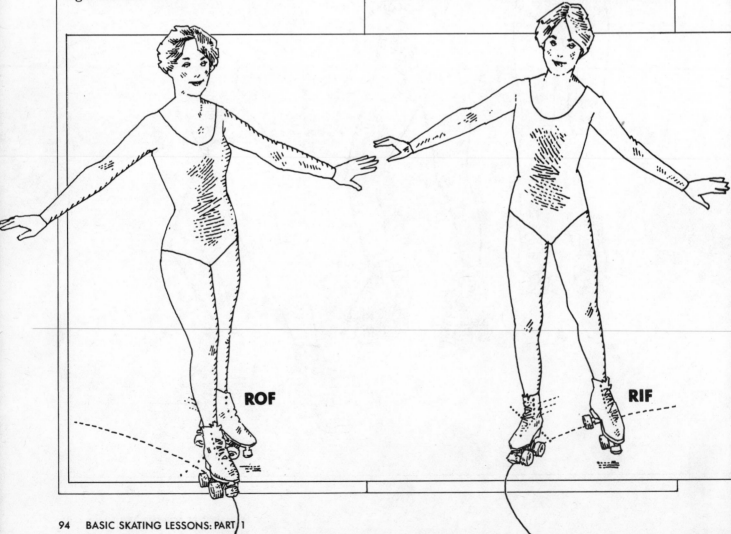

ROF

RIF

inside edge of your employed skate (LIF). You will curve to the right.

2. Next, glide forward on your right leg. Put pressure on the inside edge just as you did in Step 1. You will curve to the left. You've just learned how to do both the LIF and the RIF edges.

3. The outside forward edges are next. Skate forward on your left leg and put pressure on the outside edge of your skate (LOF). You will curve to the left.

4. Next, skate forward on your right leg while putting pressure on the outside edge of your skate (ROF). You will curve to the right. You've just learned your fourth edge used while skating in a forward direction.

Tips on style:

● Keep your arms out from your sides about waist height with your employed shoulder forward and your free shoulder back.

● Hold your hands and fingers in an attractive, graceful position, not clenched or spread.

● Hold your body erect as you edge, never stiff.

● Bend your employed leg slightly, at first, to help maintain balance. Later, as your skill improves, keep it straight.

● Keep your weight centered over the middle of your employed skate.

● Keep your free leg extended in a graceful position, with your toe pointed down and turned out.

● Stay relaxed. Your goal is to be natural-looking. Avoid stiff, angular, and unnatural looking positions. Shoot for smooth and flowing movements.

● Your skate boot should fit snugly in order for you to "feel" your edges. Your heel should not move up and down inside your skate boot. The "truck action" (see Chapter 14 to learn to adjust truck action) of your skate must be flexible in order to learn edges. Ask the skate mechanic at your rink or rental shop to show you how to adjust the action on your skates.

● Learning to edge takes time, practice, and patience. As your balance improves, first on two skates and then on one, edging will be easier.

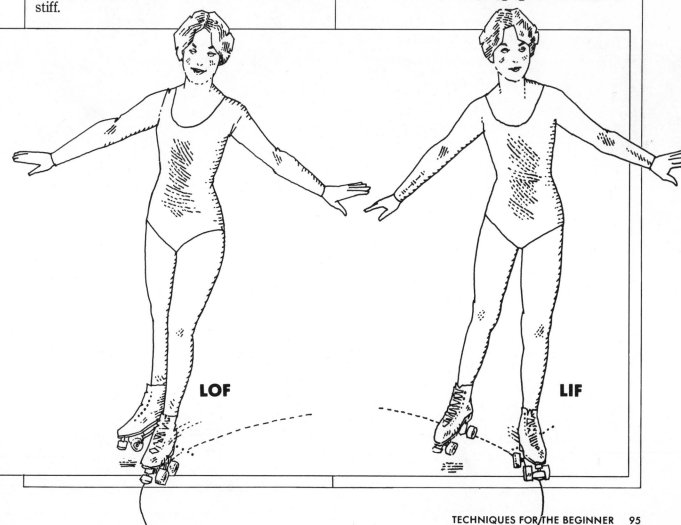

LOF   LIF

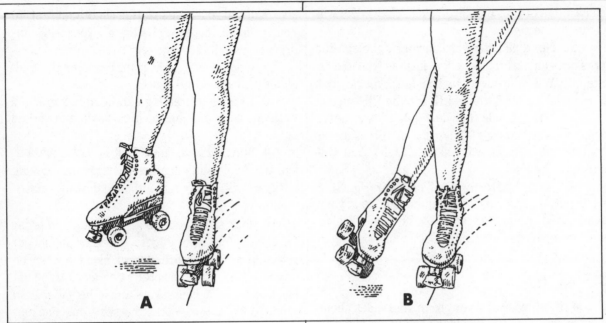

A   B

LESSON 8

FORWARD CROSSOVERS

This is a more advanced way of turning a corner while skating forward in a counterclockwise direction.

How to do forward crossovers:

1. Push off on your LOF edge (A).
2. With your knees bent, bring your right foot forward across your left, while at the same time, push under (behind) your right foot with your left. This is accomplished by straightening the left knee (B).
3. Bring your left foot alongside and begin the sequence again. Repeat as many times as necessary to complete the corner.

Tips on style:

- Keep your right knee bent slightly as you crossover to improve your balance.
- Because rink traffic during open sessions moves in a counterclockwise direction, the beginner skater will usually learn forward crossovers to the left only. Aim to learn crossovers to the right also. If necessary, take group classes and avoid crowded sessions. Then you can practice forward crossovers in both directions. Advanced freestyle and dance movements all require that you be able to crossover to the left and also to the right.

- It's easiest to learn crossovers on a smooth, clean skating surface like a rink floor. Once you've learned them indoors, try crossing over outdoors on a smooth surface.

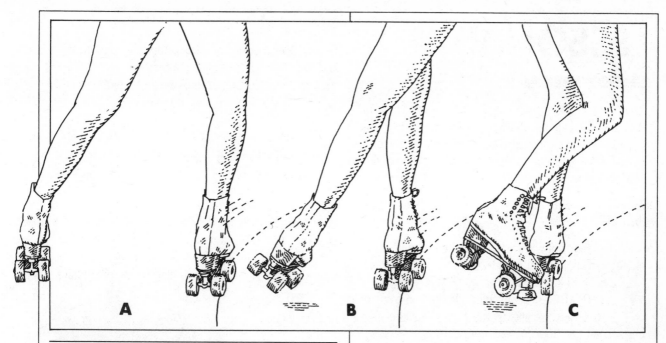

A   B   C

LESSON 9

BACKWARD CROSSOVERS

Backward crossovers are a more advanced way of turning a corner while skating backward in a counterclockwise direction.

How to do backward crossovers:

1. Push off on your ROB edge (A).

2. Bring your left leg back across the front of your right leg while keeping the right side of your body leading and the left side trailing (B and C).

3. Now push from the LIF edge to the ROB edge and start the movement again by cutting under the left foot with your right and crossing over the right foot with your left.

Tips on Style:

● Backward skating is difficult to practice during rink sessions because many rinks don't allow backward skating at all. Consider taking a group class in order to learn this basic skating skill. Then there will be less traffic on the floor.

● Backward crossovers, just like the forward ones, should be practiced in clockwise as well as counterclockwise directions. Both are necessary to learn advanced freestyle and dance movements.

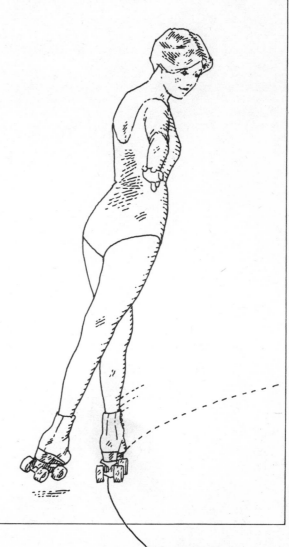

LESSON 10

SHOOT THE DUCK

Shoot the Duck is a good exercise to improve your balance as well as a stunt to show off to your friends. You have to have strong stomach muscles in order to Shoot the Duck. If you're overweight, skip this lesson.

How to do The Dip (stage one of Shoot the Duck):

1. Glide forward in a straight line with both skates parallel and alongside (A).

2. Do a deep knee bend as you are gliding forward (B). Extend your arms directly in front of you. Keep them parallel to the floor. You'll be gliding across the floor in a sitting position.

Tips on Style:

● Keep your head up with your back straight and your weight slightly forward.

● Avoid letting your ankles wobble in or out.

How to Shoot the Duck:

Once you're comfortable in the dip position you're ready to learn to Shoot the Duck.

3. Begin by gliding forward in The Dip position. Extend one leg straight out in front of you. If you have a hard time keeping your balance, hold your extended leg off the floor with both hands (C). Don't let the extended skate touch the floor. Practice Shoot the Duck by first skating on your left leg, then on your right. You can also do it rolling backwards.

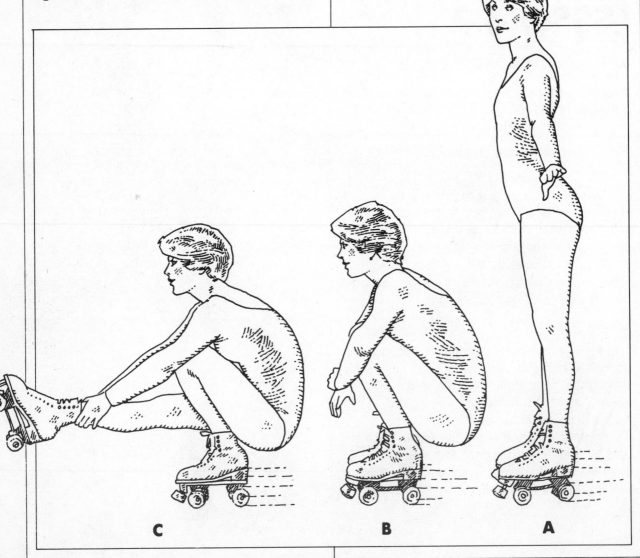

C   B   A

5. ROLLER DISCO

WHAT IS ROLLER DISCO?

From Los Angeles to Brooklyn, Miami to Detroit—just fill in the places in between—skaters are rolling to the disco beat. It seems like such a natural combination that to many it's no surprise.

In its most popular form, roller disco is a very loose, non-technical style similar to disco dancing. It expresses each skater's interpretation of the music. In its purest form, roller disco is a derivation of a style of skating that's been popular among black people for decades. There are steps, but technique is nowhere near as important as it is with artistic skating.

Skating to popular music is nothing new. It's been a regular feature at rinks, especially in the Midwest, since the '30s when hits were played on the organ. But black skaters were jamming—not waltzing—to blues, swing, rhythm and blues, soul, and now disco. The last of these provided the perfect combination of mood and beat for roller dancing. The result of this fabulous mix—roller disco—has won over skaters all around the world.

Roller skating made the bigtime with the introduction of disco music to the traditional rink scene.

All photos: Ann-Victoria Phillips

ROLLER DISCO STYLES OF SKATING

Roller disco classes are starting up throughout the United States, but the whole phenomenon is still so new that, thus far, few styles have gone national. If you do give roller disco a try, here are a few of the styles you'll see.

Doing the bounce—the basic movement of disco skating.

The Bounce Step: This is simply the most basic, natural, and popular way to skate to disco music while keeping time to the beat. It's something everyone can do, once they've mastered the basic skating stroke. Glide forward, bending your leg slightly at the knee in time with the beat of the music. It looks as though you're bouncing up and down, and that's how this simple style got its name.

The Bounce is so easy, most skaters can manage it their first time out. Just watch other skaters and you'll pick up the beat. It's relaxing and fun.

Roller Acrobatics: As the more experienced skaters roll by you, you'll notice them doing radical acrobatics on skates, all without missing a beat. High kicks, split kicks, full splits, half splits, heel splits, and heel and toe splits are only a few of the maneuvers.

The Line Dance: This looks just like a descendent of the '50s style strolls and hand jives, except on wheels. The modern day version features a line of skaters performing intricate steps all in unison. The Line Dance looks just like disco dancing's version of the "Bus Stop."

Fleurette Arseneault and Dan Littel, roller skating's 1978 World Champions in International Dance, bopping at Xenon—a Manhattan discotheque.

Bopping: Both this form and the Line Dance are styles of *dancing* on skates as opposed to *skating* on skates. The Bop looks like the jitterbug, the lindy, or rock 'n' roll (depending on whether you grew up in the '40s, '50s, or '60s). Usually danced by couples, this Bop is performed in the center of the rink or the dance floor so as not to interfere with the flow of traffic.

Rexing: This is seen only on the West Coast, where it is performed in both official competition and, informally, in hundreds of the states' rinks.

Rexing steps are skated in a *backward direction only*. Backward skating of the more ordinary variety, popular in roller discos all over the United States, is considered an intimate style, a way to skate with the one you love.

Jammin': Bill Butler, king of roller disco in New York, has designed an advanced skating style he calls "Jammin'." Jammin' is a product of different sources—a bit of artistic skating, some from styles developed in black rinks, and other movements that are so unique that they only can be called a product of Bill's rich imagination. Bill's style is improvisational yet has a firm foundation in technique. Popular in the east and in the Midwest, this style is the kind of roller disco you're most likely to see today.

DISCO SKATING AS EXERCISE

Disco skating can be an extremely vigorous cardiovascular, as well as athletic, exercise that will develop more aspects of total body fitness than other roller sports. Disco rollers are on the move almost continuously for hours at a time. In addition, just skating in time with the disco beat in-

Chic Skates—the party people on wheels.

All photos: Ann-Victoria Phillips

THE MUSIC

spires extra speed, while the particular way the skater interprets this music stylistically (more upper body movement than is generally seen in regular roller skating plus steps that require unusual flexibility and strength in the legs) produces an unusually fit skater.

For the beginner disco skater, flexibility warm-up exercises are recommended for preventing day-after aches. In addition, you will find it is easier to keep your balance while skating if your body is loose and relaxed. Warm-ups will help keep you limber as well as increase your potential range of movement, all without causing muscle

First you find yourself snapping your fingers, then your body begins to move to the beat, and, in no time, you're on your feet dancing. When you roller skate to disco music, it becomes even more seductive and irresistable. The already hypnotic stroke-glide flow of skating combines with the disco beat and creates a super-natural vibration. Some have called the unusual atmosphere of the roller disco club a type of "tribal cooperation." Others have described the effect on the individual skater as "hypnotic meditation." Whatever it is, one thing is for sure—fears and anxieties are thrown to the winds in order to experience a relaxing and natural high.

While the disco beat keeps people moving together with a certain predictability, most skaters develop their own personal style. Because the way skaters interpret music is basically improvisational, movements are as personal as a signature. But, unlike dancers at a discotheque, all skaters look sensuous and graceful on the roll, even if they're awkward and self-conscious off skates.

strains or soreness. (See Chapter 3 for an explanation of the warm-up and cool-down sequence.)

PROCEDURES AND PRICES AT ROLLER DISCO SESSIONS

Prices vary from rink to rink from 2 dollars to 4 dollars for a four-hour skating session. Skate rental is included. Skating costumes range from casual to glamorous. If you're in doubt about what to wear, phone ahead.

The one item you should take along is a pair of heavy cotton socks. Rental skates may not fit your feet as perfectly as your shoes.

Of course, if you haven't gone skating since you were a kid, take it easy. First practice by rolling along the edge of the floor until you've got your skating legs.

Remember, disco sessions feature fast skating. True, it's exciting, but you might gain confidence more quickly by skating at first either during a slower weeknight session or during a regular day session.

All photos: Ann-Victoria Philips

ROLLING THE NIGHT AWAY

Chances are that if you love disco music and want to get in on the latest roller skating craze, roller disco will be your first choice. If so, be prepared for some pleasant surprises.

If you haven't roller skated since you were eight years old, you'll be amazed to see changes in the skating environment. True, most disco skating is still done in the rink, but today roller discotheques are being built in former warehouses, gymnasiums, or bowling alleys—in short, *anywhere* a builder can lay a hardwood floor.

Both the avid disco dancer and the traditional skater are likely to find the unexpected at a roller disco rink or club. For one thing, dancers will find that it's difficult to duplicate on wheels the steps

they are used to doing, and traditional skaters will find a whole different rhythm and flow in roller disco.

ROLLER DISCO VS DANCING DISCO

Contrasting the typical disco dancing scene with that of roller disco helps to pinpoint the differences more precisely. An urban disco club can be an individual's narcissistic, costumed, orgiastic quest for an alternative identity. You can spend many whole evenings in a dance discotheque and never really meet anyone—anonymous escape can be appealing. You choose a regular disco club for its atmosphere—student hangout, young professional, black, gay, or the glamour crowd. In contrast, one of the first things you notice at a roller disco is that the crowd is mixed—it cuts across age and all ethnic and economic lines.

Another surprising thing is that even though the atmosphere at most roller discos is primitive and unsophisticated compared to the 50,000 dollar light shows and other special effects seen in many chic dancing clubs, the skaters don't seem to notice; this group doesn't need strobes, drugs, or alcohol to get where they are going. They've got wheels.

Although boutiques are featuring glamorous and extravagant skating costumes (satin hats, visors, ballet-type tutus, shorts, skirts, and skin-tight lycra pants), most of the roller disco crowd dresses very casually in T-shirts and jeans. Though the skaters enjoy themselves thoroughly, the atmosphere is neither a freak show nor an all-out costume ball like in many of the dancing places. You don't need a special outfit to have fun at a roller disco.

The astonishing openness, generosity, and cooperativeness of the experienced skaters toward beginners is another characteristic of a roller disco. No one cares *who* you are, *what* you wear,

or *how* you make a living. All they ask is "Are you a skater?" Drugs, alcohol, therapy, or page-one news items are rarely discussed at a roller disco. Cigarette smoking is very uncool. Pure apple juice and granola cookies are more typical of a skater's between-sessions snack.

You'll find a roller disco club to be a stimulating half-fantasy world where people know how to play and make dreams come alive. In addition, the cooperative loving feeling the skating and music generate makes you feel good about yourself and others. No one feels left out. Everyone is involved, becoming animated in the whirling play of

lights. It's a giddy world filled with natural energy. When you first start out, your skates may seem heavy on your feet. Once you've been skating for a while, you will feel a surprising lightness.

WHAT YOU CAN EXPECT

Suppose this is the first time you've been on skates since you were eight years old and you find that you can barely make it from the skate room to the dance floor. Since you don't know how to skate, stop, turn, or slow down, terror may define your mood. Everyone else looks like they're whizzing ahead at 30 miles an hour or faster as you creep onto the floor, clutching the railing for stability. All you can think of is falling down and that

would just be too embarrassing.

So you wait for a gap in the traffic, then cast yourself into the flow. After a few hesitant steps, you find that you're actually rolling while hardly lifting your feet. You just shift your weight from side to side and it's as if the energy and momentum of the other skaters is pulling you along. Now, you're speeding and that's when you get scared again—will you survive the first turn?

Skaters speed past—no one is falling, no one is crashing. Slowly you coast around the first bend, leaning in slightly. After that, you begin to shuffle along, shifting your weight from side to side so that you hit the second corner on your own power. After a few times around, it's a joy to

realize you can stay on your feet and even start to skate with the crowd. The place is supportive. People look wonderful; graceful, gliding forms cut through tiny, flickering lights that dance over the floor. You decide you want to be a part of this sensational experience.

Next, you allow yourself to feel the beat and relax, and a miracle takes place—you forget about falling. As you keep rolling, roller disco becomes as easy as floating down-river with the current. You may be a person who normally feels awkward dancing, but here at a roller disco you feel you've got half a chance. One thing's for sure: if, a year ago, anyone had predicted you'd be roller skating

and loving every minute, you'd have probably thought they were crazy. Now, an hour after you've arrived, you're already planning your next trip out on the floor. If you should feel yourself falling, hands reach out from nowhere to catch you and help you up while others block oncoming traffic until you can navigate on your feet again. Happily, you'll find this camaraderie an everyday experience at a roller disco.

GETTING THE FEEL OF THE WHEEL

Toward the end of the evening, you're not fighting your wheels anymore. You're just rolling and flowing along like everyone else. No one taught you

how—the music took over and you picked up the beat. Even though you still don't know how to stop, it doesn't seem to matter. You just allow yourself to slow down to a halt. No one is put off by your inexperience; they all glide past you. You feel safe and relaxed by the flow of movement around you because the effect of roller disco is a kind of spiritual massage as well as a physical sensation. For you, skating has become sheer pleasure.

The overall rhythmic glide of a roller disco is very different from the chaos of an ordinary discotheque: the action on the floor is one continuous movement that snakes, floats, and swirls around the room. Some skaters do very individual steps as they glide by, even leaps and spins right in the middle of traffic, but few skaters collide. It's as if you're a part of a beautifully choreographed dream. The vibes are unreal but you don't think about it until later. Some skaters dart and dodge or curve and cut from side to side as you all ride out the music, but most simply boogie around, keeping in step with the beat. Your speed builds, yet you're not conscious of it until the music stops. Then, suddenly, you realize how fast you've been skating. No problem. It's been said that you're safe within the beat, and you are. You're breathless, but feel ecstatically happy.

BILL BUTLER: KING OF ROLLER DISCO

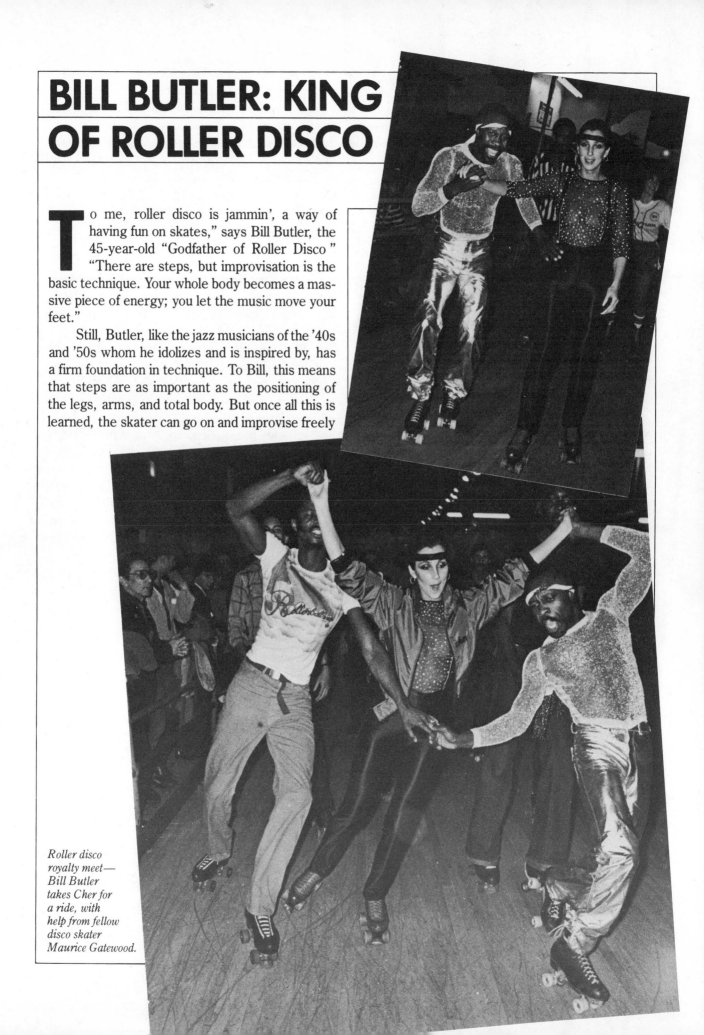

To me, roller disco is jammin', a way of having fun on skates," says Bill Butler, the 45-year-old "Godfather of Roller Disco." "There are steps, but improvisation is the basic technique. Your whole body becomes a massive piece of energy; you let the music move your feet."

Still, Butler, like the jazz musicians of the '40s and '50s whom he idolizes and is inspired by, has a firm foundation in technique. To Bill, this means that steps are as important as the positioning of the legs, arms, and total body. But once all this is learned, the skater can go on and improvise freely

Roller disco royalty meet— Bill Butler takes Cher for a ride, with help from fellow disco skater Maurice Gatewood.

to the music, creating his or her own unique look.

Although it would seem that Bill is describing what most artistic dance skaters do every day as they set up their routines, this is far from the case. In its most refined form, roller disco *never* looks like traditional artistic skating, nor is it skated the same way. The two styles have only one thing in common, the edges. After that, the two forms are as different as night and day.

A major difference is that disco is expressive and improvisational. Roller disco has its roots in the black experience of gospel, blues, jazz, and expressive interpretive dancing, while artistic skating has its roots in classical music, ballet, and ballroom dancing.

Body positions used in the two styles are noticeably different. Roller disco steps require skating in a bent knee position while maintaining a loose and flexible body stance. Artistic skaters move more straightleggedly with their upper body held upright. In artistic skating, as in the world of ballet, a long, straight, refined-looking body line, which takes years to develop, is considered the ideal. Butler's style, and disco skating in general, is sensuous, emphasizing free-flowing movements. Generally, roller disco is thought to be

Butler displays the dynamic style and innovative movements that characterize his brand of roller disco.

exciting but crude, while artistic skating is seen as sophisticated. But what others think doesn't faze Bill. "Skating is a very intimate thing. I listen to the music, close my eyes, and feel the beat. I can bring about a calmness, a tranquil state of mind through skating."

Ironically, people who watch Butler at the Empire Rollerdrome in Brooklyn describe him and his style of skating quite differently. Bill, who lunges around the floor like a raging tiger, hardly looks tranquil. His skating may relax him, but it inflames and energizes everyone else. Butler commands attention on skates. His every movement says, "Watch this. Don't you dare take your eyes off me or you'll miss the show." Dynamic in his own right, when Bill skates to equally fiery music, the resulting vision is unforgettable. Butler is not pretty, mellow, relaxed, nor does he give the impression of airy lightness as he skates the floor. Instead, he transforms himself into pure energy, and becomes an accelerated mass that hurls itself through space. "I'm concerned with movement—it's a science," he says. "Everything has to be in the right place. Your legs, arms, and body position have to work together or it doesn't look right. You've got to hook it all up."

Bill has two different looks when he skates—both involve precise timing, balance, and complicated footwork. When he skates what he calls "full-time," he does individual steps on every beat of the music at the same time as he rolls forward and backward and cuts from side to side. Butler, his legs pumping like an eight-cylinder engine, looks energetic and powerful. He draws energy from his "center" and channels it through his legs down into the floor. Gliding and shuffling one foot at a time, he weaves, bobs, and zigzags around the floor. As quickly as he sets one skate down, he picks the other up. While continuous progressive steps are the foundation of his style, the variations are provided by hops, jumps, spins, rolling splits, and grapevine steps.

At other times Butler skates to what he calls "half-time," that is, he does a different movement on alternating beats of the music. This way, Bill's skating look has a smoother quality to it; his footwork is not so frantic.

How Bill looks when he skates depends on how he feels about the music and how he wants to interpret it on that particular day. Whatever he does, it's always a surprise. He may skate alone or

Bill Butler (right) and Maurice Gatewood jammin' to the beat.

with his partner Janet Burrows, or with his best friend, Maurice Gatewood. Sometimes he skates trios or in fours.

Remembering that his style, like all true roller disco, is improvisational, he has developed a way of communicating with a partner that approximates the spiritual. The effect of it is that Bill keeps people on the edge of their chairs wondering what will happen next. He says, "All my choreography is on the spur of the moment. That's what makes things interesting."

Butler's body shape dictates his visual style. He's athletic, strong, and beautifully muscled. At 5 feet 9 inches, 165 pounds, he has the kind of body typically seen in top-rank gymnastic competition.

"Skating with Bill is not like skating with anyone else," says Bill's 26-year-old partner, Janet. "He skates with his whole body, bending forward, backward, and to the side. He can flow like water. Bill skates how he feels. He tells us, 'if you feel like a hop, split, or a jump, do it. Do it with

Bill Butler and The Goodskates put on a show at an outdoor disco contest in Central Park.

rhythm, class, and style. Just do it.'

"Bill skates like a continuous line, never broken, always flowing up, down, and around. A kid would draw Bill's style like a scribble because Bill gets very excited when he skates.

"In Bill's style, the hockey stop is essential. We have to be able to do it to the right or to the left. You must be able to stop on a dime and, just as fast, pick up and get going again.

"Bill fascinates me," declares Janet, with a laugh. "He's 45 years old and can still twist his body into a pretzel. I can't get over this man. He skates for hours. You'd think he'd get tired. Never. I have to tell Bill I'm tired. He understands."

Diana Moore, another of Bill's group, has her own way of describing what happens. "People have a tendency to skate one-sided so one side of the body gets stronger than the other. Bill teaches you to skate with both sides. It feels funny at first, like being right-handed and trying to write with your left hand." Diana, who partners with Maurice

Janet Burrows, Rosalyn Scott and Diana Moore model the new skating fashions.

Gatewood, nonetheless always watches her mentor. "Bill has fitness at top speed. He does no-touch skating. He spins, jumps, and cuts across the corners. There are 800 people on the floor and he never touches a soul."

Randy Higgenson, a man who has watched Bill for years and is also one of his students, says, "Bill is what we call a very serious skater. He's the best. Nobody does it better. Bill moves across the floor like a bouncing ball or a ricocheting bullet. He can move sideways as fast as forward or back. Like a roadrunner, he never misses a beat."

Amazingly, everyone who watches Bill skate sees something different. Anthony Forde, a student of Bill's for ten years, feels that "What Bill does is a science. His style? It's like slide, slide,

The opening of the roller disco boutique at Macy's department store in Manhattan provides Bill and The Goodskates another opportunity to dazzle an admiring crowd.

pull, pull. There's no stop-and-go. It's smooth. You have to breathe properly, just like a singer. He can cut to the left or cut to the right. He has perfect ground control. Bill's style is very strenuous," adds Tony. "He's skating for hours in a crouched position, curving and dipping every minute. Bill's power comes from the center part of his body and then from his legs. He skates with short

tight steps with his arms tucked in at his sides. He's a mass of power." Balance is a key to understanding Bill's skating ability. He is "centered," that is, movement is generated from his abdomen area, just below the navel. Centering, a well-known physical principle widely used in other sports, is a way to find the body's center of gravity. If a person is also in a relaxed state, this process can result in unusual athletic feats.

Because Bill and many other disco skaters remove their toe-stops, there's no toe drag to prevent full leg extension while skating. This makes many new movements possible. For example, disco rollers can do heel-and-toe splits either at a standstill or on the roll. One- or two-foot spins on the front wheels are also possible once the toe-stops are removed. Additionally, skating up on the front two wheels, known as the "grapevine," presents no problem. Although these steps are commonly associated with roller disco today, skaters from Detroit, Cleveland, Chicago, and Columbus have been doing them for the past 40 or 50 years. Bill's style is unique because he does these advanced maneuvers at full speed. These are complicated steps that require extraordinary balance and muscle control, yet they have all become a regular part of the progressive flow that characterizes Bill's skating. His genius is executing them so smoothly that other skaters can only dream of duplicating him.

Watching Bill brings an awareness of the relationship a skater can have with the floor. While others float, Bill pounds the boards. He is "grounded." "Grounding" is the feeling of being connected to and supported by the floor. Butler, as a skater, is aware of the relationship between his mind, body, skate wheels, and the maple floor, and he uses it to his advantage. He appears to test himself against every inch of the skating surface. He bends his knees and relaxes into his skating posture. His skates become an extension of his legs and then connect to the floor. His legs are tight but bent, never rigid. Because he's centered, he has the freedom to do radical interpretive skating movements with great ease and assurance.

Bill is one of the best role models in the skating world. Just watching him skate does the beginner, as well as the advanced skater, a world of good. The reason many people find skating, especially advanced disco skating, difficult is that they keep their legs too stiff. Bill teaches what he

A bodybuilder for years, Bill's muscular physique is an integral part of the look of his skating style.

practices, a style of skating that allows one great freedom of movement and the potential for total body and mind relaxation.

Butler has taught hundreds of people how to skate and has influenced thousands more. Although most people don't realize it, he is directly responsible for initiating much of the roller disco craze that is sweeping the country. Even though skaters from black rinks in the Midwest have been doing the steps for years, Bill is and has always been, their most visible spokesman.

He's organized his own hand-picked team of exhibition skaters to spread the word. This group, known as Bill Butler and The Goodskates, has performed all over the East Coast, on network television, and even as far away as Sweden. Being associated with Butler now has so much prestige that, according to Butch Ford, a skater from New York, who is close to the inner circle, yet not one of The Goodskates, "People will just do anything to be a part of Bill's group. Many are called, but few are chosen."

The Goodskates, a group of one-time regulars from Empire, follow Bill's training program much more diligently than many world-class artistic skaters. This includes a strict diet and breathing and flexibility exercises. Butler initiated this program because his style is so physically demanding, you need every ounce of energy and flexibility you can get. The ability to concentrate while remaining relaxed is another element that puts this group apart from the rest of the pack.

Additionally, Bill's style appears very natural for the body. Interestingly enough, the rate of injury for those skaters who train with him is almost zero. In contrast, the injury rate for competitive skaters who use a straight-legged style similar to that of ballet dancers, is very high.

Butler encourages his students to focus on their inner feelings. It may seem unusual to hear skaters talk about things that are "spiritual," but it's familiar to Bill's skaters because he talks to them about "feelings" every day. To him, "skating is a way to make you feel better." Also, Bill, like many other sports people, is aware of Eastern philosophy, religion, and attitudes usually associated with self-awareness movements. Through these, he attempts to incorporate spiritual elements into his approach to roller skating.

Says Butler, "I'm not a performer. I'm not an entertainer. I'm a skater." Butler's attitude is understandable considering that he has spent the last 35 years of his life skating to please only himself. But, today, Bill is experiencing some of the biggest changes in his life. As manager and skating director of The Good Skates, he regularly performs demonstrations and skates at exhibitions that are connected with the promotion of the rental shop of the same name. He performs at press events, fashion shows, outdoor exhibitions. Being in front of a camera does not necessarily synch with Bill's skating style, which is more personal than commercial. He can come off as stiff and overly technical while skating in front of strangers. But at Empire, his home turf, he skates so joyously that it's hard for people who have seen him on different days and in different settings to reconcile the two images.

Bill is widely respected. His circle of influence extends far beyond the geographic limits of Brooklyn. He is roller disco's most articulate spokesman. His technical style, like a cosmic jigsaw puzzle, provides an infinite number of ways to put the pieces together. The elements include steps, arm movements, and general body positioning, all of which combine according to the music and the body of the skater, each time in a different way. Unlike artistic skating, you never stop learning with roller disco. It allows the skater to develop a highly individualistic style. This partially

accounts for why roller disco has caught on so quickly and has such a wide appeal. What establishes Bill Butler as a leader is his degree of credibility. Skating is a way of life to him, always was, and most likely, always will be. He is actively concerned with exploring the potential for movement as well as challenges in his own life. "Remember, I don't choreograph routines," Bill insists. "I'd rather be surprised. That's the challenge of my style. It keeps me vibrant, keeps me from getting bored."

Technique as an end in itself is not complementary with Bill's outlook. More is involved: he uses technique to build a foundation and then goes beyond, exploring life through music, his feelings, and his skating. This approach is his key to spiritual awareness in his own life. Rather than being a performer, Bill Butler is a true artist. Says Bill, "Skating is personal freedom to me."

Judy Lynn, owner of the Goodskates rental shop, and her skating director, pose with his latest award.

DISCO FOR DOLLARS

At Empire Rollerdrome, roller dancers got a chance to put on their moves for the judges. Skaters young and old, amateurs and professionals, used the contest to show where their enthusiasm for the new beat is taking them.

All photos: Ann-Victoria Phillips

EMPIRE ROLLERDROME, BROOKLYN, NEW YORK

Empire Rollerdrome, the hub of New York City's roller disco scene, is old fashioned, even spartan, compared to the plushness of modern-day disco design. The lighting effects consist of colored outdoor screw-in bulbs, eight-foot-long fluorescent tubes, and small studio spotlights that are directed on four revolving balls that hang from the ceiling. There are no computers, strobes, or lasers at Empire.

As plain as it is, Empire still has a distinct personality. Its most unusual feature is the park-style playground set right in the center of the rink floor. Surrounded by a wrought iron fence, the area is an oasis, complete with neon palm trees that surround eight picnic tables and benches. Especially on Wednesday evenings, Empire's club night, the center court serves as both a protected practice area for learning as well as an all-natural foods

Saturday night crowds jam the Brooklyn street outside the birthplace of roller disco.

All photos: Ann-Victoria Phillips

Club night at the Rollerdrome. The center of the rink is a good place for skaters to practice steps or take a breather.

snack bar. Club skaters carry in their own fresh fruit and drinks and create an all-night picnic. It's this down-home atmosphere plus the people (some of the friendliest skaters in the US) that inspire crowds of Manhattanites to take the ride to Brooklyn. But this is nothing new. Empire has been one of New York's most popular rinks for a long time.

Empire, at first called the Brooklyn Roller Rink, was designed and built for championship speed competition in 1920. Empire also featured competitive artistic skating as well as a full program of recreational skating. In addition, the rink hosted roller skating vaudeville acts, boxing and wrestling matches, and served as a practice rink for a cele-

Wednesday night regulars find their groove in the disco beat.

A relaxed atmosphere and casual dress are part of the appeal of the current rink revival.

brated Roller Derby team, the New York Chiefs. More importantly, the Empire, almost from the very beginning, gained a reputation as New York's finest roller ballroom.

Bill Butler discovered the Empire in 1956, while he was stationed with the air force in Brooklyn. When Bill first arrived, Empire's skaters danced waltzes and fox trots to tape recorded organ music, but he persuaded the rink's manager to play popular music, at first once a week, then on

an exclusive basis. Bill, who skates at the rink regularly, immediately began teaching his unconventional style to fellow skaters and, it is said by some, was the first person to coin the words, "roller disco," in 1976.

Today, after 23 years, Empire is Bill's home and the site of the most unorthodox skating school in the United States. Although the rink hosts large numbers of very proficient skaters, Bill remains the dominant force and Empire the most exciting roller disco rink in the United States.

All photos: Ann-Victoria Phillips

6.
SHOW SKATING

THE HISTORY OF SHOW SKATING

Although ballet and opera companies and actors and mimes used roller skates in their performances as far back as the early 1800s, it wasn't until the American ballet master Jackson Haines gave exhibitions in the 1860s that a roller skating act came to be widely accepted as entertainment.

After Haines, fancy skating acts came and went until the turn of the century which heralded the heyday of the professional show skater. From about 1900 until 1950, the use of roller skaters as part of a variety act, either in the rink, club or on a vaudeville stage became an American institution and was also popular in England and Australia. The spectacular professional roller skating show, Skating Vanities, was created and produced in 1942. But this roller popularity was short lived; the '50s spelled a decline for both Skating Vanities and other professional skaters on the RKO Vaudeville circuit when all show skaters lost their audience to television.

Famed entertainers Helen Carlos and Howard Fielding (top) perform their version of the "Merry Widow Waltz" in 1908.

From the earliest days a show skater's costume has been an integral part of his or her act.

All photos: Courtesy of Chicago Roller Skate Company

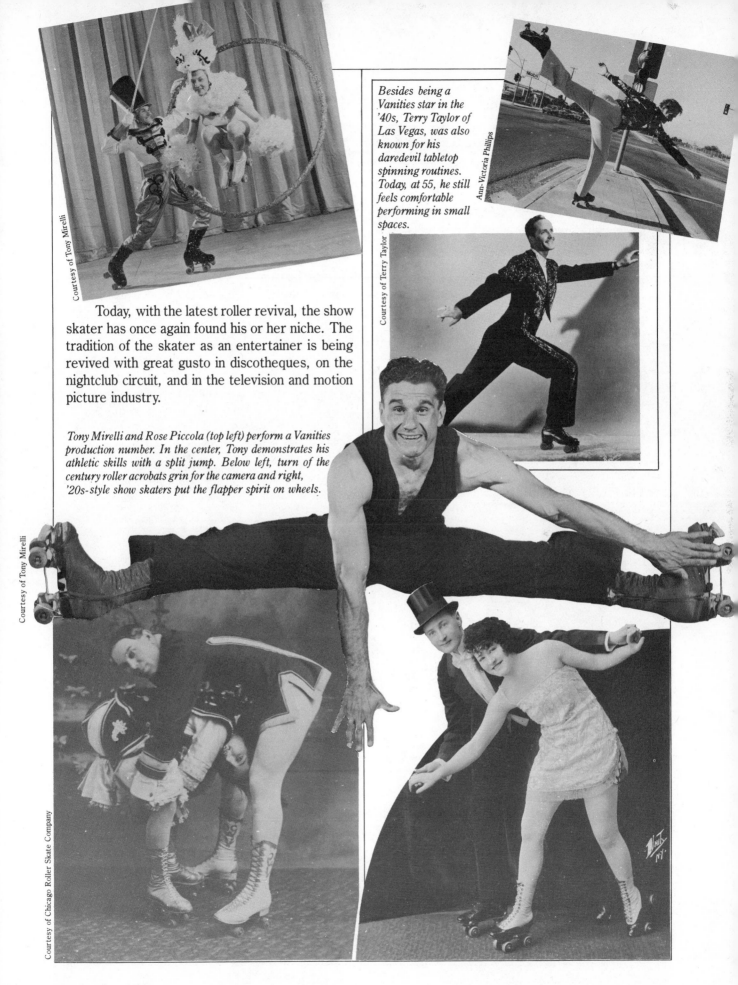

Today, with the latest roller revival, the show skater has once again found his or her niche. The tradition of the skater as an entertainer is being revived with great gusto in discotheques, on the nightclub circuit, and in the television and motion picture industry.

Tony Mirelli and Rose Piccola (top left) perform a Vanities production number. In the center, Tony demonstrates his athletic skills with a split jump. Below left, turn of the century roller acrobats grin for the camera and right, '20s-style show skaters put the flapper spirit on wheels.

Besides being a Vanities star in the '40s, Terry Taylor of Las Vegas, was also known for his daredevil tabletop spinning routines. Today, at 55, he still feels comfortable performing in small spaces.

Courtesy of Tony Mirelli

Ann-Victoria Phillips

Courtesy of Terry Taylor

Courtesy of Tony Mirelli

Courtesy of Chicago Roller Skate Company

GLORIA NORD AND SKATING VANITIES

From 1942 to 1954 the name Gloria Nord, meant glamour and artistry on wheels. At 5 feet, 2 inches the blue-eyed elfin Gloria was the roller skating world's answer to Sonya Henie and the star of Skating Vanities, the most fabulous and extravagant roller skating show of all time.

On January 7, 1942, the Roller Follies, a lavish production with a cast of 85 skaters opened in Baltimore, Maryland. At first everyone associated it with Roller Derby, so four weeks later in St. Louis, the show's name was changed to Skating Vanities. "Business picked up right away," Gloria recalls. "People couldn't picture a musical show on wheels; that was the problem. But the Vanities was exotic and we got rave reviews."

Vanities toured constantly and stayed a week at a time in cities throughout the country. Every Sunday night after the last show the stage hands disassembled the enormous masonite portable stage and packed 36 tons of equipment onto a train or truck to travel to their Monday destination.

Gloria, as beautifully radiant today as ever before, lives near Newport Beach, California, recalls her life with the show: "I was always prepared and things sort of happened for me. I was excited, yet I got nervous or jumpy. For me Vanities was a magical life."

Gloria Nord was a roller skating superstar during the '40s and '50s; a glamour queen on wheels who brought spirit and show-stopping style to every Skating Vanities performance and eventually to the whole entertainment world. At far left, she takes Charlie McCarthy's place on Edgar Bergen's knee, and chats with Betty Grable, her co-star in the 1944 movie "Pin-Up Girl."

JAN AUJAY AND JERRY NISTA'S DISCO ROLLERS

At the 1978 Pacific Coast Roller Skating Championships held Labor Day weekend at the Runway Skatepark in Carson, California, a 17-year-old amateur roller skater named Jan Aujay hooked up the most electrifying skating routine of her life. Dressed in a

Jan, like most show skaters, has a firm foundation in dance and warms up at the barre (right) before she practices her routine.

Bruce Hazelton

Ann-Victoria Ph...

Ann-Victoria Ph...

NEW HORIZONS

In a roller world now flooded with disco skaters, New Horizons stands out. At the Los Angeles International Film Exposition where the group performed a special roller exhibition, the 10,000 strong audience liked their act so much they demanded more and more until the event's director finally pulled the plug on the sound system to quiet down the crowd. Encouraged by this response, New Horizons has been booked in clubs, on TV shows, and other special events, and are now planning a coast-to-coast road show.

day-glo orange leotard and shorts and moving to the sound of "Disco Inferno," Aujay dazzled the crowd with her fiery and unusually expressive skating.

Jan Aujay is one of the most dynamic skaters in the United States. It's her degree of personal magnetism that wows people. She does a kind of ecstatic skating—she communicates feelings of excitement and joy so intensely that, when first seen, it's breathtaking. No matter whether she skates alone, with her partner Jim Sallenbach or with other members of her coach's group (called

Jerry Nista's Disco Rollers), she projects a degree of vitality unmatched in the roller world today.

Jan's coach, the innovative Jerry Nista, poses with his wife, Elayne, (left) also a member of his professional skating troupe. Elayne, a former national dance champion, demonstrates a showy number with partner, Mike Kirkpatric (right).

MAURICE COOKE: THE ENTERTAINER

A long time ago in a galaxy far, far away, a great adventure took place." The narrator's voice booms across Venice Beach in California. Trumpets blare while the familiar "Star Wars" movie theme introduces a new act. Fifteen hundred people are gathered together surrounding a make-shift beachfront dance floor watching the First Outdoor Roller Disco Championships.

The sight of the villainous Lord Vader, played by veteran skater, Maurice Cooke of Los Angeles, is both shocking and humorous. Cooke, dressed in quilted shirt, vest and pants, cape, utility belt with red lights and mini-computers plus roller skates with a patent-leather sheen, is high kicking, heel splitting and grapevining his way through an acrobatic routine set to a disco beat.

Cooke, a professional entertainer who has roller skated his way through cabarets, TV shows, motion picture sets, and dance hall audition studios for the past fifteen years, is finally coming into his own. He says. "I know I'm good and that I offer something special. I have performed in front of so many audiences, both young and old. I get a joyous response."

Maurice Cooke in character as Roller Vader (top), and Mr. Bojangles, (bottom, far left).

All photos: Ann-Victoria Phillips

7. ARTISTIC SKATING

DANCE, FIGURES AND FREESTYLE

Although many people enjoy artistic style roller skating as a recreational sport, it primarily attracts skaters who are interested in competition. Artistic skating is divided into three basic styles: figures, freestyle, and dance. Both the figures and basic dance movements are made up of set, formalized movements and steps, while the items used in freestyle and free dance routines are choreographed for each individual skater or couple.

Figure skating: Figure skating movements were first developed in 1863 for ice skaters by an American ballet teacher, Jackson Haines, who

Earl and Inez Van Horn of Mineola, New York, were influential in popularizing dance skating in the 1940s.

Courtesy of Chicago Roller Skate Company

lived in Vienna. After watching their local skaters, he decided to combine ice skating technique with ballet and music. Once combined, he taught this new-style ballet to others. One student, Louis Rubenstein, brought the new method of ice skating to North America, where he helped found the Amateur Skating Association of Canada. Since roller skaters imitated everything their counterparts did on ice, the Haines method was eventually assimilated into the roller world.

Both ice and roller skating contestants had to prove their mastery of standard edges and turns, called "school figures." The skater's form while executing these figures became an important criterion for judging during competition. This new emphasis on "manner of performance" led to the separation of artistic skating into its three forms. Jumping and spinning movements were gradually added to the "free figures" category. They became known as "freestyle skating." Figure skating retained the rigid upright postures derived from ballet and eliminated the music. Roller dance skating kept the music and prescribed dance steps, but in its looser form, called free dance, skaters were able to incorporate a popular dance flavor into their routines.

Freestyle skating: This is one of the most dramatically spectacular forms of artistic skating. Although a lot of creative freedom is allowed, skaters also must prove their technical proficiency by performing specific maneuvers, known as "items," that score points with the judges. All movements are choreographed into two, three, four or five minute routines (depending on the division) and set to music. Skaters are free to develop their own personal on-floor style—and to choose the items in their routine, their music and their costumes as well.

Laurene Anselmi Patton of Pontiac, Michigan, won more US amateur championships than any other skater in history.

Freestyle is different from figure skating. While figures require a machine-like consistency and the ability to concentrate, freestyle, on the other hand, demands high-level athletic skill and strength, showmanship and pure guts. In addition, a freestylist must interpret the tempo and mood of the music during the routine. Each skater is judged by his or her virtuosity—the speed and height of jumps and speed and sureness of spins and connective footwork.

Dance skating: While roller dance skating has been an American tradition since the 1880s when rinks hired professional teachers to give exhibitions and teach fancy steps, it was not a competitive sport in the US until 1939. Actually, roller dance skating was far more popular in England where, as early as the 1890s, that country's National Skating Association standardized steps modeled on existing ice skating figures in order to promote world-wide competitions. This became known as the "International Style."

During the first two decades of this century, the only artistic skating seen in the US was performed by professionals during special rink exhib-

itions of "novelty" and "fancy skating." Artistic skating was also a popular theme in musical comedy acts and other productions for the stage.

In the '30s the Winter Olympic Games were held in Lake Placid, New York, and provided glamorous ice skating role models like Sonja Henie for roller skaters to emulate. All that was needed was a leader to join the different skating styles together and popularize the new product—roller dance skating. This leader was Perry Rawson, an American rink owner.

Rawson attended England's national championship in 1933 and brought home movies of roller dance competition to show his colleagues. He convinced rink owners that promoting dance skating would be a very good investment. The group hired the English national champion dance skaters, Joan and James Lidstone, to make a 60-day exhibition tour of American rinks. This tour launched competitive dance skating in the United States. Later, Rawson, using the Lidstones' style as a guide, added his own techniques to develop an "American style" of dance that he believed was better suited to roller skating.

Although many people take private lessons, join a skating club and practice regularly for recreation, there's another large group who do it because they want the added challenge of competition. If you decide amateur competition is what you want either for yourself or your child, you will have to search out and study the available competitive programs. There are at least three factors to

ART WALTERS: THE DOCTOR WHO DOES DOUBLES

All photos: Ann-Victoria Phillips

At the end of a busy day, Dr. Walters is ready to skate.

"Medicine is my most serious commitment," says Dr. Art Walters, a 35-year-old neurology resident at King's County Hospital in Brooklyn, New York. "Next on the list would have to be scientific research. The third most important thing to me is my political activist role as a doctor. (Walters is a delegate to the city-wide union called the Committee of Interns and Residents.) After that, there's my roller skating."

Walters, who learned to skate while he was a student at Kalamazoo College in Michigan, later started taking private lessons in freestyle from skating instructor Bob Tabacchi while he studied medicine at Wayne State University in Detroit. In 1974, Art, who was by then finished with medical school, accepted a research fellowship at Columbia University and moved to New York.

"One of the first things I did when I got here was look for a new place to skate," recalls the young doctor, "and the closest place was the Wal-Cliffe Skating Rink in Elmont, New York, a 30-minute drive from my house."

Dr. Walters started freestyle lessons again, first with instructor Betty Marcus, and perfected single jumps like the Mapes, Salchow, and the Axel, plus some of the simpler spins. His present coach is Gail Keicher, a former Senior American Dance champion before she turned to coaching six years ago. She has Art working on more advanced jumps: the Double Axel, Double Mapes, and the Double Salchow—challenging freestyle maneuvers that require two complete revolutions in the air.

"My goal," says Art, "is to get out on the floor and skate a competitive routine at the regional meet. My coach, Gail, is very supportive, but I'm not yet at the point where I know enough items and feel comfortable doing them. My biggest problem is finding the time to practice at the rink—that's what is holding me back."

Walters works at one of the busiest hospitals in the world and the largest in the city of New York. "As a doctor, I'm on call," he explains, "for 36-hour shifts. For example, I might start at 8 o'clock Tuesday morning and work until Wednesday at 8 PM. That means, I would miss Tuesday evening practice at the rink. Most weeks, I work 80 to 120 hours. I must force myself to make time to get over to the rink to practice."

"I have a lot of good things to say about Art." Skating instructor Gail Keicher smiles as she watches her student warm up. First, Art does cross pulls and then single jumps, in preparation for his lesson. "Most people think 35 is way too old to start learning advanced freestyle. I have to give him credit. He struggles, he concentrates, and he tries very hard. His heart is really in it. When I see someone like him working at 100 percent effort, I'll give 200 percent to back him up.

"Falling is a big part of learning freestyle and Art takes some pretty bad spills. But he's never gotten hurt and he always gets up smiling. Art doesn't care what people think. He has a very strong self-image. He believes in himself.

"The kids at the rink don't bother me much," says Walters, as he looks around the large arena. People are practicing every different kind of skat-

evaluate: the rink, the club, and the coach.

Rink: The rink should have practice sessions available every day of the week, with extra hours, upon request of the coach, during April, May, June, and July in order to prepare for state, regional, or national meets. Ideally, the existence of other programs like speed and hockey at the same rink would be a plus. The combination of speed and freestyle develops some of the best-conditioned skater/athletes.

ing on the rink floor—some are getting figure lessons while others practice freestyle or dance routines. "The adults are the ones who kid and tease me a lot. Surprisingly, I get quite a bit of negative feedback. They are always trying to shuttle me into figures or dance skating. That's where they think I have a better chance of winning.

"Their basic feeling is that freestyle is for kids and that once you're over 21 you can't learn anything new, especially not advanced freestyle. People tell me I should give up and that I'm wasting my time.

"I disagree with them. I'm determined to do freestyle. It gives me exercise and it's more of a challenge.

"Most people ask me why I'm involved in such a strenuous skating program," says Art, as he rests on the rail for a moment. "I used to play tennis before I skated. In fact, I was very good and a ranked player in my home state of Michigan. But now skating is the only thing that appeals to me, and I'm really serious about it. It's relaxing and it

takes me away from the pressures of the hospital. I treat a lot of gunshot wounds, fractures to the spine, and comas of all kinds," he continues. "I have to deal with critically and seriously ill patients every single day. I have to make life and death decisions in the middle of the night on my own.

"Medicine will always be my top priority, but I have found that one serious commitment helps me relax from another. Skating is the 'funnest' thing I do."

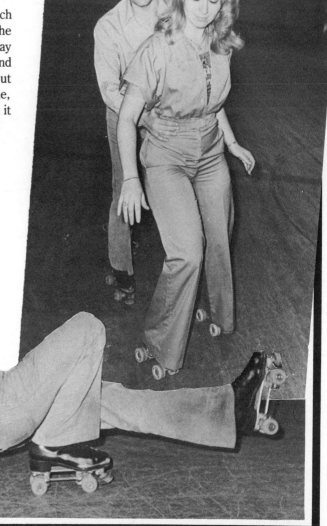

Former dance champion Gail Keicher clowns around with her student, and then demonstrates a fine point of freestyle form.

Club: Look for a club membership that is fairly constant from year to year. Being involved in a figure, freestyle, or dance program represents a sizable investment in effort, time, and money. Most skaters and their parents are interested in long-term programs. Seek a club that has skaters of all ages (including the over-30 group) in every division. Find out if the club participates in inter-club and league competition as well as invitational meets. Becoming a "seasoned" skater means getting competitive experience wherever you can, as frequently as possible. Go where the best compe-

titive skaters are. You'll probably learn more quickly just by watching them. Friendly rivalries on the club level help condition and sharpen competitive instincts.

Coach: Seek a coach who recognizes artistic skating as a high-level competitive sport and who sees his or her skaters as athletes. Find out if the coach recommends a well-rounded training program, including flexibility exercises, strenuous workouts, and perhaps diet management (this is often the most neglected part of the artistic skater's training program).

You should also be looking for a coach who is

Dawni Coan takes advantage of the superb facilities at her rink, Warnoco Skating Center in Greeley, Colorado. First, she warms up with gymnastics coach Theo Digerness (left), then gets set to practice multiple revolution jumps with skating coach Jay Norcross (right).

Ann-Victoria Phillips

World-class freestyle coach John Dayney of East Meadow, New York, with students (from left to right) Lisa Vickers, Linda List, Janine Hand and Thumper Smith.

free from pre-conceived ideas about what is masculine and what is feminine in terms of skating styles. Look for one who demands equally strenuous practice sessions for women and men skaters and takes the time to know the skaters well enough to help them achieve their personal goals as well as maximize their contribution to the club. Find out if he or she has a good record of achievement in competition. Also, try to find a coach who

Coach Jane Puracchio of Euclid, Ohio with International Senior Dance skaters Alicia Kisner and Rick Kisner.

has good relationships with other athletes, trainers, and the sports community at large. Ideally, your coach should be open-minded and receptive to new concepts and ideas as they are introduced to the sport.

IMPROVE YOUR SKILLS : TAKE A PROFICIENCY TEST

Any skater can take a RSROA (Roller Skating Rink Operators of America) proficiency test. Such tests are administered by officially commissioned judges several times during the year at most RSROA rinks. Member rinks offer tests in figure, freestyle, and dance (both American and International styles).

The tests are not a competition. You will simply be testing your skill against the style book. As you progress, you can earn Bronze, Silver, or Gold award medals, depending on your level of skill.

Much practice is required to pass a proficiency test, and many rinks have adult classes during weekday nights for just this reason.

The roller skate proficiency testing system is extensive and best explained in the RSROA rule books. These are available, for two dollars each, from RSROA, 7700 "A" Street, Lincoln, Nebraska 68510. The books are: *American Roller Dance Skating I, American Roller Dance Skating II, International Dance Skating, Roller Free Skating,* and *Roller Figure Skating.*

STARTING OUT IN COMPETITION

Before competing, you must join your local skating club and get your amateur card (see box on this page) from USAC. Beginning skaters who are interested in competition start out in local, inter-club meets. League meets are those in which a number of area rinks get together on a regular basis and hold competitions. Invitational meets are those in which a host rink invites other local skating clubs as well as those from other parts of the country.

You and your instructor will decide together what your training and competition schedule will be. It's usually planned a whole year in advance. Don't enter a meet unless you're really ready. Once you are, local competition is the best way for you to measure your skills. Entering local meets has another benefit—social. You will meet other skaters and, just by watching them, get new ideas.

Figure skating: Skaters must know how to do all the figures. The judges will choose five out of the group to be used in competition. The figures that are chosen will differ from meet to meet.

Freestyle: As a freestyle skater you must work up a "routine," a choreographed sequence of movements that is set to music. The routine is made up of freestyle items that are within your skating ability. You will get points for content (your choice of items and their degree of difficulty), and for performance (skill). You will perform your routine in front of an audience and, depending on your age, it will last from three minutes (young skaters) to five minutes (older skaters).

Dance: If you dance, you can choose compulsory dance divisions or those for free dance or both. A free dance routine is choreographed much in the same way as freestyle and, of course, set to music.

Costs of competition: Competitive skaters buy the finest equipment. The skates, complete, cost around 300 dollars. Skating costumes can range from 50 dollars for men to 100 dollars for women. Besides the cost of lessons, you will also be required to pay for club dues as well as transportation and other expenses connected with entering the meets. Costs of competition for an artis-

THE USAC AMATEUR COMPETITION CARD

Every amateur competitor entered in USAC-sanctioned roller skating contests must apply for and obtain a USAC Amateur Competition card in Artistic, Speed or Hockey. An amateur may hold a card in more than one discipline. The price is 5 dollars and you can get it through your local skating club. Although you can take private lessons, join a skating club and practice without it, you must have the amateur card if you want to compete, even on a local level.

For further information about amateur skating in the United States contact:

> USAC
> 7700 "A" Street
> Lincoln, Nebraska 68510

Ann-Victoria Phillips

Jill Manning of Dublin, California, practices her figures under the watchful eye of coach Jim Pringle.

Performing their routines at the US National Meet are International Senior Dance skaters Larry Chopp and Judy Landau of Livonia, Michigan, (left) and International Senior Ladies competitor Colleen Daly of Toledo, Ohio (right).

tic skater will range from about 1,000 dollars to as high as 10,000 dollars a year (for a top-ranked world-class competitor).

Seamstress Ethel Bond fits World Champion Dance skater Fleurette Arseneault for a new costume.

ARTISTIC SKATING AS EXERCISE

Figure skating: This requires excellent balance and coordination. Although skating figures is difficult, it does not require strenuous physical activity and, by itself, does not produce high level cardiovascular health nor aid in losing weight—you just won't burn up enough calories.

Figure skating will improve your posture and balance. Since figures do not involve taking hard falls, it is good for adults who have been physically inactive for a long time. Furthermore, it is an excellent way to learn your edges, skills that are also necessary for freestyle and dance skating.

To get the maximum physical benefit, figure skaters should practice another aerobic-style exercise, such as jogging, bicycling, or racquet ball.

Freestyle skating: This is an extremely athletic style of roller skating. It qualifies as an aerobic exercise if practiced under certain condi-

UNITED STATES AMATEUR CONFEDERATION OF ROLLER SKATING

The first official US amateur roller skating championship was held at the Arena Gardens in Detroit in 1937, but from the years 1942 to 1972 competitive skating in the United States was controlled by two different sanctioning groups. This caused confusion because both groups held championships and sent their own top skaters to the World Meet. The existence of two groups instead of one was a major reason roller skating only recently achieved recognition by the US Olympic Committee.

In 1972, with an eye towards acceptance as an Olympic sport, the two amateur groups merged forming the United States Amateur Confederation of Roller Skating (USAC). USAC is now the only amateur group in this country recognized by the Federation Internationale de Roller Skating as well as the US Olympic Committee. In 1976, USAC was accepted as a class "A" member of the US Olympic Committee so it appears that roller skating's inclusion in 1979 Pan Am Games may prove to be a stepping stone to the 1984 Olympics.

Courtesy of RSROA

tions. You must skate vigorously and continuously to get all the benefits.

Skating freestyle, even for short periods of time, burns up a lot of calories. Weeks or even months may be spent mastering simple single or double revolution jumps so it will help to keep you slim and trim if you practice regularly.

Falling down is an accepted part of learning intermediate and advanced freestyle items so skaters who want to meet the challenge must have great determination and also a flexible and physically strong body.

Ann-Victoria Phillips

Heidi Pringle of Dublin, California, limbers up (left), while world class skater JoAnne Young of Virginia Beach, Virginia (right), stretches out with the help of coach Millie Funda.

Freestylists will fatigue easily if they are overweight or if skating freestyle is all they do. Choose a complementary aerobic exercise to practice along with your freestyle skating. This could be another skating sport which does develop cardiovascular endurance, such as speed or dance skating, or else an off-rink sport such as bicycling, running, or cross-country skiing.

Roller dance skating: This is an excellent form of aerobic exercise, yet you don't need to be a super-athlete to be able to do it. Dance is a good choice for people who *hate* to exercise because it's also an enjoyable social sport.

If you skate regularly and strenuously, you will burn up calories, lose weight and also increase your cardiovascular health. Dance skating, however, does not develop flexibility. Remember to do warm-up and cool-down flexibility exercises before and after you skate. Other complementary forms of exercise would be modern dance, ballet, yoga, disco dancing, and gymnastics.

SPECIALIZED COMPETITION COACHES

Figures and Freestyle:

Joe Baker
Golden Glide Skateport
Decatur, Georgia

Jack Breen and Elaine Breen
Roll-Land
Norwood, Massachusetts

John Dayney and Barbara Dayney
Levittown Arena
East Meadow, New York

Randy Dayney and Petra Dayney
Ohio Skate
Toledo, Ohio

Omar Dunn and Delores Dunn
Kern County Skateland
Bakersfield, California

Ron Jellse and Nancy Jellse
Harp's Rollerdrome
Cincinnati, Ohio

Jay Norcross
Warnoco Skating Center
Greeley, Colorado

John Olsen and Millie Funda
College Park Skating Center
Virginia Beach, Virginia

Sue Rendfrey
Cherry Hill Skating Center
Cherry Hill, New Jersey

Elmer Ringeisen
Skyline Rollarena
San Diego, California

Beverly Schien
Rollhaven Skating Arena
Flint, Michigan

John Viola and Dee Dee Viola
Wal-Lex Rollerway
Waltham, Massachusetts

Adolph Wacker
Ann Arbor World of Wheels
Ann Arbor, Michigan

American Dance:

Ron Jellse and Nancy Jellse
Harp's Rollerdrome
Cincinnati, Ohio

Bob LaBriola
Holiday Skating Center
Fountain Valley, California

Al Thompson
Rollero Skating Club
Phoenix, Arizona

John Viola and Dee Dee Viola
Wal-Lex Rollerway
Waltham, Massachusetts

International Dance:

Jack Burton and Honey Burton
Levittown Arena
East Meadow, New York

Warren Danner
Skateland-Rosedale
Baltimore, Maryland

Jim Dunlop
Livingston Roller Rink
Livingston, New Jersey

Joe Gaudy and Marie Gaudy
Cherry Hill Skating Center
Cherry Hill, New Jersey

Jane Puracchio
Euclid Rollerdrome
Euclid, Ohio

Pairs:

Tim Abell
Rollerama
Brighton, Michigan

Gene Buell
Skateland Frayser
Memphis, Tennessee

Ron Fitzgerald
Seabrook Roller Rink
Seabrook, Maryland

Don Gates
Ann Arbor World of Wheels
Ann Arbor, Michigan

Pamela Cornwall Morris
Airline Skating Rink
Houston, Texas

Tom Panno
Holiday Roller Rink
Orange, California

Lou Pannuzio
Brookpark Skateland
Brookpark, Ohio

Jim Pringle
Rollarena Dublin
Dublin, California

Jerry Waters and Darlene Waters
United Skates of America
Parma Heights, Ohio

VICTOR HERNANDEZ: DUAL ROLLS

Like many amateur athletes, Victor Hernandez, a top-ranked International Senior Men's competitor, has a schedule that includes both a full-time job and many hours of strenuous practice. His two worlds seldom meet, but one day Victor's co-workers at Regional Transit in Sacramento, California, asked to see his skating form—so Victor washed down the floor, put on his roller wheels, and dazzled the crew with some of the items from his freestyle routine.

All photos: Ann-Victoria Phillips

THE NATIONAL MEET

Backstage: Billy Vickers, American Junior Men's competitor, warms up (left); Isha Green and Stacy Cantrell, Juvenile Girls' skaters, cluch good luck charms (right); Dana Minor, Senior Dance skater, touches up (bottom left); and coach Dee Dee Viola sews Senior Dance skater Lori Walsh into her costume (bottom right).

International Senior Men's Competition: *The three top men in the division are Fred Morante (left center); Lex Kane, defending his title (right center); and Rick Elsworth who also skates in the Pairs competition with Danette Sullivan (top center). At bottom left, Rick stands with coach Bev Schien; at bottom right an excited and exhausted Fred dries off; and center—the moment of glory on the winner's platform, with Lex taking top honors.*

All photos: Ann-Victoria Phillips

International Junior Dance; Early in the week, David Golub and Wendy Galante practice under coach Jack Burton's direction (top center). At top left, David puts the finishing touches on his outfit before skating, and at top right he and Wendy perform in the compulsory half of the competition. Later in the week, the two skate the free dance portion (bottom left), and when their scores for the two events add up to a first place finish, they share a congratulatory kiss.

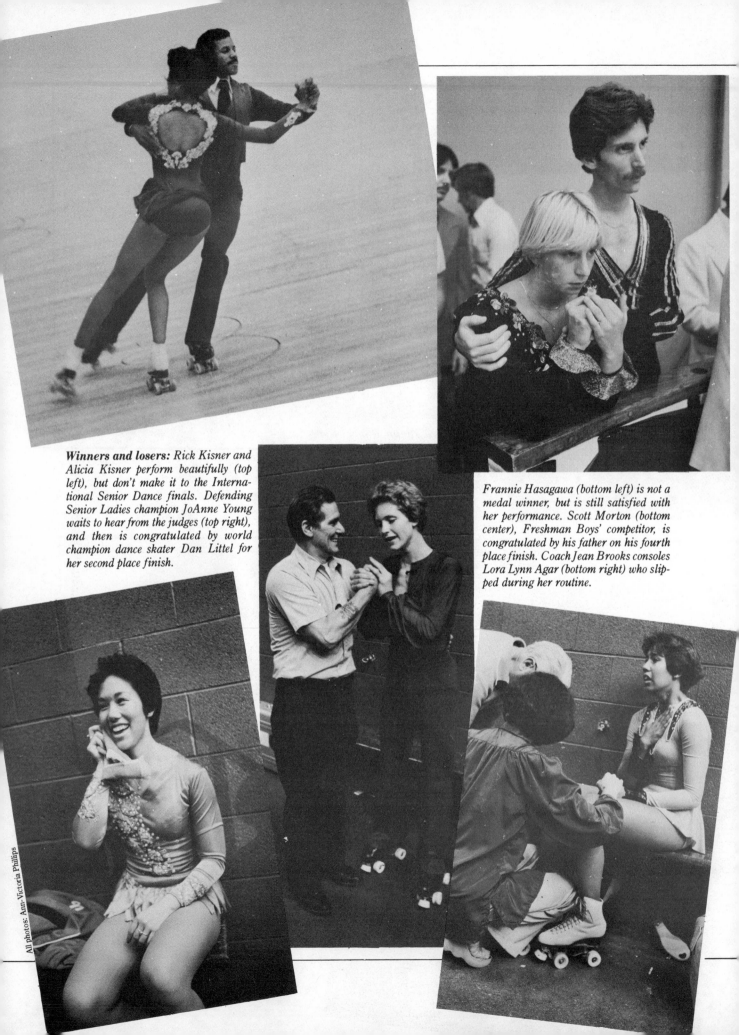

Winners and losers: *Rick Kisner and Alicia Kisner perform beautifully (top left), but don't make it to the International Senior Dance finals. Defending Senior Ladies champion JoAnne Young waits to hear from the judges (top right), and then is congratulated by world champion dance skater Dan Littel for her second place finish.*

Frannie Hasagawa (bottom left) is not a medal winner, but is still satisfied with her performance. Scott Morton (bottom center), Freshman Boys' competitor, is congratulated by his father on his fourth place finish. Coach Jean Brooks consoles Lora Lynn Agar (bottom right) who slipped during her routine.

1979 PAN AMERICAN GAMES

*Coach Jack Burton
poses with his four powerful International Senior Dance teams for the traditional post-meet photo.*

Fleurette Arseneault and Dan Littel on the winner's platform, having successfully defended their International Senior Dance title.

Although roller skating has not yet been accepted as an Olympic sport, it has been accepted and will be included in the 1979 Pan American Games in Puerto Rico.

United States Artistic Roller Skating Team

Coach: Jane Puracchio,
Cleveland Heights, Ohio

Figures and Freestyle Skaters:

Natalie Dunn; Bakersfield, California; age 22

JoAnne Young; Norfolk, Virginia; age 18

Lex Kane; Pontiac, Michigan; age 22

Fred Morante; Plainview, New York; age 19

Dance Skaters: Teams

Fleurette Arseneault;
Cambridge, Massachusetts; age 21
Dan Littel; Farmingdale, New York; age 26

Cindy Smith; Petersburg, Virginia; age 18
Mark Howard; Richmond, Virginia; age 18

Pairs Skaters: Teams

Robbie Coleman; Memphis, Tennessee; age 17
Pat Jones; Germantown, Tennessee; age 20

Tina Kneisley; Marion, Ohio; age 15
Paul Price; Howell, Michigan; age 17

PAUL PRICE AND TINA KNEISLEY: IN COMPETITION

Why are you the best?" Coach Tim Abell, 29, of Brighton, Michigan, huddles with his young Pairs team, Paul Price, 17, and Tina Kneisley, 15, at the 1978 United States Amateur Roller Skating Championships being held in Lincoln, Nebraska's Pershing Auditorium.

"Our Double Loops are the best," answers Tina.

"What else," demands Tim.

"Our Back Loop Lift is the best," says Paul, "because of its speed and sureness."

Although Tina and Paul are seasoned competitors—they won the US Junior Pairs title the year before and have each won national titles in individual freestyle events—they still need a last minute pep talk with their coach. A lot is at stake: winning the US Senior Pairs title means a ride to the World Meet, held in Lisbon. In addition, first- and second-place finishers will qualify to represent the United States at the 1979 Pan American Games in Puerto Rico.

All photos: Courtesy of Price/Kneisley

Their training regime, and in fact, their entire life-style, are typical for top-ranked competitive roller skaters. Both have been skating since they were very young: Tina since she was 10 months old.

Although neither of their parents were top competitive skaters, Tina's mother and Paul's father skated well enough to enter a few local meets. Both brought their children to the rink with them almost every time they skated.

Tina and Paul were matched as a team by Tina's mother when Paul was eight and Tina six. Both were cute kids who looked alike, were built similarly and had the same athletic skating style. They got along well together, loved competition, were hard workers, and looked good out on the floor—all prime requirements for Pairs skaters.

When pairing their children, parents have to make extraordinary commitments to each other once it's agreed that the two young athletes will skate as a team. Parents, skaters, and coach all work together toward the common goal.

Most times, all involved become the closest of friends. The parents share the responsibility of escorting the young skaters to practices and meets, sewing costumes for both skaters, and even sharing traveling expenses once their children qualify for the National Meet. The coach many times agrees to take on one or both skaters as a house guest every weekend and sometimes full-time during the summer months.

The trouble Paul, Tina, and their families go through for the weekly, four-day practice is mind-boggling. Every Tuesday and Thursday, Paul and Tina "meet in the middle," at a rink in Findlay, Ohio, a halfway point between Howell, Michigan and Marion, Ohio, that means a twice-a-week, 250-mile round trip for both skaters. They practice together without their coach for four hours, then each drives home.

That's only the beginning. On Saturday morning every week, Sharon and Tina Kneisley drive to Brighton, Michigan and the Rollerama rink (Abell's headquarters) where the two young skaters practice extensively in the afternoon and early evening. The Kneisleys stay overnight at Tim's house, practice all day Sunday, and drive home Sunday night.

The commitment between the two young skaters is even more complicated and personal. Not only does the team work require close physical contact, but also emotional and spiritual harmony. Once matched, the two must skate together as one.

They commit themselves to working with each other for at least one competitive year—

Tina and Paul, like most championship skaters, began in competition as small children— individually and then as a pair. They've had to sacrifice a lot but the hard work has paid off in their development as world class athletes.

Ann-Victoria Phillips

Paul uses meditation to calm jittery nerves before going out on the floor.

that's the minimum, but many Pairs teams skate together year after year, especially if they win.

Other responsibilities, as Tina sees them, are, "making sure I'm not too tired to give it my all in practice. I also have a responsibility to Paul to experiment, to try new things. That's why we have worked so well together."

There is also the responsibility that Tina has to control her body movements precisely during complicated maneuvers so that she doesn't hurt Paul.

She has to be alert and aware at all times. Most people think that the woman, who's up in the air a lot, stands the greatest chance of injury, but that's not necessarily true. It's Paul who often gets hit in the face, the head, and the groin. Says Tina, "One time we were practicing an Airplane Lift in a new position. I swung my leg around and kicked Paul in the head with my wheel. I knocked him out. One minute, he was holding me in the air; the next minute, he fell and dropped me.

I flew through the air, landing on the floor on my stomach, still in the Airplane position. It knocked the wind out of me. I didn't know what had happened to him. When I looked back, I thought I'd killed him. But it wasn't that bad. We were back practicing the next day."

Both Tina and Paul must be on time for all practice sessions. This may not sound like much of a problem except when you consider that competitive skaters sometimes fly or drive hundreds of miles to work with a top coach. Lessons cost a lot of money, not to mention the traveling expenses. Missed practices are considered a serious issue, from a financial point of view, and also as a reflection of the skater's lack of commitment to a serious training program.

Tina and Paul, in spite of their tightly scheduled lives, still find time to enjoy off-skate activities. Since she spends so many nights away from home, Tina goes to great lengths to guarantee herself a social life. Astonishingly, she has a dizzying schedule of school activities—she's a varsity cheerleader, plays the flute in the high school concert band, runs track in the spring (100-yard dash and 440-yard relay team), and takes once-weekly lessons in advanced gymnastics to help her with her skating. Tina is also an excellent student.

Paul, a senior and straight-A student at Howell High School, has a heavy course schedule that includes calculus and human anatomy. His goal is to major in physical therapy when he gets to college. He wants to be a skating coach and feels that this supplemental degree will help him in his profession. Paul loves to play pool, poker, and pinochle—in fact, any kind of strategy game. He relaxes by going to movies with his girlfriend and listening to music. Not as involved in school activities as Tina, but just as busy, Paul works in the skate shop at the rink almost every night.

For a long time, most of Tina's and Paul's friends had never seen them practice and had no idea what a competitive roller skater did. "When my girlfriends finally came to the rink and saw me fly through the air they were dumbfounded," reports Tina. Paul's classmates had a different reaction. "My friends thought roller skating was a sappy thing to do, until they found out that I lift the girl. To them, that was okay. That straightened them right out."

As Paul, Tina, and Tim huddle, the Senior Pair's event begins. The first team is called out onto the floor but the trio doesn't watch or listen. Instead, Tim, his arms wrapped protectively around his skaters, gives final instructions.

The first team, from California, finishes their routine to applause from the crowd, and skates off the floor. Paul and Tina wait at the gate. The announcer's voice begins, "From Brighton, Michigan, team number 1086, Paul Price and Tina Kneisley." They skate out onto the floor and stand still for a moment, posed hand in hand, under the bright lights. They look at each other, smile, and squeeze hands.

Tim, after wishing them good luck, has left the gate area and sprinted backstage. He reappears on stage near the music steward's table where he will watch the routine and supervise the playing of the music.

The young team's music, lively Eastern European folk tunes that are Tim's favorites, will provide a unique tempo and beat throughout their routine. As the music starts, the sound of Russian guitars fills the auditorium and Paul and Tina skate toward the five judges who are seated at the end of the floor.

Ron Robivitsky and sister Gail of Detroit, Michigan, were five-time World Champions in Senior Pairs.

Courtesy of Penny Money Miller

WHAT IS PAIRS?

Pairs is an advanced, freestyle event skated by two people who move as one. The event, a favorite of the crowd, is exciting, athletic, dangerous, and full of surprises. It features all the jumps and spins seen in Singles events except, since there are two people skating, Double Spins, Throw Jumps, and the spectacular lifts create a unique feeling of suspense.

A Pairs routine maintains a constant relationship between the skaters throughout the program. This is accomplished through mirror movements (the skaters perform the same movement facing each other as in a mirror) and shadow movements (the skaters skate side by side and do exactly the same jumps and spins).

In competition, a routine is judged by choice of items and how difficult and well executed they are, how expressively the team interprets the music, and how creatively the different items in the routine are linked together to make up the total program. The quality of this connective footwork can often make the difference between winning and finishing in second place in a National Championship.

Pairs skaters must be physically strong as well as highly skilled freestyle skaters in their own right before they can even attempt this advanced form of competition. In addition, the woman must have unusual strength and flexibility as acrobatic skills are also helpful to perform the lifts and jumps that characterize this unique skating event. The man must be strong and skilled enough to lift the woman into the air and support her. Lastly, both must have an unusual knack for showmanship, all-important for winning over a crowd.

In the next five minutes, Tina and Paul will perform item after item to both fast and slow music. The routine includes more than 16 individual items: lifts, throw jumps, double spins, as well as individual jumps and spins. Connective footwork with which the young skaters hope to impress the judges is another important part of the routine. "This is a one-shot deal," explains Tim, looking out at his skaters. "It's no time for mistakes. You don't get a second chance."

Skating together and backward around the floor, Paul lifts Tina up in the air with a quick, snapping movement that awes the crowd. He holds her, first with two hands until she's stable in the air, then, he lets one supporting hand drop away as he rolls forward and revolves at the same time. Tina, sitting in the palm of Paul's hand as if she were in a chair, sails through space, nine feet above the floor. Smiling, her arms outstretched, she looks radiant and totally secure. After three complete revolutions, Paul sets Tina down so

smoothly that the audience can't hear her wheels hit the floor.

Tim, who describes himself as a "basket case" while he watches final events, smiles and says, "Look at those two, how casual they are. They'll talk to each other throughout the whole routine. They can't afford to get uptight. They talk to relax and encourage each other."

Next, the skaters will attempt side-by-side double loop jumps. Skating close, but not hand in hand, they hurl themselves into the air, make two revolutions and land simultaneously, skating in a backward direction. Tina's arm, hand, and body position are an exact shadow of Paul's movement.

"Take it easy," Tim whispers to himself. "The Double Loop is hard enough for one person, but Tina and Paul do it perfectly *together*."

The young skaters, who use up every inch of the floor as they skate, collect themselves for another crowd-pleaser—a Throw Double Loop. "Take it easy Paul," yells Tim. Even though the

All photos: Ann-Victoria Phillips

Tina and Paul's routine consists of connective moves, at left, and specific items, like the Face Camel Spin at right.

auditorium is crowded his skaters can still hear his instructions because no one in the crowd is talking. They're all holding their breath. "Don't throw her too hard." Tina wraps for the jump and, at the same time, Paul assists her by lifting her three to four feet straight up (much higher than she would ever go by herself) and throwing her outward. Tina flies through the air, landing the jump backward, 20 feet away. Comments Tim, "Sometimes Paul throws Tina like, 'Hey, folks, watch this.' Paul gets carried away and starts showing off. This is a spectacular jump but hard for Tina to control. We have to remind him to take it easy every single time."

Tina and Paul criss-cross the floor to the sound of quick-moving Russian guitars which contribute to the creation of a distinct on-floor identity characterizing the work of all of Tim's students.

Another strength and balance item is next on the program. "This one will wow the crowd. Just watch," says Tim.

Skating backward, Tina jumps as Paul lifts her over his head. She does a Split Cartwheel over his shoulder. For a fraction of a second all motion is suspended; it looks like Tina is doing a handstand on Paul's shoulder, her feet pointed straight up into the air.

"We call this a True Cartwheel Lift," says Tim. "It's a novelty item used to wake up the crowd, just like the headline on a newspaper. Tina and Paul are the only ones who do it in the world. When we put together a routine, we face the problem that most people (sometimes even the judges) don't know which items are the hard ones. Sometimes my students do extremely difficult movements so smoothly that the item looks easy. This doesn't help them win the crowd. This Cartwheel Lift is easy to do, yet it looks scary. In pairs, we choose items that attract people's attention."

Next, Tina and Paul do side-by-side spins. First, each skater revolves on one foot, and then switches quickly to the other foot with a snap—all of it in perfect synchronization. Tim, coaching from the sidelines, mutters, "That one's gonna help us score."

The beat of the music picks up and Tim adjusts the volume, making it louder. Hand in hand, Tina and Paul skip and skim diagonally across the floor past the judges. They flash brilliant smiles as they move by as quick and light as ballet dancers.

Tina landing a Throw Double Loop—one of the hardest items for her to control.

All photos: Ann-Victoria Phillips

Tina and Paul's True Cartwheel Lift is unique in Pairs competition.

The team skates back to the center of the floor. Paul, holding Tina's hand and pivoting, swings her around him in a circle. She circles faster and faster and relaxes down into a backbend position, her head inches from the floor. This item, called a Death Spiral, looks shockingly dangerous. According to Tim, "It's easy, but hard to make it look nice. Tina has to have a nice arch in her back and get down as close to the floor as possible. This movement is easier on ice than it is on rollers. So far they're perfect. No slips, no misses. I'm keeping my fingers crossed."

The next item, called an Impossible Sit Spin, is one of the most difficult movements in Pairs skating. Only two other teams in the world can do it. Tina and Paul separate and skate in opposite circles to build up speed. They join together again and merge into a Camel Spin. Still spinning, at top speed, Paul picks Tina up in his arms, holding her under the small of her back with one hand and under her leg with the other. Tina, still in his arms, is as stiff as a board. Holding her, Paul sinks down into a Sit Spin position. (It looks like Paul is doing Shoot the Duck, carrying a 100-pound weight.) This is known as a strength movement, in Pairs lingo, because after making three revolutions in this position, Paul will rise up on one leg still carrying Tina in his arms. Paul supports Tina as she drops one leg back to the floor and they shadow one another's movements with a second Camel Spin, revolving three more times together. The transition is executed smoothly and at top speed. They look perfect. A few beats of the music are lost to the ear while the fans *ooh* and *aah*, and scream encouragement to Paul and Tina.

The young pair jumps and spins through four more items, looking calm, smiling at each other as if they were doing a routine practice. Paul and Tina move through their repertoire with amazing precision and speed. Observers wonder how they can manage to pull off many complicated movements in such a short time. Only two minutes and thirty seconds have gone by—they're only halfway through the routine. Every time the skaters move in a backward direction, the crowd is cued to an upcoming lift, usually something spectacular. Those are the crowd's favorites. All eyes focus on the small figures skating across the auditorium floor.

On the edge of their seats, the audience watches Paul assist Tina up into an Inverted

Airplane Lift, first holding her with both hands, and then just with one on the small of her back. This looks fast, sensational and scary. The crowd gasps. Tina, who gazes at the ceiling during the item, arches her back. Paul rolls forward while, at the same time, doing Mohawk turns across the floor. As he revolves, Tina also turns in the air. Spinning so quickly that she almost blurs out, she looks more like the revolving blade of a helicopter than a woman.

"This one is very dangerous," says Tim, an anxious look on his face. "Paul is holding her on only one point, the small of her back. If he loses control, it would be hard to save her. She's really helpless up there. Inverted, Tina loses orientation with the rink and the floor. She only sees blurs. She has no control over what happens and sometimes tells me that she doesn't even know where she is.

"It's a thrill for her because she goes weightless. She can't even feel Paul's hand under her back. This excites her—it's as good as a ride in an amusement park.

"On the bad side, if she falls Paul could only hope to break her fall with his body. She could never save herself."

The young champions execute an Airplane Lift, right, and impress the judges with a forward run.

The crowd, behind Tina and Paul all the way, watches every movement. "They're wondering, 'Will he drop her?'," says Tim. "Not too many parents will let their daughters do this one."

Paul reaches up and grabs Tina's free hand, and quickly assists her down to the floor. "She's

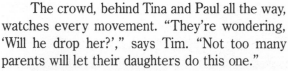

safe," says Tim. "Paul's never dropped her where she's hurt herself. There's never been any blood. We're very careful about these things."

Across the floor, Paul and Tina smile at each other and the crowd in a self-congratulatory way. "We don't worry about accidents," says Tim. "These two get hurt more goofing around than when they're skating. Tina pulled a ligament in her leg playing baseball. Paul has been known to walk into doors. They're both *klutzes* off skates."

The fact that Tim's team can pull off such a demanding move so late in the routine is remarkable. Other skaters perform their difficult items as early in the program as possible. Otherwise they'd "die" (come close to physical collapse) at the halfway point. The typical five-minute Pairs routine is so strenuous that few skaters have the energy to do complicated maneuvers placed at the end. Tina and Paul don't look tired. In fact, they've stepped up the pace in synch again with the music. To show the judges how versatile they are, they skip and shuffle, hand in hand, side by side, forward and backward across the floor. The rhythm of the music has gotten them going and the audience loves it.

The young team executes another difficult lift cleanly and perfectly. They close their program with simple side-by-side spins. It's all over. Tina and Paul, spotlit in the center of the floor, hold hands over their heads, victoriously acknowledging the cheers of the crowd. Last year's Junior Pairs champions, they look as fresh at the end as when they first started.

Tim rushes off the stage, meeting his skaters back in the pit. The three of them stand close, their arms wrapped around each other's shoulders.

"Tim, what do you think?" Tina, misty eyed, looks happy and anxious at the same time. She tries to catch her breath. "You did a super job," compliments Tim. "Win or lose, you couldn't have done any better. So far, you're first."

Ann-Victoria Phillips

Paul and Tina make the Impossible Spin, one of the toughest items in skating, look easy as they float across the rink floor.

Two more teams have yet to skate. The last one, Robbie Coleman and Pat Jones of Memphis, Tennessee, are stiff competition, they're favored to win the event. While his young skaters, busy with family, friends and fans, ignore the action, Tim watches. A few minutes later they regroup as Tim critiques their competitors' routines. "You're still in the contest," he says.

Although Senior Pairs is the climax and the last event of the eight-day meet, the three of them will have to wait 10 to 15 minutes longer while tabulators work out the judges' score. Tim explains how the winner is chosen. "Each of the five judges gives each team two different marks, rating them on a scale from 1 to 100. One mark is for technical merit (what they did), and another for artistic impression (how they look when they did it). The scores are added together. The team that has the highest score gets a one, the next highest gets a two, and so on. The placement of each team is determined by the judge's agreeing on at least three or more scores."

BORN TO WIN

Courtesy of Price/Kneisley

Tina Kneisley, a world-class Senior Pairs competitor, started walking when she was 8 months old and started skating at 10 months old. This strange history is familiar enough among competitive roller skaters, especially national and international champions. Skating parents often fit their children with roller skates at the same time as they first learn to walk. They start out on baby shoes mounted on small aluminum plates with trucks and wheels. Not only do these youngsters quickly learn to skate, they learn to walk and do a whole variety of other physical activities better and faster than non-skating children.

It is widely acknowledged that skating develops balance, advanced motor skills, confidence, physical strength, and a good self-image at an early age. This same story is heard over and over again. As extraordinary as it may seem, there is also a group of skaters whose parents claim that roller skating has corrected emotional problems as well as minor physical disabilities.

Melissa, daughter of coach Tim Abell, walked and skated when she was not yet a year old. Tim, who gives lessons at the rink during the day while his wife also works, wanted Melissa with him instead of with a sitter. Once at the rink, his young daughter demanded skates. Tim says, "It's important that the child really wants to learn. They must decide to do it for themselves. The parents should never push their child into anything, especially not skating."

Tim, busy much of the time giving lessons, didn't have to teach Melissa to put on her skates and lace them up by herself. At 18 months, she learned it by herself. About the same time, she showed off her first freestyle items—Shoot the Duck and a Waltz Jump. At three years old, Melissa, who now trains with another skating instructor at the rink, understands most technical points about elementary-level figure skating and freestyle.

Tim has seen the good effect skating has had on very young children by watching other people's kids as well as his own daughter. He mentions some advantages in starting children at a very young age. "They are super-coordinated and strong. When Melissa went in for her three-year-old examination, the doctor said he couldn't believe she was so young. She has the muscle definition of a much older child because of roller skating."

Skating can help children in other ways. Says Tim, "It helps them socially. Being at the rink everyday, they meet skaters of all different ages. Their vocabulary increases very quickly too."

As they wait, awards are presented to the winners of the preceding event—Senior International Men's Singles. The pit is swarming with skaters, coaches, officials, mothers, fathers, fans, and hangers-on, all of them in different emotional states. Some stand still; others sweat; a few cry; one is happy and another disappointed. It's a confusing scene: skaters crowd near the rail to watch the award ceremony on the floor.

Five judges walk back onto the floor single file and stand in a line. The skating floor is crowded with officials. The crowd waits for the announcement.

"The ordinal placement for Team number 952, Brown and Grossi, please," says the announcer. Five small children, called caddies, walk to a box and select appropriate cards with large numbers, hand one to each judge. The judges hold up the numbers for the announcer, the skaters, and the audience to see. This time the cards are all fours.

Tim, standing near the rail with Tina on one side and Paul on the other, strains forward. "Everyone watches the kids carrying the numbers," he says. "You don't have to wait for the announcer to know what you got."

"The ordinal placement for Team number 1086, Price and Kneisley, please." The announcer's voice is soon overpowered by the noise of the crowd, not waiting to hear the numbers.

"That's it. You've done it," exclaims Tim. He hugs both skaters close. They watch the cards as the judges calmly hold up the numbers. Tina and Paul scored five ones. A perfect score.

In the pit, Paul jumps straight up in the air screaming, "We won, we won. I feel out of breath," he says, "but I could do it all again. My heart is pumping like crazy. We knew we did good." He kisses and hugs Tina. He thanks her. She thanks him. Paul, flushed and elated, looks like he's floating on air. "Oh God, we enjoy this so much."

Competition is very close at the top of the Pairs skating world—at the National Meet Tina and Paul (right) beat out Pat Jones and Robbie Coleman for the Gold Medal. Two months later at the World Meet in Portugal the tables were turned, and it was Pat and Robbie who finished in first place (left).

Courtesy of Price/Kneisley

Courtesy of RSROA

TIM ABELL: A TOP-NOTCH COACH

Tim Abell, at 29 years old, is one of the youngest top-ranked competitive roller skating coaches in the US. His specialty is Pairs and, although at one time he also skated this event in competition, today he concentrates on teaching and coaching at Rollerama, a rink located in Brighton, Michigan. His students admire him enough to travel from as far away as Detroit, Cleveland, Columbus, and Chicago to take his lessons.

Most people know his name because of the success of his two star Pairs teams: Ray Chappata/Karen Mejia and Paul Price/Tina Kneisley. Ray and Karen won the US Championship and the World Championship in 1977 but, due to illness, were not able to defend either title in 1978. (They will return to competition in 1979.) His "little team," as he calls them, of Price and Kneisley were US Champions in 1978.

To work with Tim requires a high level of awareness. He likes a lot of feedback. He wants to know what his students think about everything they do, how they feel doing it, and how they think it will help them achieve their goals. Although Tim's always in charge, he underplays the coach-athlete relationship to a degree that's unusual in the skating world. Because of his young age and also his attitude, he's more like a brother than a teacher. He makes his home available to all his away-from-home skaters, especially on weekends and during the summer. Known affectionately as "Abell's Hotel," the house is furnished with extra couches, and is always overbooked. Accommodations even include a fully-equipped weight room. Tim encourages a wide variety of stretching exercises before practice to make sure his skaters stay limber.

Although all his students take lessons regularly, Abell believes that his two "world-class" teams deserve extra attention beyond what they pay for. He offers them a totally supervised practice during the summer months and just before the national meet. Says Tim, "They deserve more.

Coach Tim Abell (center) with one of his teams, Frannie Hasagawa and Matt Olszewski of Melrose Park, Illinois.

They're giving everything they've got for skating."

Abell has a number of attitudes about training, conditioning, and competition that set him apart from most of his colleagues. For one thing, he describes himself as a choreographer. Other coaches confirm his skill as an innovator who is constantly searching for new eye-catching movements that can be incorporated into competitive routines. If Ray and Karen, who Tim refers to as his "aesthetic team," see Baryshnikov do something they like, he'll encourage them to incorporate a similar movement into their program. "I try to keep an open mind," says Abell. "My philosophy is, there's no movement too feminine for a man and no movement too masculine for a woman. Unlike most other teachers, I put no limitation on the kinds of movements my skaters use. The only time I throw something out is if it doesn't fit their personality or isn't right for the music."

Abell does not consider long hours of practice to be an indicator of how hard his skaters are working or how fast they are progressing. "I'd rather see my teams practice hard for short, concentrated periods of time—30 minutes or so and then rest. They should never practice if they're tired. Only when they're physically and mentally alert."

Although to an outsider he may seem easygoing, Abell has finely tuned competitive instincts. He tells his students, "After first, you've lost. Second place is not winning." Like the late Vince Lombardi, one-time coach of the Green Bay Packers, Abell can be a hard task master. Always a realist, Abell does not believe in luck when it comes to winning, no matter whether it's on a beginner level or in world-class competition.

"If you want to be the best, you have to work hard, practice, and *really* want it. I tell them if *their* best happens to be *the* best on that particular day, they'll win. I never try to fool the kids about where they're at. My approach is to be honest. If they want to get better, they'll have to improve their form, skate faster, or put harder content in the program. There's no luck in this thing."

Courtesy of Mejia/Chappatta

Former World Pairs champions Karen Mejia and Ray Chappatta of Melrose Park, Illinois, are also coached by the talented Abell.

DESTINED TO SUCCEED

Young, competitive roller skaters are nearly always straight-A students. This story is so familiar that one can almost create a profile of these young athletes.

For one thing, the discipline of an everyday practice teaches competitive skaters, at a very young age, how to organize their time. This responsibility carries over into many areas of their lives. Young skaters express themselves well and are sophisticated, yet modest. They're unusually sociable and have friends of many ages, including older skaters. Often, they've traveled all over the United States.

Although "rink mothers and fathers," who pressure young skaters to compete, do exist, most young athletes skate primarily because they love it. They like the experience of competition and winning.

Young competitive skaters have a set of physical and mental attitudes that set them apart from their classmates. For one thing, they appear to have an unusually high energy level. While many other young people today seem unfocused, alienated, insecure, self-conscious, physically passive, and perhaps inarticulate, top skaters as well as other prominent sports figures, are goal-oriented. They feel lucky they've found something they like at an early age. Acknowledged and accepted by their peers and authorities, they know their own minds—what they want in life and how to get it.

8. BASIC SKATING
LESSONS PART II

FREESTYLE TECHNIQUES FOR THE BEGINNER

O nce you have mastered the basic lessons in Chapter 4, try some of the basic freestyle items which follow. Before starting, review the abbreviations below. They are used again here in helping to explain technique.

The four edges used when skating on the right foot are:

ROF: right foot skating forward on the outside edge

RIF: right foot skating forward on the inside edge

ROB: right foot skating backward on the outside edge

RIB: right foot skating backward on the inside edge

The four edges used while skating on the left foot are:

LOF: left foot skating forward on the outside edge

LIF: left foot skating forward on the inside edge

LOB: left foot skating backward on the outside edge

LIB: left foot skating backward on the inside edge

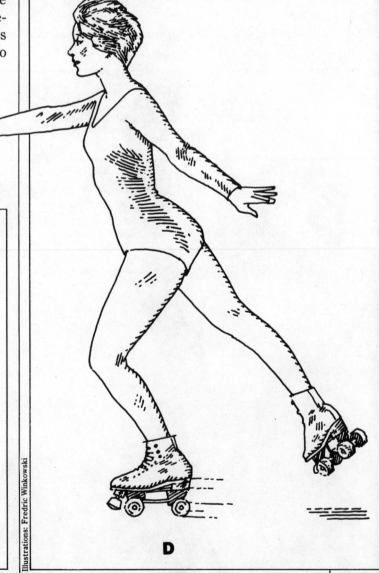

Illustrations: Fredric Winkowski

D

LESSON 11

THE BUNNY HOP

The Bunny Hop is a forward leap with no revolution.

How to do the Bunny Hop:

Start: Skate forward on your left foot (A) and . . .

Takeoff: . . . as you leap, swing your right leg (free leg) through (B).

Landing: On the descent, bring your right foot down, *landing on your toe stop* (C).

Finish: After landing on the toe stop, immediately *push* and *stroke* onto your left foot on your LOF edge (D).

C   B   A

LESSON 12

THE SPREAD EAGLE TURN

The Spread Eagle is the simplest kind of turn to use when changing direction from forward to backward. In this turn, your weight is evenly distributed. The Spread Eagle turn, as explained below, is done in a counterclockwise direction.

How to do the Spread Eagle turn:

Start: Stroke forward on your RIF edge (A). Your weight should be on the heel of your right foot.

Preparation: With your left rear wheels slightly off the floor, turn your left side, hip and leg into an open position (as in ballet) (B).

Spread Eagle position: Place your left foot on the floor with your toes out, heels together (this is the Spread Eagle position, C). Your right skate will travel forward as your left travels backward.

The Turn: When you feel ready, take your right foot off the floor. Now, you'll be rolling backward on your left foot (D). Keep your back straight. Don't bend forward.

Finish: Now that the turn is completed, stroke onto your right foot and continue to skate backward (E).

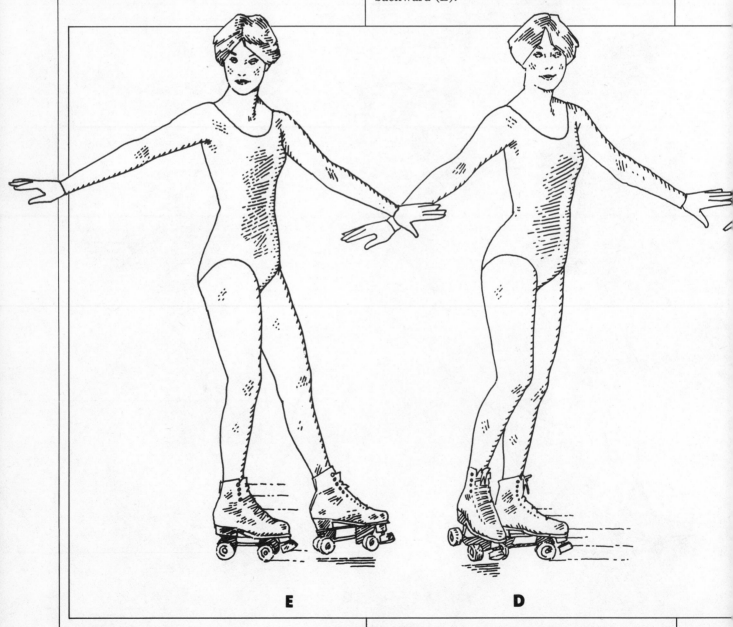

E   D

Tips on style:

- Keep your head up.
- Keep your back straight and your legs straight. Your arms should be held in a graceful position.
- When using the Spread Eagle position for a turn, keep your heels close together. The Spread Eagle can also be used as a beautiful position for a glide. For a glide, keep your feet spread wide, your legs stretched and your back well arched.

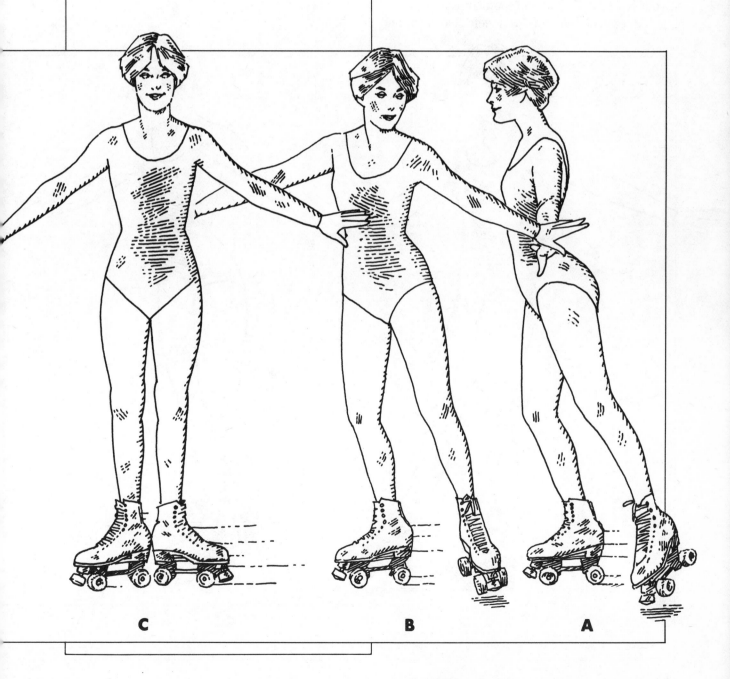

C   B   A

LESSON 13

THE MOHAWK TURN

The Mohawk is another basic turn like the Spread Eagle, except in this turn, your weight is placed on one foot at a time. The Mohawk Turn, as described below, is done in a counterclockwise direction.

How to do the Mohawk Turn:

Start: Stroke forward on your RIF edge with your left skate slightly off the floor (A).

Preparation: Turn your left side open and bring your left foot close to the heel of your right foot and at a right angle to it (B and C).

The Mohawk Turn: As you put your left foot down, simultaneously pick up your right foot.

Finish: Now that your turn is completed, stroke onto your right foot and skate backward (D).

Tips on style:

● Keep your body straight and your head erect. Don't watch your feet.

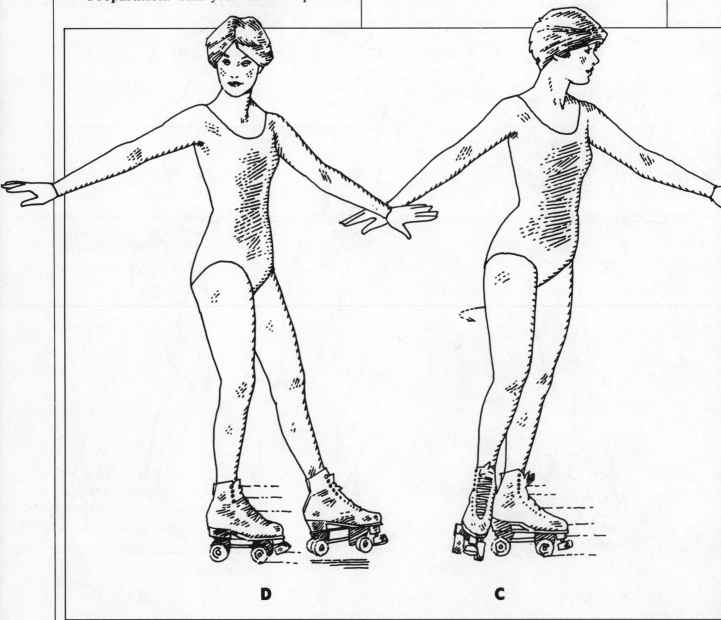

D   C

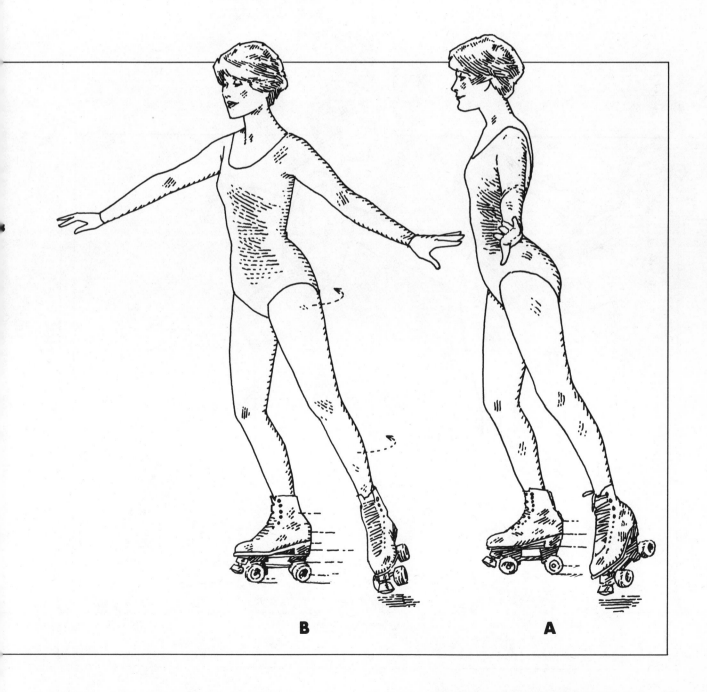

B   A

LESSON 14

THE ARABESQUE

The Arabesque is like the ballet movement of the same name. The instructions, as described below, are for an Arabesque in a forward direction.

How to do the Arabesque:

Start: Skate forward while balancing on your left leg. Keep your weight on your heel (A).

The Arabesque: Lift your right leg straight up behind you and into the air, with your hip, leg, and toe turned out. Keep your body horizontal to the floor and arch your back (B). The Arabesque can be skated on a flat or a curved edge.

Tips on style:

• Keep your head and your right foot up while you arch your back. Your foot should not be held lower than your head.

• Keep your chin erect.

• Extend your arms and hands out in a graceful position. This will also help maintain balance.

• While doing the Arabesque, lock your free leg straight.

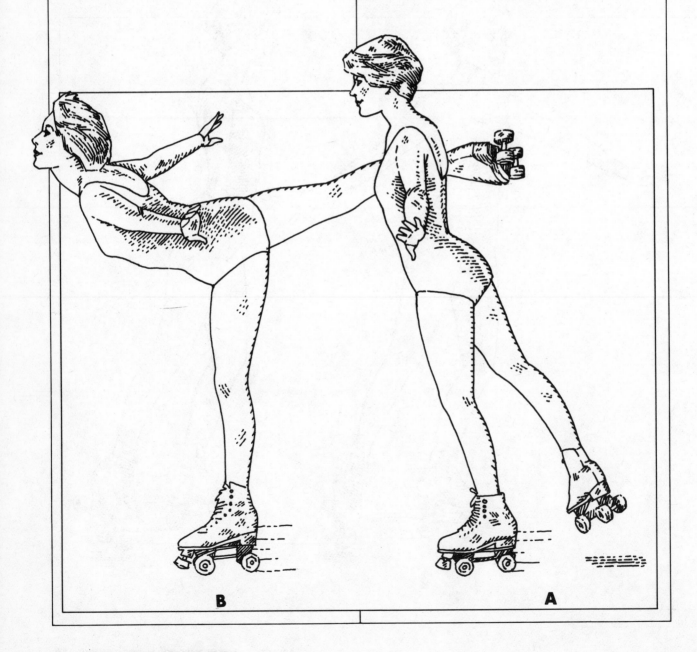

B

A

LESSON 15

THE THREE TURN

The Three Turn got its name from the shape the skate traces on the floor—similar to a numeral "3."

There are eight possible Three Turns. Because skating in most rinks is done in a counterclockwise direction, the Three Turn, done on your LOF edge is usually the first one learned.

The Three Turn is another basic turn used to change directions from forward to back or back to forward. Unlike the Mohawk Turn, Three Turns are done on one foot. The Three Turn, as explained below, is done in a counterclockwise direction.

How to do the Three Turn:

Start: Skate forward on your LOF edge keeping your weight on the heel of your left foot. Extend your right leg (free leg) slightly back and keep it turned open (A). Lock your hip and keep your calf and thigh muscles firm. With the exception of slightly rotating your shoulders counterclockwise, hold this position throughout the turn.

The Three Turn: To make the turn, press forward onto the ball of your left foot, transferring part of your weight forward (B). Do it in a pushing-type motion and this will start your skate turning in a counterclockwise direction.

Finish: After you are turned backward, your weight should be distributed toward your toe while your right shoulder is back. Your body should be facing the inside of the curve.

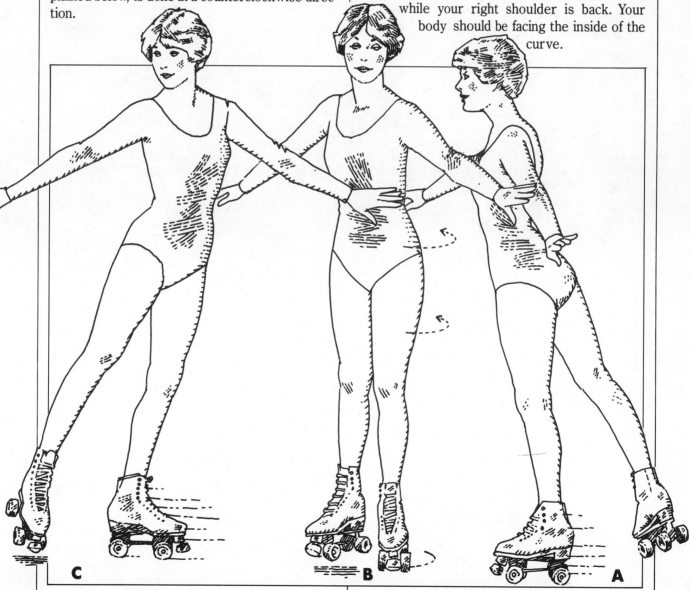

C   B   A

LESSON 16

THE WALTZ JUMP

The Waltz Jump is a simple freestyle jump with a half revolution. The approach is similar to that used in the Bunny Hop except, this time, you'll make a half-turn in the air and come down backward landing on your right foot. The Waltz Jump, as explained below, is done in a counterclockwise direction.

How to do the Waltz Jump:

Start: Skate forward on your LOF edge (A).

Takeoff: Swing your right foot (free foot) forward past your left leg (B) . . .

The Waltz Jump: . . . and, at the same time, leap into the air and start your half-revolution (C).

Landing: Stop the rotation by extending your arms sharply outward at your sides, and, at the same time, land backwards on your right foot on your ROB edge (D). Bend your knee as you land.

Finish: Bring your left leg (free leg) back and extend it outward in a semi-Arabesque, graceful position (E).

Tips on style:

● Movements should have a graceful flowing quality. Avoid jerky motions.

E   D

- If you bend the employed knee as you land the jump, the impact will be softened.
- Once the jump is completed and your free leg is extended back, your toe should be pointed and slightly turned out.

C   B   A

LESSON 17

THE TWO-FOOT SPIN

The Two-Foot Spin is one of the simplest spins. In it all eight wheels will remain on the floor. The spin, as described below, is done in a counterclockwise direction.

How to do the Two-Foot Spin:

Start: First, learn the spin at a standstill position. Your left arm should be forward, your right arm back. Stand in a slightly pigeon-toed stance while putting pressure on your left toe and right heel at the same time (A).

The spin: To begin the spin reverse the position of your arms (in other words, left back, right forward) and at the same time, turn your torso in a counterclockwise direction (B). This will cause you to spin.

Gaining momentum: Draw your arms inward and close to your body (C). You will automatically gain momentum and spin faster.

Finish: As you finish the spin, step onto your right foot in a backward skating, semi-Arabesque, graceful position (D).

Tips on style:

• Keep the body and head in an upright position. Avoid bending at the waist.

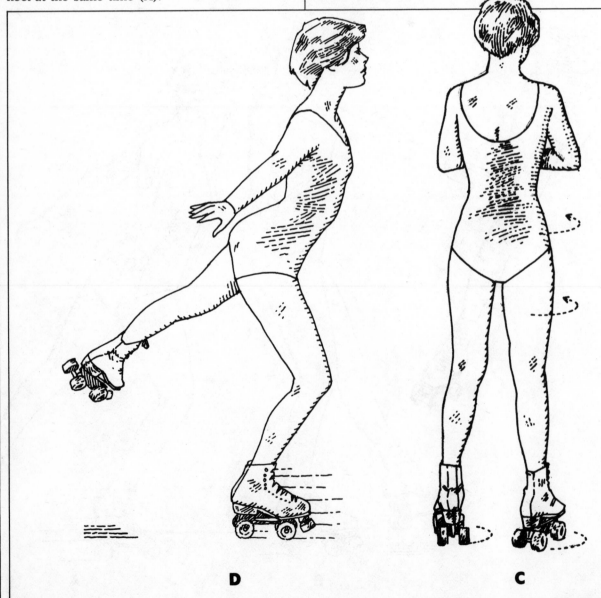

D   C

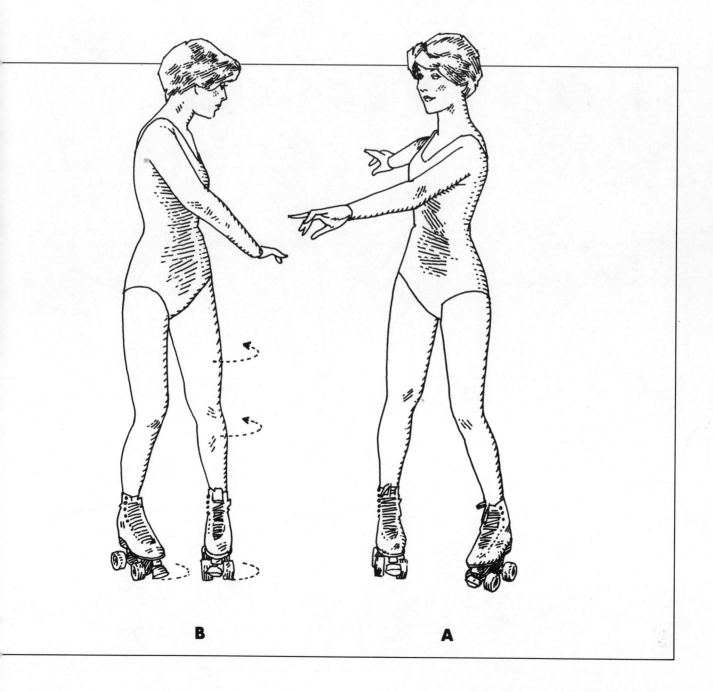

B   A

LESSON 18

THE MAPES

A Mapes is a simple, one-revolution *toe jump* (done off your *toe stop*). You take off from your right foot and left toe and then land the jump on your right foot. The jump, as described below, is done in a counterclockwise direction.

How to do the Mapes:

Start: Skate backward with your weight on your ROB edge with your left leg (free leg) extended in front of you (A).

Preparation: Bring your left foot (free foot) back and *jab your toe stop into the floor* (B). Look in the direction you're coming from, not where you're going.

Takeoff: As your toe stop hits the floor, start to bring your right foot off and in toward your left leg (C) and . . .

The Mapes: . . . jump from your left toe while turning your body in a counterclockwise direction (D). Make a complete revolution in the air (E).

Landing: Stop the rotation by extending your

F   E   D

arms sharply outward to your sides, and at the same time, land backward on your right foot on your ROB edge (F). Bend your knee as you land.

Finish: Bring your left leg (free leg) back and extend it outward in a semi-Arabesque, graceful position.

Tips on style:

• Movement should have a graceful flowing quality. Avoid jerky motions.

• If you bend your employed knee as you land the jump, the impact will be softened.

• Once the jump is completed and your free leg is extended back, your toe should be pointed and slightly turned out.

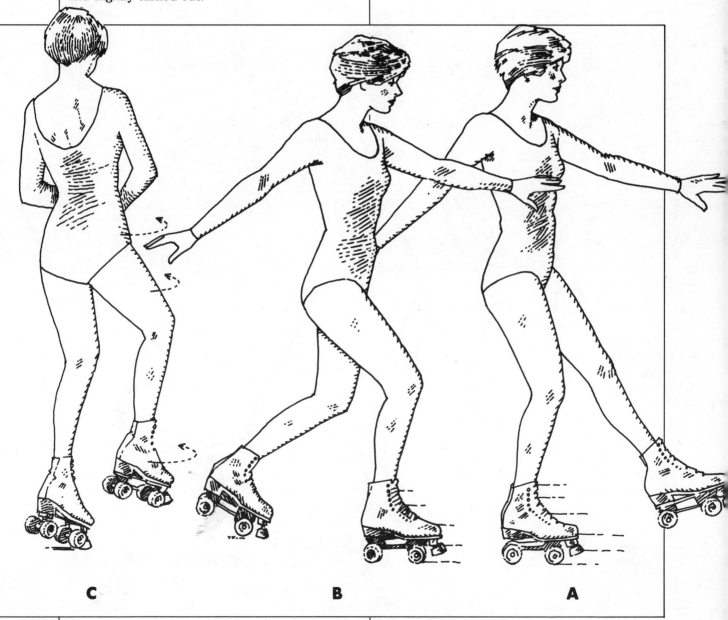

C   B   A

LESSON 19

THE SALCHOW

A Salchow (pronounced "sow-cow") is another basic one-revolution jump similar to the Mapes, except this jump is done off the *wheels*. The Salchow, as described below, is done in a counterclockwise direction.

How to do the Salchow:

Start: Skate backward on your LIB edge with your right foot stretched out behind (A).

Preparation: Bring your right foot (free foot) around and slightly to the front (B). Keep your left knee (employed knee) slightly bent.

Takeoff: Now that your free leg is slightly forward and around, bend your knee quickly and leap into the air from your left skate (C) . . .

The Salchow: . . . draw your right leg and arms in (D). This will assist you in making one complete revolution in the air.

Landing: Stop the rotation by extending your arms sharply outward to your sides, and, at the same time, land backward on your right foot on your ROB edge (E). Bend your knee as you land.

Finish: Bring your left leg (free leg) back and extend it outward in a semi-Arabesque, graceful position (F).

F   E   D

Tips on style:

- Movements should have a graceful flowing quality. Avoid jerky motions.
- If you bend your employed knee as you land the jump, the impact will be softened.
- Once the jump is completed and your free leg is extended back, your toe should be pointed and slightly turned out.

C   B   A

LESSON 20

THE UPRIGHT SPIN

The Upright Spin is done on one foot instead of two.

How to do the Upright Spin:

Start: When first learning the spin, begin at a standstill position. Your left arm should be forward, your right arm back. Stand in a slightly pigeon-toed stance while putting pressure on your left toe and right heel, all at the same time (A).

Preparation: To begin the spin, reverse the positions of your arms (that is, left back, right forward) and, at the same time, turn in a counter-clockwise direction (B).

The Spin: As you first start to turn, immediately shuffle your right foot and leg forward off the floor (C). Spin on your left foot only.

Finish: To finish the spin, set your right foot back down and come out of the spin skating backward in a semi-Arabesque, graceful position (see Finish, Lesson 19).

Tips on style:

● To gain momentum, draw your arms and your right leg in close. The tighter your position, the faster you'll spin.

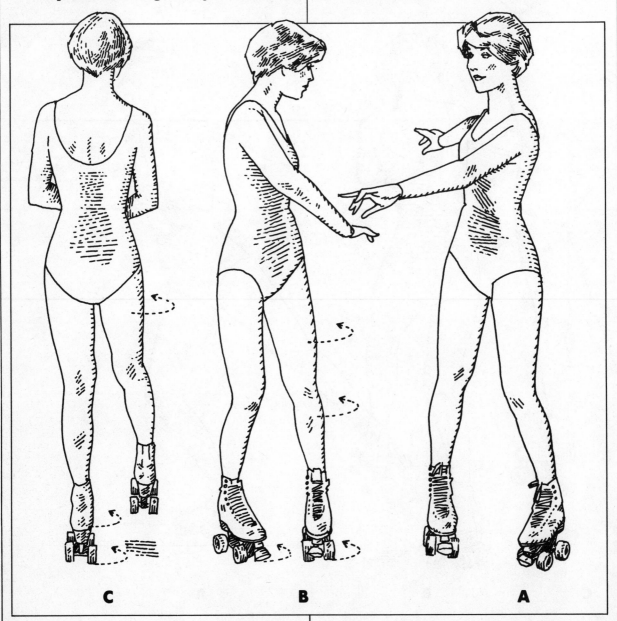

C   B   A

9. SPEED SKATING

SPEED ON WHEELS

S peed skating is a simple, primitive, competitive event. Skaters race in a pack; there is body contact. Ultimately it doesn't matter how good or bad your form looks as you race, just as long as you're first over the finish line. Coaches emphasize physical and mental conditioning rather than technique because speed skating takes a strong endurance, a fearless fighting attitude, a super will to win, and a refusal to quit.

Youngsters sprint off the line in a Depression-era outdoor race.

National Archives

Courtesy of Chicago Roller Skate Company

Although speed uniforms have changed little since the '30s, racers no longer wear tights.

SOME BACKGROUND

Before 1939 practically all roller speed skaters in the US were professional. Many races were organized by skate companies who gave cash prizes to the winners. One-mile sprints and five-mile endurance races were the most common, with every race attracting thousands of spectators.

Early speed champions were all-around athletes who sometimes held world titles in other sports as well. For example, a skater named Harley Davidson was not only a world champion roller skater, but a first-class ice skater and cyclist as well. He won over 2,500 prizes by competing in these three sports between 1884 and 1928. He drew crowds by telling spectators he represented Harley-Davidson, a motorcycle manufacturer, even though he did not. (The Harley-Davidson name was, in fact, made up by combining the names of the founders.) In 1909, Davidson set a world record for skating the mile in two minutes, 51 seconds.

In 1911, on the same track, another American, Allie Moore, beat Davidson's record by skating the mile in two minutes, 49 seconds. Moore was also a world champion boxer, a swimmer, and an oarsman. Ten years later, Frank Klopp of Philadelphia established a new world record by skating a mile in two minutes, 45 seconds. From the '20s through the '40s American skaters dominated many world-class contests.

Speed skating moved outdoors in the '20s. The New York City Department of Parks and Recreation sponsored speed tournaments for adults and children in Central Park. In 1925 as many as 8,000 applicants skated qualifying heats at different city playgrounds. The winners, representing each borough, were sent to the annual major race.

In the '30s Harley Davidson teamed up with a younger partner, Roland Cioni of New York, and they traveled around the country together, challenging local speed teams. They supported themselves by splitting the admission profits.

A world-class professional speed skating champion in 1914, at the age of 15, Roland Cioni held the title undefeated until he left racing in 1954. Roland and his wife Margaret, an artistic skater, became national dance skating champions in 1944 and then world-class in 1948. They then retired from competition, but continued to coach young skaters well into the '50s, first at the Fordham Skating Palace in the Bronx and later at the Park Circle Rink in Brooklyn. Peggy Wallace, a well-known Skating Vanities star, was one of their students.

FRED "BRIGHT STAR" MURREE: THE FASTEST MAN ON WHEELS (IN 1876)

Courtesy of Chester Fried

Fred "Bright Star" Murree, a Pawnee Indian speed and figure skater, set the world's speed record on roller skates, in Boston, Massachusetts, when he was 18 years old. That local rink race was the start of his professional career in roller skating, which lasted for the next 63 years.

Murree, born in 1861 in a tiny wilderness village outside Omaha, Nebraska, came to Massachusetts as a child with his father, three brothers, and one sister (his mother died when he was five). The US government had been trying to herd all Indian tribes onto one reservation in Oklahoma in 1875 and, in response to this, Murree's father, who neither liked the idea nor the proposed resettlement location, drove his family East in a two-wheeled cart drawn by a pony. When they arrived in Boston, they sold their horse and cart in order to pay for furniture and a place to live.

A local youth, who was employed at the neighborhood roller rink, asked Fred if he'd like to work there as a skate boy. He tried out the job and liked it. Eight months later, the rink staged a five-mile race open to anyone under 18. Fred not only beat the 18 other competitors, but also broke the speed record. (The record for the five-mile race was 16 minutes. Fred Murree did it in 15 minutes and 52 seconds.)

No sooner did the newspaper story hit the streets than Frank Clayton, manager of the Argyle Rink in Boston, called to sign the youth to a contract which promised him 1,000 dollars when he reached 21. Fred Murree won 284 five-mile races during the next three years but he never received any money from his manager. Just before his 21st birthday, Murree refused to race until Clayton agreed to pay him a weekly wage of 100 dollars, plus all expenses. For this salary, Fred skated exhibitions twice a day, dressing 15 minutes later, for speed skating in order to race any and all challengers—seven days a week.

In 1880, Fred Murree obtained a pair of newly-manufactured ball bearing skates, the Skinner racing skate. He promptly skated five miles in 15 minutes flat, on the same rink track as his first victory. When he finished out his contract with Clayton, Fred Murree began racing on his own and won 50 percent of all races he entered. In 1890, the Raymond Skate Company hired Murree to represent them on an international tour, but he got as far as England and then decided to go it alone. He toured Italy, Germany, and France for eight months and performed in front of many European crowned heads as well as hundreds of thousands of people.

Returning to the United States, he married Frances Alice Crews and made his permanent home in Red Lion, Pennsylvania. Murree continued to perform in rinks throughout the country. In 1939 (the last report found of this astonishing skater), at age 78, he skated 19 exhibition dates on a 7,000-mile tour, including an engagement at the Hollywood Roller Bowl.

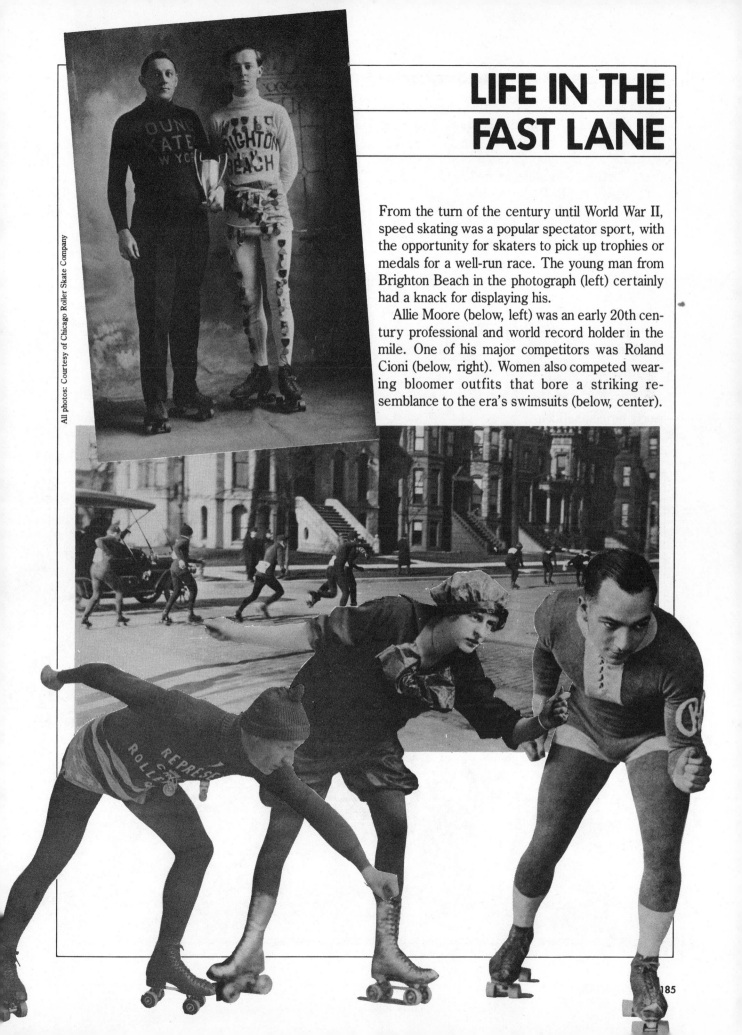

LIFE IN THE FAST LANE

From the turn of the century until World War II, speed skating was a popular spectator sport, with the opportunity for skaters to pick up trophies or medals for a well-run race. The young man from Brighton Beach in the photograph (left) certainly had a knack for displaying his.

Allie Moore (below, left) was an early 20th century professional and world record holder in the mile. One of his major competitors was Roland Cioni (below, right). Women also competed wearing bloomer outfits that bore a striking resemblance to the era's swimsuits (below, center).

THE AMATEURS GET ORGANIZED

Speed skating was organized, in 1937, as an amateur indoor event by the Roller Skating Rink Operators of America (RSROA, see box on page 140 of Artistic Skating). This signaled the end of professional speed skating as well as any outdoor competition. The RSROA joined the Amateur Athletic Union the following year and added artistic skating to its program as well. By the '40s, amateur contests were established all over the country and the pattern was set for present day national championships.

Today, amateur speed skating competition includes both individual and relay races. Skaters compete in many divisions ranging from Primary (eight and under) to Senior (over 18), the same for both men and women. Races are skated in a counter-clockwise direction around a flat, oval, 100-meter track. Skaters wear jersey shirts and shorts for competition.

Over the past 40 years, the only major equipment change has been in the skate wheel.

Originally, the wheels were made of maple; later, a softer, pressed-wood composition of sycamore and pine was used because it gripped the wood floor better. The reason the wooden wheel held the floor so well was that rink operators powdered the skating surface with rosin. That created excellent traction, but was a health hazard. Whenever the skaters raced, clouds of this white powder would fill the air. In 1977, rosin was declared an environmental threat and banned from use in competition. That meant the end of the wooden wheels because, without the rosin, they didn't grip the floor. In 1978, wood wheels were replaced by urethane for all US competitions, however, international-style speed skaters still use wooden wheels on their outdoor tracks.

THE UNITED STATES IS DISADVANTAGED

The change in the wheel is just an added problem for US competitors. The way things are now, 35- and 40-year-old European and South American

America's world-class speed skaters traveled to Mar del Plata, Argentina in 1978 and scored a 4th place team finish—their best effort to date.

athletes can skate rings around 18- to 22-year-old US champions. They've been doing it for years, and the reason is basic. Although speed skating is one of the best organized competitive programs it is still inadequate when it comes time to train our athletes for world-class competition.

One thing that holds our skaters back is that the US is the only country in the world that trains and races on indoor tracks and on plastic-coated, wooden floors; the rest of the world trains and races outdoors exclusively. The World Meet and the Pan American Games are both run outdoors. Skaters run on wooden wheels and usually race on large, 200-meter, banked tracks. Furthermore, while the longest race skated in US competition is 5,000-meters, 10,000- and 20,000-meter races are common in international competition.

Another difference is that US speed skating features individual-style racing while team-style racing is used by all other countries. In other words, even short races are run according to a pre-arranged plan. Each country's speed skating team knows in advance which one of their skaters will attempt to win the race, and the whole team will work together to make it happen. Winning as an individual is not as important in international competition. What is important is that the team skates and wins for their country.

US skaters come to a World Meet and are at a severe disadvantage from the very beginning. The US team, unlike its European and South American counterparts (who may work out together almost every day), trains together only once a year and usually just before the meet. It should be noted that this brief training session takes place on the host country's track, because there is not one active outdoor speed skating training facility in the entire United States.

Training for an outdoor meet is similar to conditioning programs used by track and field

athletes. It is completely different from training for indoor meets. While quickness is important in indoor events, endurance is the way an outdoor World Meet is won. Few of our coaches have any idea how to condition their star athletes, male or female, for a big international race. Our best skaters are sometimes left entirely on their own when designing a suitable outdoor training program. They can expect very little help or advice from anyone.

Generally, US skaters don't train as thoroughly as does the rest of the world. Skaters from other countries, similar to all top athletes, do warm-up stretching exercises and weight training. Some are involved in other competitive sports.

It has been suggested that our top speed skaters might be better off training with their local high school or college track coach. A track coach, at least, would know how to condition skaters for the long-distance races that make up a big part of every World Meet.

Another factor is that indoor racing creates a protected environment for the skater. Outdoors, speed skaters must contend with the elements. Wind, temperature, and debris on the track all play a part in the way a skater runs his or her race. For many US skaters a World Meet is their first experience with these factors.

Additionally, the style of skating outdoors is quite different. Because the track in international competition is two times as large, skaters use a different skating stride on the straightaways. Also, while being fast in the corners is important for an indoor competition, this skating style doesn't work well in long-distance races where endurance and strategy are more important.

Lastly, US skaters, who have been taught to skate a "clean" race since they were five to six years old, are shocked and further disadvantaged when they compete in their first international event. All sorts of procedures which are illegal in US competition appear to be tolerated in international racing. Blocking, punching, and jabbing maneuvers, sure in US skating to get one disqualified from a race and maybe an entire meet, are not sanctioned in international races, but seem to be permitted.

UNDERSTANDING SPEED SKATING COMPETITION IN THE UNITED STATES

Roller speed skating is "pack racing." As many as eight skaters may be on the track at one time. There are both individual races and relay races, and both are run on an indoor, 100-meter flat track.

Individual skaters accumulate points by skating three to four different races in their division. Tom Peterson, for example, won the 1978 US Senior Men's title by high placements in one sprint race (1,000 meters), one middle-distance race (1,500 meters), and two long-distance races (3,000 and 5,000 meters). The women's events are run the same way. Younger skaters race only three distances, all of them over a shorter course.

In relay division, teams win the title on the basis of one heat and one final only. There are relay divisions for all-men, all-women, and mixed couple teams.

Skaters in the individual divisions qualify for events by placing either first, second, or third in preliminary heat races. Skaters take their position in lanes on the starting line. When the starter fires the gun, they sprint off the line and race each other into the first corner. Skaters then settle into stride and plan who they will pass and when. The skater who crosses the finish line first wins the race.

In relay races, skaters from each team race for either two laps or five (depending on the division). At that time, they're tagged by their teammate who will skate the same distance again. The anchorperson (the member of the team who skates last) who crosses the finish line first wins the race for the team. Any racer whose skate crosses the starting line before the starter fires the gun is penalized. He or she gets pushed back behind the starting line four feet the first time it happens, four additional feet the second time, and is disqualified the third time.

Other grounds for disqualification include both personal and team fouls. Personal fouls include tripping, holding, shoving, and any other kind of rough behavior. Blocking is also illegal in American speed skating competition. Officials signal a disqualification by flagging a skater off the track.

Courtesy of John Gustafson

Leading the pack in a 10,000 meter event are the US's Ken Hutter, Chris Snyder, and Ken Sutton.

A LOOK TO THE FUTURE

Up until 1978, US skaters did poorly in international competition. In that year, in Mar del Plata, Argentina, Ken Hutter and Chris Snyder, working as a team, placed third and fourth, respectively, in the 10,000-meter race. Their finish helped the US team achieve a fourth overall placement. That's the best the US has ever done in top-ranked competition.

While the achievements of these fine athletes, who both trained hard outdoors, were acknowledged and even received some media attention, so far nothing has changed. There are still no outdoor training facilities in the United States.

In addition the United States Amateur Confederation of Roller Skating (USAC), who governs all speed skating competition in the United States, has been negligent in designing and implementing new international speed divisions for Junior and Senior men and women. At least four new divisions are needed. These skaters would train mostly outdoors, competing in US outdoor events. They would focus, if they qualify, on world-class competition. Both banked track and open road racing would be featured in these new international divisions. This way, our finest US skaters would not be continually frustrated in their efforts to train for two radically different styles of racing.

THE DECISION TO RACE

Speed skaters are the thoroughbreds of the roller world. Their two-hour practice sessions are extremely strenuous and mental toughness is a prime requisite. Most US speed skaters are between the ages of five and 25 but coaches will take a youngster as early as age three, if the child already knows how to skate. Some clubs have local and regional divisions for those over 30 as well.

Coaches are demanding and prefer to work with skaters who make every practice, train hard and refuse to quit, no matter how tired they are.

WHAT TO LOOK FOR IN A SPEED SKATING PROGRAM

When you choose a speed program examine the rink, the club, and the coach. The following list of criteria will help you evaluate a total program.

Rink: This must be available for at least two practice sessions a week. Extra sessions must be scheduled during April, May, June, and July in order to prepare for the state, regional, and national events.

Ideally, the rink should have other competitive programs, such as freestyle, dance and figures, or hockey. Participating in more than one kind of skating is a good way to condition yourself for speed competition. For example, artistic skating increases flexibility. Hockey is good for building cardiovascular fitness as well as muscle strength.

Club: Look for a group that has a fairly constant membership from year to year. Committed athletes often race for years and so will want a

Senior women scramble off the starting line at the National Meet held in Lincoln Nebraska's Pershing Auditorium.

Ann-Victoria Phillips

Ann-Victoria Phillips

Young skaters
limber up before a relay heat.

long-term
program. Look to see that the club has
both a beginner (B-Team) and an advanced (A-Team) group. After all, when you are just starting out, you won't want to learn the basics racing against the division's top regional or national competitor. Choose a large club when possible—the more members, the more partners you will have for relay races.

Check the club's participation in league competition as well as invitational meets. Does it participate in closed meets between several rinks in your area? Does it host regional or national events? If you have the chance to race frequently, take it. Skating as many different tracks as possible is an important part of becoming a "seasoned" racer.

Look for cooperative attitudes among club members. Do they train on their own? Do they skate outdoors, cycle, or do other aerobic-style exercises together, in addition to the regular practice sessions?

Choose the club with the most competitive skaters. It's a known fact that skaters of near-equal ability enjoy friendly rivalries with each other during practice sessions. Competitive attitudes within a club sharpen one's aggressive instincts, a plus when one is shooting for a regional or national title.

Since there are now over 300 clubs in the US

with more than 10,000 registered speed skaters, it should not be difficult to find one. Call your local rink and ask if they have a speed club. You could also call or write USAC (see the box in Chapter 7, page 140).

There is no professional-level speed skating at this time in the US—all registered clubs are amateur.

A speed club requires that you know how to skate, pay your membership dues on schedule, buy your own equipment, pay your way to meets, and that you attend every practice. Coaches are very strict about this. The only excuse for missing practice is illness.

Coach: Look for one who is a real trainer and wants to win. Competitive attitudes start at the top. Find a coach who recognizes speed skating as a high-level, competitive sport, and sees his or her skaters as athletes.

The coach should be knowledgeable enough to recommend a balanced training program, both on- and off-rink, and also have a knowledge of flexibility exercises, weight training, diet control, and the value of complementary aerobic exercises, such as cycling and jogging to provide a change of pace. He or she should plan equally demanding training sessions for all skaters—the girls and women as well as the boys and men. The coach should take time to know the skaters well enough to help them achieve their individual goals, in addition to those of the club. Furthermore, the coach should support league and other local competition especially for beginner-level skaters or those of average ability. Look for a coach who has the experience to train you for a world meet and other international events should you qualify.

TWO GREAT COACHES

Both Mike Dorso, Jr. and RoLores "Skip" Peterson coach skaters who win many national singles and relay team events. They draw some of the best skaters to their clubs and develop many into regional and national champions. The fact that both also own their own rink aids the speed program. It guarantees that the maximum amount of practice time will be available to their skaters. Both coaches maintain very high athletic standards for their skaters and have superior knowledge of training techniques.

Twenty-five-year-old Mike Dorso started speed skating when he was three years old. Since then, he has accumulated 19 years of racing experience. A professional coach for the last three years, he is presently training two well-known athletes: his sister, Linda Dorso (who qualified for both the World Meet and the 1979 Pan Am Games) and Marcia Yager (who has won more national placements than any other woman in speed skating history). His relay teams are also nationally prominent.

Dorso is a hard trainer, one reason he gets such superior results. His practice sessions are three hours long, five times a week. In addition, club skaters also do off-rink complementary exercises such as baseball and bicycling.

Skip Peterson, from Tacoma, Washington, is considered by other coaches to be the toughest trainer in the speed sport. Her skaters currently hold five national titles: Senior Men's, Junior Ladies', Senior Two-Man Relay, Senior Four-Man Relay, and Senior Mixed-Couple Relay. Skip has 50 skaters in her club including two world-class contenders—her son Tom, and her daughter Lin. Both qualified for the World Meet and the Pan Am Games. Skip describes how she runs her club. "If the kids leave practice and they're not tired, I feel I've failed. My club is very strict. I want skaters who will make a total commitment. They can't miss practice and think they will keep up. To be outstanding, you must put in the time."

Coach Mike Dorso, Jr. believes in beginning skaters at a tender age. Here he watches his eight-and-under-group practice their starts.

A family dedicated to skating: Tom, RoLores, and Lin Peterson.

Courtesy of RSROA

Courtesy of RoLores "Skip" Peterson

THE COSTS OF COMPETITIVE SPEED SKATING

As a registered amateur, you cannot accept any gifts, sponsorship or money. That means you and your family will be footing the bill. The following is a summary of expected costs:

1. Your club dues will range from 12 dollars to 24 dollars each month. This comes to around 2 dollars per practice. Being a member of the speed club is less expensive, per practice, than open skating sessions at most rinks.

2. Your USAC amateur card is 5 dollars per year.

3. Your equipment costs will vary. All competitive racers buy their skates piece-by-piece and assemble different components. Top skaters may have as many as six different sets of wheels, one for each different track condition. Each coach has his or her own favored skate set-up. He or she will tell you what to buy. A pair of leather speed boots, including plates, trucks, wheels and bearings ranges from 150 dollars to 180 dollars. Extra sets of wheels are optional and cost extra. Club uniforms run about 30 dollars.

4. Speed skaters must pay for their own traveling expense to meets, but USAC pays the way, should one qualify, for the World Meet or any other international race. For local competition, usually a one-day meet, expenses will include meals and transportation only. Regionals are two to three day meets and nationals last for five days. At the national level, expenses will soar as the costs of plane tickets, hotel rooms, and rental cars are added on. In addition it is common for nationally prominent skaters to travel hundreds of miles each week to train with top world-class coaches. All these additional expenses are paid for by the skater and his or her family.

HOW SPEED SKATING RATES AS AN AEROBIC EXERCISE

A typical speed practice, held at least twice a week for an hour-and-one-half to two-hour period, is a continuous and strenuous physical activity. Speed skating has been evaluated as a high-level aerobic exercise by Dr. Kenneth H. Cooper, in his book, *The Aerobics Way*. It has more than triple the point value of normal rink skating.

Dr. Cooper's point system was developed to determine how much exercise done within a cer-

TOP-RANKED SPEED SKATING PROGRAMS IN THE UNITED STATES

Coaches and skaters rank these speed clubs as being the best because they fulfill the previously mentioned program requirements. The following are the most prominent clubs, rinks, and coaches in the United States.

Club	Coach
Bonaventure Speed Club Bonaventure Skating Center Farmington Hills, Michigan	Virgil Dooley
Dorso's Speed Club Colerain Skateland Cincinnati, Ohio	Mike Dorso, Jr.
High Point Skating Club Rol-A-Rink Skating Arena High Point, North Carolina	Bob Byerly
Skate Ranch Speed Club Skate Ranch Santa Ana, California	Grady Merrell
Tacoma Speed Club Tacoma Roller Bowl Tacoma, Washington	Skip Peterson

tain amount of time is necessary to maintain cardiovascular fitness. Cooper suggests that a person earn a minimum of 30 points a week, and that these points should be accumulated over a three- to four-day period, each week. Speed skating, rated as an exercise, comes out way ahead of the others because one single-practice session satisfies over half of the week's requirements. Since speed skaters practice at least twice a week, they can easily earn their aerobic points each week. In addition, many competitive skaters supplement their practice with other aerobic exercises such as cycling, running, and cross-country skiing. These additional activities also improve cardiovascular fitness by improving heart and lung efficiency. This may give a skater an advantage on the race track. For some point values for speed skating, see Chapter 3, page 69.

FUNDAMENTAL SKILLS OF SPEED SKATING

The start of the race, is the most important part and also the most confusing. A mad scramble, often a collision ensues as all battle to be at the head of the pack when rounding the first pylon. The start requires total concentration, lightning reflexes, good balance and precise muscular coordination. Mental attitude is just as important; you must really want to win and have total belief in your physical abilities.

CHECKING YOUR EQUIPMENT

Make sure your laces are in good condition and that they are tied securely. Double-knot them for safety. Adjust or tighten your toe-stops. If they are too low you will scrape your skates against the floor and slow down your start. If they are too high, you won't be able to run on them easily at the start. Raise up onto your toe stops to check their position. Your back wheels should be about three to four inches from the floor when your toe stops are adjusted properly. Don't use brand new wheels in competition because they won't grip the track. Use wheels that are already broken in.

THE RACE BEGINS

The start consists of four parts: starting position, the toe-stop run, the Duck Walk, and rounding the first corner marker.

Starting position on the line: Different skaters favor different starting positions. There are no rigid rules; you must find the position that works best for you.

When your event is called, go from the "ready area" up to the four-foot setback line in your lane.

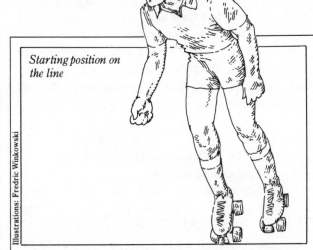

Starting position on the line

Illustrations: Fredric Winkowski

At the command of "To Your Mark," advance to the starting line. Take your preliminary starting position. At the direction "Set," take your final starting position and don't move until you hear the gun. Any movement before the gun will be considered a false start and you will be penalized. At the time of the final starting position:

1. Face directly forward and distribute your weight evenly between your front and rear foot toe-stops. Place your rear foot a bit to the side of the front one so you don't trip coming off the line.

2. Concentrate totally. Keep your body forward and lowered so that your head is about three or four inches higher than your hips. Don't bend from the waist. Instead, lean from your toes up. Your lean should be so far forward that when the starting gun goes off, your body actually falls forward off the line. Your hips are over the front leading skate which supports 50 percent of your weight. Since the first toe-stop step is dependent on body position, you must practice this stance thoroughly.

Springing off the line—the toe-stop run: Your power and reaction time on your first step, as well as the next three or four steps, are often the most important part of the start, especially in a short race. These first steps are run entirely on the toe-stops but the number and length of steps depends on your own preference. Because skaters start from a standstill, the object of the run is to build up to maximum speed quickly. Generally skaters run on their stops until they are about to fall forward; then they change to the Duck Walk. To learn how to run on your toe stops:

1. Find a partner who is willing to help you. Face your partner and hold on to his or her arms just below the shoulders. While running forward on your toe stops, push your partner backward as fast as you can. Be sure you are running on the stops, not your front wheels.

2. Repeat this until you are able to do it on your own. Then practice getting from your final starting position into the toe-stop run.

The Duck Walk: This is the third part of your start. It is used as a transition from the toe-stop run to the extending racing stride you will be doing on your wheels. The transition must be done quickly and smoothly:

1. In the Duck Walk, turn your toes outward at about a 45-degree angle. The angle will prevent you from slipping or rolling backward.

2. Drive your skates hard into the floor, as though you are trying to push right through the wood. Keep your stride extended to attain maximum power.

3. The number of Duck Walk steps you take depends on your personal preference. It can vary from a few steps to the length of the entire straightaway. You will have to experiment to find the style that suits you best.

4. Arm swing style differs from coach to coach but speed skaters generally swing their arms from front to back keeping their shoulders square and facing forward.

5. As you near the first corner marker, change over from running to a full racing stride.

Rounding the first corner: Rounding corners was easier and quicker when skaters had wooden wheels and tracks were powdered with rosin. During the 1977-78 season, both rosin and wooden wheels were banned from official competition. Now US speed skaters use plastic wheels on plastic-coated wood floors. Good cornering technique is more essential than ever in order to keep your balance and round the corner markers.

Try to round the first (and all) pylons as tightly and quickly as possible so that opponents cannot pass you on the inside. Don't knock them over, however, or you will be disqualified.

1. As you round the corner, put slightly more weight onto your right foot. This will give you

Toe stop run

The Duck Walk

Rounding the first corner

TRISHA HILLER

Thirteen-year-old Trisha Hiller of Orange, California, is the only US skater to hold national titles in both speed and freestyle. Nicknamed "Carrot Top" for her red hair, Tricia received a perfect score for her artistic skating performance in Elementary Girls Singles and also won the Elementary Girls Speed championship at the 1978 National competition.

To hold two national titles is an extraordinary athletic accomplishment. Together these two sports involve every component of physical fitness. Speed skating develops endurance and quickness while freestyle increases flexibility and strength. Trisha is one of the best examples of an all around, well-conditioned skater. Her speed coach, Ted Patterson, says she's "a natural."

Courtesy of RSROA

better balance and support you as you round the pylon.

2. Keep your shoulders square with your hips, and your arms swinging from front to back to help increase your speed.

INTO THE RACE

Forward Crossovers: This is the same technique you learned in Chapter 4, page 96, except in racing it is done faster.

1. Push off on your left outer forward (LOF) edge.

2. With your knees bent, bring your right foot forward across your left. At the same time, push under (behind) your right foot with your left by straightening your left knee. Repeat the sequence as many times as necessary to complete the corner.

Sprinting: This is skating at top speed. During a short race, skaters may sprint almost the entire distance but they would burn themselves out if they did so for long ones. Distance races are alternating periods of sprinting and pacing.

1. When sprinting, keep your body as low as you can, bending at the knees and leaning forward from the hips.

2. Establish a smooth rhythm. Momentary pauses can drain your energy and cause you to lose ground.

Pacing: This is skating at a smooth, constant rate to conserve energy needed for the all-out

sprint at the finish of a long-distance race. It is also used as a conditioning exercise in practice to build endurance. In a long-race, the whole field will pace; lap after lap will show little change in positioning.

During a race, get as close to the skater in front of you as possible and match his or her stride.

Passing: Always be alert for an opportunity to pass. The best places to pass are halfway down the straightaway and at the halfway points around the pylon when the skater in front of you leaves a slight gap as he or she rounds the corner. There are two strategies:

1. Taking advantage of any mistake or break in stride by the skater ahead of you.

2. Sprinting and passing your opponent in a burst of superior speed. This is particularly useful if you are familiar with the track.

Avoid passing until you know you can do it successfully, without fouling and disqualifying yourself from the race. When you think you are ready to make the move:

3. Get in close to the leading skater and match his or her stride. This will help you to know if you do, in fact, have enough speed to make a pass and will also give you a chance to observe the leader's habits closely.

4. When you are ready, sprint before the leader can react and speed up. Move to the inside of the leader in order to pass.

5. You can also make an outside pass on the

straightaway, but this takes more time, speed and quickness than on the inside pass. Use it only if absolutely necessary.

6. In order to avoid being passed yourself, sprint as you come out of corners and round the pylons tightly.

THE RELAY TAG

Relay races have teams of either two or four skaters apiece. One skater from each team skates the track for either two or five laps (depending on the division) and then is relieved by another team member.

A relay in speed skating is completed much the same way as in track, except skaters do it by tagging and, at the same time, pushing off the next member of the team. No whip-style relays are permitted.

There are many relay divisions for men and women on both a Freshman and Senior level: Two-Man, Four-Man, Two-Lady, Four-Lady, Two-Mixed Couple and Four-Mixed Couple.

MARCIA YAGER: CHAMPION SPEED SKATER

"Who is our fastest woman speed skater? That would have to be Marcia Yager of Cincinnati, Ohio," answered Chris Snyder, when he was asked. "Marcia trains by running up and down the stadium steps at the University of Cincinnati and she skates outdoors 15 miles a day. She's a tiger!"

Marcia, who until she was 14 had never skated, began her training at Castle Skateland, in Loveland, Ohio. In 1971, the first year she ever skated, she qualified for the National Meet in a relay division and finished last. After that, "I decided to get with it," says Marcia. "I started running, lifting weights, and getting seriously involved with training."

A year later, Marcia, with barely a year's worth of competition experience under her belt, came back to win the 1972 Sophomore Ladies national title as well as the Senior Two-Lady relay event with teammate, Brenda Haggard. New speed records were established for both events. All Marcia's hard training had paid off. She decided to double the pace and triple the pressure.

After winning six more national titles, Marcia became a known and feared competitor. She ran away with every Senior event title in 1976 at the US Amateur Roller Skating Championships held in Ft. Worth, Texas.

In spite of knee surgery in November, 1976 and a time-consuming weight training and rehabilitative program to regain her racing form, Marcia came back in 1977 and won her third, successive Senior Ladies title.

Although Yager represented the United States in the World Meet in May, 1978, in Mar del Plata, Argentina, she took the rest of the competitive year off from skating and continued with school at the University of Cincinnati studying Physical Education. She then started back on a full-time training program with Mike Dorso who says her goal for 1979 is "to win Nationals for the fourth time." Coach Dorso predicts, "The women who usually skate against Marcia at Nationals will go crazy, knowing she's coming back and that they'll have to race the fastest woman in US speed skating history. They think she's retired. We were keeping it a secret, but she will be there. I guarantee it."

Courtesy of RSROA

A DAY AT THE RACES

You've got to have gravel in your gut to get out there and speed skate," says Jim Hughes of Spokane, Washington. Jim must shout at the top of his lungs to be heard over the ear-splitting racket in Pershing Auditorium. Roller speed skating is not for the weak-of-heart. The combination of the starter's gun, the howling of the fans, and the constant "clomp" and "thonk" of hard, plastic wheels striking the maple floor would drive the average spectator crazy. But speed people are a hardier breed.

What would faze most everyone else only fuels up the average speed fanatic. Speed skating is in their blood. It's addictive. They live it, they love it and, at the second day of competition at the 1978 United States Amateur Roller Skating Championships in Lincoln, Nebraska, they want more of it.

To an outsider, this four-day speed meet would seem disorderly, even chaotic. But all 750 skat-

All photos: Ann-Victoria Phillips

ers from the youngest six-year-old boy skating in the Primary division, to the oldest woman, a 29-year-old who skates in the Senior Ladies division, seem to know where to be at what time for their heats, relays, or finals. First-, second- and third-place medals, roller skating's gold, silver, and bronze awards, are offered in 26 events.

Speed skating is as primitive a sport as you can get: It's pack racing with body contact. A form of wheel-to-wheel combat, it's surprisingly, as someone suggested, "like stock car racing, strategy-wise, yet much more personal." Speed is enormously athletic and chancy as well, for no one can predict when a skater will slip, trip, or fall head-over-wheels, a whole year's training down the drain.

The crowd of 3,000 hollering, rail-slapping, foot-stomping coaches, skaters, and parents who are here to watch a full day's schedule of racing events, are jampacked into front row seats all around the auditorium and shoulder-to-shoulder on the floor near the gates. They're skating the race themselves from the sidelines and the stands. Some—coaches acting as pit crew with wrench in hand—are even out on the floor near the track, ready to perform first-aid during the upcoming relay event, should a skate break or a wheel fall

Speed skaters are an emotional breed. They train all year for the big event, the National Meet—so it's do or die every time they hit the track. Ecstasy, tears, and the camaraderie of top-rank competition make this a trying yet rewarding four days for the best skaters in the US.

*Winners of the Freshman
Four-Girl Relay event. Left to right:
Jill Bantin, Tracy Ashby, Gina Remer, Karlene Dooley.*

off. The excitement is contagious. There is nothing laid-back about speed skating—everyone is totally involved.

Rita and Rick Dooley are on their feet. "Go for it, baby: Pass! Pass!" Like many speed skating parents, they are quiet people who, once at a meet, go completely bananas and start screaming for their pretty, brown-haired daughter, Karlene, hoping she can blow the socks off the other skaters and run them right into the ground.

"Come on, Karlene!" Coach Mike Dorso, Jr. of Cincinnati screams encouragement as his orange-and-black-uniformed, 13-year-old skater streaks by, her body low to the ground, almost pitched forward. Her arms and legs are pumping wildly. Little Karlene Dooley, the "starter" on Dorso's Freshman Four-Girl Relay team, rounds the number 3 corner marker, a day-glo orange pylon, and powers down the straightaway, sitting right on the leader's tail.

"And Washington is in the lead," announces Tony Braswell, who is calmly calling the race. "Ohio is challenging, followed by North Carolina." Karlene has skated past the start/finish area and is coming around again. "Pass," commands Dorso. Even as he says it, the slender skater from Cincinnati quickens her pace, ducks inside on the corner, rips past the leader and sprints toward her teammate, Jill Bantin, who is waiting up ahead for the

first relay. "And Ohio takes the lead," states Braswell. People in the crowd are going berserk, screaming directions and encouragement to the skaters on the floor.

"You just have no idea what hard work it is out there," says a Washington-based coach who is watching from his position near the rail. "These are the kids who love to go fast. 'Thrill me,' they say. They've worked hard all year long. They know they're the best in the nation. Nobody out there wants to get beat."

By now, Tracy Ashby, the third skater on Dorso's relay team has taken over from Jill and is out on the track, struggling to hold second. Dorso, who is crouched on the floor 15 feet back from the action, nods to Gina Remer, his fourth skater, who is positioned in the infield, ready to start the final (anchor) leg of the relay.

A small, thin girl who looks out of place on this racetrack, Gina is the captain of the team and Dorso's powerhouse skater. Strategically placed in the anchor position, this quick sprinter is Cincinnati's sure-shot. Either she will win the race for the team or save them a placement. For her, this means real pressure. Only the three top relay teams will advance to the finals.

Gina skates into the relay zone, looks over her shoulder for her teammate, and abruptly springs off. Tracy, closing fast at near top-speed, catches Gina from behind and, pushing vigorously with her hand flings her into the fast lane. Gina proceeds to skate her heart out and, two laps later, there's hooting, clapping, and cheering by her fellow Ohioans as she romps over the finish line, an easy winner by five yards.

The girls' race is over. They leave the floor, arm-in-arm, kissing and hugging each other and the coach, while 24 top men skaters file onto the track for a short warmup.

The announcer's voice is startlingly loud, "Senior Men who will skate in the 5,000-meter final, check in, please. Senior Men, final call." Tension levels in the vast auditorium shift quickly. Now, the high-strung crowd has quieted down, recharging their batteries for the next round of combat.

Out on the starting line, the Senior Men line up eight-abreast, three rows deep. The 5,000 meters is an individual race and the highlight of the meet. Unlike other events where skaters qualify

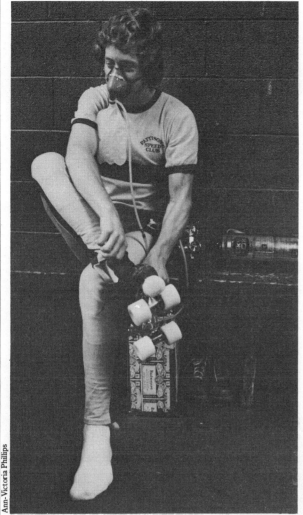

Curtis Cook takes oxygen before the Senior Men's 5,000 meter final.

by first winning heat races, this 5,000 meter race is a final—it's man-against-man for 50 laps, a real battle down to the last yard. While Seniors run three other distances—1,000, 1,500, and 3,000 meters—this 5,000-meter final is the real test for these older, experienced skaters. Because of the long distance, a skater must have great endurance plus the ability to use strategy in order to win. Not only is the US Senior Men's title up for grabs, but also the rights to go to the 1979 Pan American Games in July and the 1979 World Speed Meet in Rome in September.

"To your mark!" shouts the Assistant Referee. Chris Snyder, the defending Senior Men's National Champion, moves to the pole position on the starting line. Snyder is officially ranked number one in the US and number four in the world. In addition, most top coaches agree that the heavily muscled, sandy-haired speed skater from Euless, Texas, is the United States' strongest contender to win the 1979 Pan American Games.

Snyder, already a seasoned racer in world-class competition, is the most experienced man on the track, but he is having serious problems at this meet. So far he has finished back-of-the-pack in the already completed 1,000- and 1,500-meter heats. Earlier in the season, Chris with seven other skaters, represented the United States at the International Roller Speed Skating Championships (Worlds) in Mar del Plata, Argentina. Upon his return, Chris plunged back into an intense program that left no time for rest. As Clay Briggs, Snyder's coach, sees it, "He trained harder last spring than he's ever trained in his life. He skated 15 miles to work every day for five months, worked out three hours a day at a health spa, and then skated two more hours of freestyle at night. (Chris also competed in the artistic portion of the National Championship Meet in Junior Men's Singles and placed fifth.) That is very, very hard work, plus he came to my regular, Mid-Cities Speed Club practice held at my rink three times a

Senior men round a pylon in the 5,000 meter final.

week. There is no one in roller skating today who is more dedicated to fitness than Chris Snyder," says Clay, a worried look on his face as he watches his 23-year-old star athlete. "He trained for Worlds and was out of the country for over four weeks. He's tired. He's under so much pressure here with interviews and people asking him questions. We're not making any excuses," repeats Clay, referring to Chris' back-of-the-pack finishes, "but he is very tense."

"Set!" The skaters crouch in ready position. The Starter fires the gun. Chris springs off the starting line on his toe-stops, Duck Walks another 20 feet, and settles into stride, his eyes fixed on the first corner marker. Being in second or third position rounding the first pylon is best in order to avoid accidents and pileups. Trouble is inevitable because everyone has the same goal at the same time. Twenty skaters mash together in a space meant for three, skates slash, wheels touch. "Someone's down." The crowd gasps. But Chris, pumping at top speed, vaults a fallen skater, rounds the number 2 marker, and opens up down the straightaway. He's not in first place, but he's in the clear. Just what he planned.

"I don't know all the details of Chris' training program," says Mike Dorso, himself a well-known

Defending champion Chris Snyder prepares to pass.

competitor before he turned to coaching three years ago, "but I can guess. What happened to Chris infected the entire World team. Chris peaked in late May, just before going to Argentina. He killed himself with brutal practices, skated the World Meet, and then burned out. Without a rest, there's no way a skater could make it back in time

All photos: Ann-Victoria Phillips

Chris Snyder (second from right) and Tom Peterson (far right) struggle for position during the final laps of the race.

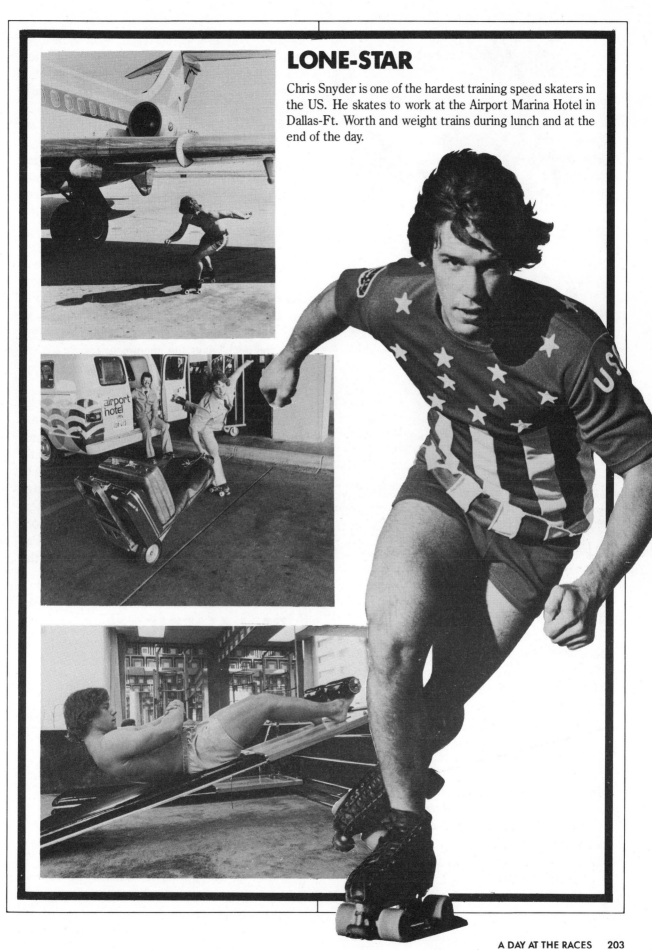

LONE-STAR

Chris Snyder is one of the hardest training speed skaters in the US. He skates to work at the Airport Marina Hotel in Dallas-Ft. Worth and weight trains during lunch and at the end of the day.

Chris Snyder is leading the 5,000 meter pack during the race's final moments, but challenger Tom Peterson is right behind him.

for Nationals. You'd need at least three to four weeks of rest and nobody did that. Everyone of our skaters who went to Argentina is doing poorly at this meet. You cannot train 12 months a year in this game and continue to win."

"Hey! Close it up, Chris. Move up!" A speed coach from Kansas is just one of many people calling out to favorites in the race. Across the auditorium floor, on the California side, skaters and fans from Washington State and Oregon (one of the hottest speed regions in the country) shout instructions to Tom Peterson who is leading the race. Tom is another top-ranked athlete who trains outdoors, cycles 10 miles a day, and lifts weights to complement his indoor programs. His mom, RoLores "Skip" Peterson, recognized as one of the hardest-driving and most successful speed coaches in America, paces nervously behind the rail. Her daughter, Lin, another champion, stands beside her.

The crowd is waiting. Lap after lap, the skat-

ers are flying around the track. Each time they pass, wind-waves roll across the floor chilling the fans. Goose-bumps pop up. Hair stands on end. "Pass! Pass! Pass!" Now the crowd is behind Chris as he passes. Chris, a long-distance man who has taken this event many times, is known to the crowd as a come-from-behind winner. He has thrilled them before. Now they're watching and waiting again. Who could forget what happened at Nationals in 1974, the first year that Chris won the Senior Men's title? Chris fell 880 yards out into the 5,000-meter final, and was almost lapped by the leaders. As quick as a big cat after prey, he closed the gap, and, in the last four laps of the race, made two good passes, winning the event. But now either Snyder is slowing or Peterson is gaining— the skaters are changing places on the track. Peterson strides past Snyder. "And Washington takes the lead," says the announcer calmly.

"Bang!" The sound of the gun startles everyone. "Final lap!"

Nineteen-year-old Tom Peterson, still holding first place, is drawing away as he coasts to the finish line. "And it's Washington!" Texas is second.

Tom Peterson, who just upset the event's defending champion accumulated enough points to go on and win the US Senior Men's title. Though Snyder fell short of achieving his immediate, personal goal, to win the meet for the third time, both he and Peterson have won places on the US Pan American team. They will both compete at the 1979 World Meet.

PAN AMERICAN SPEED SKATING TEAM—1979

These skaters will represent the US in the 1979 Pan American Games.

Coach: Charles Wahlig; Elsmere, Delaware

Elaine Coley; Ft. Lauderdale, Florida; age 19
Curtis Cook; Spokane, Washington; age 20
Sue Dooley; Livonia, Michigan; age 29
Linda Dorso; Cincinnati, Ohio; age 20
Lin Peterson; Tacoma, Washington; age 18
Tom Peterson; Tacoma, Washington; age 19
Chris Snyder; Euless, Texas; age 23
Ken Sutton; Muskegon, Michigan; age 18

10. ROLLER HOCKEY

HELL
ON WHEELS

One hundred years ago, it was called roller polo; today, it's called roller hockey, but no matter what you call it, or whether you play it with a curved stick or an ice hockey stick, the essential game is the same. Two opposing teams try to shoot either a ball or puck (depending on the type of hockey being played) into their opponent's cage to score. The team that scores the most goals wins the game.

Although field and ice hockey came first, as soon as roller skates became widely available, America put the game on wheels. By the 1880s, the United States had a number of roller polo leagues and the game was firmly established. It was still not officially sanctioned as an amateur sport, however, until the 1950s. By then, thousands of roller hockey leagues were established throughout the country.

OFFICIAL AMATEUR LEVEL ROLLER HOCKEY IN THE UNITED STATES

USAC (The United States Amateur Confederation of Roller Skating) sanctions all official amateur roller hockey competition. Two different types of roller hockey are played. One type is ball hockey, the official International style. It has a World Meet, and is sanctioned by the sport's worldwide governing body, the International Federation de Roller Skating (IFRS). Ball Hockey is a potential Olympic sport and has already been accepted for the 1979 Pan American Games in Puerto Rico. The other style, and the one which is more popular in the United States, is puck hockey, which is played on the National level only.

The age divisions for playing either type of amateur hockey are less restrictive than those of artistic speed and skating. Skaters as young as six years old can play as can men and women over 18. Adults can play in their respective senior divisions for as many years as they want.

TYPES OF ROLLER HOCKEY

Ball Hockey (International style): This has been described as a combination of field hockey, ice hockey, and basketball. It is played indoors with a short curved stick and a small black ball. Two teams of five members each play the ball,

Roller hockey gets in your blood. Once you start you'll probably continue playing throughout adult life.

using only their sticks, although they may stop the ball with any part of their bodies except their hands. No checking or body contact is allowed. Since these skaters use a ball instead of a puck, the emphasis is more on passing and on a zone type of defense similar to basketball. The ball is scooped up, passed with the stick, and is almost always up in the air.

Because the curved stick is shorter than the ice hockey stick used in roller puck hockey, ball hockey players skate in a more crouched position, similar to that of speed skaters.

According to the rule book, body contact is not permitted so the players use very little protective equipment—no gloves, chest protectors, or helmets—only shin guards. In fact, ball hockey skaters are so lightly dressed, they look more like soccer players. Only the goalie wears a full protective outfit.

Puck Hockey (American style): This is the only other form of roller hockey sanctioned for official competition. As mentioned earlier, although registered amateurs play roller puck hockey in inter-club competition and have their own national meets, this style is *not* played in world-class competition.

The skaters play indoors at rinks, using standard ice hockey sticks and a collapsible plastic puck. Roller puck hockey is much the same the world over and is very similar to ice hockey in the rules, dress, and manner of play. Although body contact (checking) is technically not allowed, a full outfit of protective gear is worn in official amateur competition.

Puck Hockey (League style): This semi-professional style of puck hockey, organized and played on a city-wide level at school playgrounds, closely follows the rules and regulations of the NHL (National Hockey League) and may be financially supported by local merchants. A few of the playgrounds have a specially constructed playing area that is lined with dasher boards designed to contain the puck. But the majority of playgrounds are simply that and, with the exception of boundary lines painted on concrete, have no permanent roller hockey facilities at all.

Checking is permitted; in fact, just as in the NHL, it's an integral part of the game.

League-style roller hockey has nothing to do with USAC, and virtually anyone can organize a

Ann-Victoria Phillips

Ft. Hamilton Roller Hockey League defenseman Joe DeVincenzo waits for teammates to pass him the puck.

league and solicit sponsorships. Leagues are often affiliated with church and business groups and sometimes the Police Department. Each league organizes its own teams and sets up its own playing schedule. Regulations, governing eligibility to play, vary from league to league, but generally skaters as young as six can sign up. Most leagues have Unlimited divisions—any man over 18 can play for as many years as he wants. As far as anyone knows, there are no separate women's divisions, so if a girl or woman wants to play hockey, she must sign up for a men's team.

Street Hockey: This is the most common style of roller puck hockey played in the United States. Most popular in the Northeastern part of the country, it rates high as *the* sport to play on city streets.

Street hockey may be as simple as a group of neighborhood kids getting together after school and setting up an impromptu playing field on a dead-end street. "Found objects" such as garbage cans, traffic cones, or manhole covers may serve as goals while street curbs define the boundary lines. Skaters may wear little or no protective equipment.

Sometimes street hockey fanatics may be almost as well organized as a league team—they play regularly scheduled games, have their own neighborhood coaches and referees, and also have their own goal cages.

But no matter how loosely organized a street hockey game is, and in spite of the players' reputations as fierce, stick-wielding aggressors, the game usually follows NHL (National Hockey League) rules as closely as possible.

WHAT TO LOOK FOR IN A ROLLER HOCKEY PROGRAM

Rink: Look for a skating rink that has hockey practice sessions scheduled at least twice a week. Extra sessions should also be added during April, May, June, and July to train players for the National Meet. Ideally, the rink should also offer other skating programs, such as freestyle and speed, to help the roller hockey player build up skating skills. One needs endurance, strength, flexibility, and quickness to play the game.

Club: Look for a hockey club or league that has a fairly constant membership from year to year so that you can continue to play hockey as long as you want. Ideally, it should have divisions for beginners and advanced skaters alike because it's especially important for beginners to practice with others of their same age. Also, look for a group with a senior unlimited division so you will be able to compete regardless of age. Women should find a club or league that welcomes them into all regular practices and games, especially if the club doesn't have a separate women's division. Clubs that participate in inter-club and invitational meets produce well-seasoned players.

Indoor ball hockey is a growing sport, especially among women.

Courtesy of RSROA

TOP-RANKED AMATEUR ROLLER HOCKEY PROGRAMS

Ball Hockey Clubs (International Style)	Coach
Ardmore Skateland Ardmore, Oklahoma	Gary Martin
Starlight Roller Rink Bakersfield, California	Bill Ray
King's Skate Country Sacramento, California	Tim Maher
Playland Rollerdrome Pismo Beach, California	Ural Foresee
Skate Ranch Lubbock, Texas	Kevin Baker Bill Sisson Dick Sisson
Puck Hockey Clubs (American Style)	
Capitol Skateland Olympia, Washington	Bob Hemphill Fred Lee
Carousel Skating Rink Houston, Texas	Dick Parker
Northgate Skating Center Bossier City, Louisiana	Larry Sanford Jerry Lavonte

Coach: Look for a coach who sees his or her skaters as developing athletes and can advise a well-rounded on-and off-rink training program that may include weight training, diet control, and complementary aerobic exercises such as cycling, racquetball, running, and cross-country skiing. They should plan equally demanding practices for the women players as well as the men, and help all skaters achieve their personal goals. Look for a person with a good record on a league or national level, one who clearly understands the difference between healthy aggressive play and violence. The coach should also have a basic knowledge of sports medicine as it applies to the hockey skater. Ideally, the coach should have good relations with other athletes and trainers, and be open to calling in outside consultants if necessary to help train a world-class athlete.

ROLLER HOCKEY: WHAT THE PROGRAM LACKS

The United States has never done well in world-class roller hockey competition. The reasons are many. For one, many other "amateur" teams that the United States competes against are really government sponsored. But by far the most significant reason for the lack of success is that US roller hockey coaches lack a systematic training program.

Many roller hockey coaches in this country—no matter whether they oversee a ball or puck hockey program—neglect the teaching of fundamental hockey skills. Instead, they devote most of their team's practice time to scrimmage games.

Customarily, hockey skills are developed through extensive drills that teach the skater to maneuver, stickhandle, pass, and shoot. Understanding both offensive and defensive strategies

Chris Carson, a defenseman, leaps into the game (above) while Joey Sergi, a 16-year old center takes a breather.

and practicing plays are other important parts of the step-by-step training of the typical hockey player. Off-skate exercise and weight training sessions are also used to more fully condition all athletes.

The sport of roller hockey is a demanding game. It has all the color and excitement of ice hockey, yet is less expensive and more accessible to greater numbers of people. It has all the potential to become a big-time sport but unless roller hockey coaches start their athletes in serious training programs, the sport is destined for obscurity.

ROLLER HOCKEY AS AN EXERCISE

How does roller hockey rate in developing cardiovascular efficiency in comparison to other forms of roller skating? Dr. Kenneth Cooper's Institute for Aerobic Research has prepared the following table:

	Time	Point Value
Hockey* (continuous activity)	15 minutes	2.25
	30 minutes	5
	45 minutes	8
	1 hour	11

For times greater than one hour, points can be calculated at a rate of two points per 10 minutes.

Count only the time you are *actively participating* in a practice or game situation.

Interpretation: It should be understood that practicing and playing the game of hockey is a good aerobic exercise, but only if it is played continuously and strenuously. During an actual game, it's typical to see a player skate furiously for one to two minutes and then sit on the bench, sometimes for the rest of the period or even the game. So, the players who get the most practice and playing time in are those who'll receive the greatest benefits of hockey as an exercise.

To more fully condition yourself for the game, choose another complementary aerobic exercise such as racquetball. This can be done individually or as a team effort. Pre-practice and pre-game warm-up exercises are also essential because roller hockey especially stresses an athlete's hips, knees, and ankles. Post-game cool-down exercises are also important for sustaining flexibility.

*Cooper, Kenneth H., New York, *The Aerobic's Way*, Bantam Books, Inc., 1977.

Ann-Victoria Phillips

All photos:

SKILLS OF THE GAME

Hockey involves advanced skating skills so you should already know how to skate forward, backward, and do both forward and backward crossovers before starting out. It is a physically demanding game. If you are overweight or have been inactive for a long period of time, get yourself back into shape, then *slowly* begin learning the game skills.

The style of roller hockey familiar to most Americans is puck hockey. Although there are a small number of skaters who do play the game with a ball and so their style of play looks slightly different, the two styles of roller hockey have more skills in common than those that are different.

Hockey is a stop-and-go game. A hockey player must learn to skate fast in short bursts, cut from side to side, crossover, and brake down from top speed to a stop. In addition to these skating maneuvers, a skater must be able to stickhandle the puck down the court, pass it to team members, evade the opposing team's defensemen, and shoot in an attempt to score a goal.

Defensively, a hockey player must forecheck and backcheck the opposing team's skaters and try to steal the puck back before they can score a goal.

If this sounds like a lot to do all at once, it is, and it takes years of practice to polish your skills. The following skills are applicable to both styles.

SKATING SKILLS

Three basic types of skating are used during a roller hockey game—free skating, agility skating, and backward skating, plus a method of stopping which is unique to the sport of hockey.

Free skating (also called straightaway skating): This is sprinting across an open court as you cover your position.

Agility skating: This is the ability to move in all directions quickly, smoothly, and automatically. It includes doing crossovers at high speed (see Chapter 4, Lesson 8, page 96), except, in this case, you'll crossover first to the left and then immediately to the right (cutting from side to side) in a zigzag pattern. This style of skating is used to evade opponents while dribbling the puck toward the goal.

All photos: Ann-Victoria Phillips

The sport of roller hockey demands endurance, speed, agility—and a fearless fighting spirit.

Backward skating: This is an absolute necessity for a defenseman and valuable for a forward as well. It's often the only way to deal with an onrushing opponent so you never lose sight of the puck. You also should be able to crossover while skating backward in order to cover the opposing team's attackers. Both are usually done in short bursts.

Hockey stop (also called a Jump stop): This is accomplished by pushing both skates into the floor, jumping up and making a small turn in the air. When you land, you dig your wheels into the floor. This is the most difficult skating stop to control but also the fastest way to change directions while in motion.

There are two other stops—the single-leg and double-leg stops. They are used in other types of skating as well. To make a single-leg stop, lift one skate off the floor and turn your body sharply toward your lifted leg, at the same time straightening the knee of your supporting leg and digging the inside edge of your supporting skate into the floor. Whether you stop on your right or left leg depends on the direction of play. To make a double-leg stop, rotate your body either to the right or to the left and turn both skates sharply in the same direction, either to the right or the left.

GAME SKILLS

The basic roller hockey game skills are stickhandling, passing, shooting, defensive skills, and playing goalie.

Stickhandling: This is simply using the hockey stick to move and control the puck while skating. The two basic stickhandling motions are dribbling the puck from side to side or moving it backward and forward as you prepare to pass.

Passing: This is a most important skill and also the most neglected. You can pass a puck faster across the floor than you can dribble it. Passing is one thing that gives this game so much speed. You usually pass it to a moving skater and their speed determines how far ahead of them you shoot the puck.

The Forehand Pass (also called the Flat or Sweep Pass) is moving the puck flat across the court, in one continuous sweep, without lifting the stick.

The Backhand Pass is done in the same way except that you sweep the puck off the backside of your blade.

The Push Pass (also called the Wrist Pass) is done by snapping (quickly flexing) your wrists as you hit the puck. There is no sweeping motion; the action is all in your wrists.

COSTS OF PLAYING HOCKEY

Team uniform (two sets)	$ 35 each
Hockey skates (complete outfit) . .	$150
Hockey sticks (two to three per year)	$ 20 each
Helmet/mouth guard	$ 30
Shoulder/chest pads	$ 50
Elbow pads	$ 25
Shin guards	$ 25
Ankle guards	$ 20
Gloves	$ 25
Goalie's protective gear	$200

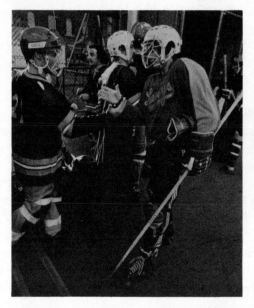

If you're a registered amateur, additional costs include: USAC amateur card (5 dollars a year), club dues (about 15 dollars per month), and the price of transportation to all league, inter-club, and invitational meets plus the annual National Meet. If, however, you're a ball hockey player and are chosen to play in the world meet or any other international event, USAC will pay all expenses.

If you play roller hockey in a city league, transportation costs will be much less. Although league teams are semi-professional and sponsored, individual team members must still buy all their own equipment.

The Flip Pass (also called a Lift Pass) is used to lift the puck into the air to get it over an opponent's stick, skate, or body. Scoop the puck up onto the heel of your blade and about a foot off the ground, and then snap your wrists, letting it fly.

The Drop Pass is not really a pass at all but a maneuver in which you leave the puck on the floor for your teammate behind you.

The Off-the-boards Pass is passing the puck to a teammate by bouncing it off the sideboards.

Shooting: This is hitting the puck toward the cage in order to score a goal.

The Forehand Wrist Shot, the most basic shot in hockey, is made with a powerful snap of your wrists. Drag the puck toward the goal, keeping it in the middle of your blade. Then, while continuing to skate forward, push your lower hand forward and up in a quick snapping motion and, at the same time, pull your upper your hand back. Follow through until your stick blade is pointing at your target.

The Backhand Wrist Shot is made the same way as the forehand wrist shot, except reversed. Hit the puck with the back of your blade.

The Forehand Flip Shot is used to lift the puck up into the air with a twisting motion of the wrists and over the goalie. The greater the snap of your wrists, the higher and faster the puck will flip.

The Backhand Flip Shot is the same as the forehand flip shot except that the puck is hit with the back of the blade.

The Slap Shot, the most powerful shot in all of hockey, has the sweep of a golf stroke. Swing your stick back and upward, keeping your eye on the puck, then bring it down fast and hard. Your blade should strike the ground an inch behind the puck. As you shoot, shift your weight to your forward foot and remember to follow through.

The Face-Off: All play begins with a face-off in the center circle. The official drops the puck between the two opposing centers. Each tries to sweep it away and pass it back to one of their players waiting outside the center circle.

Offensive Play (also called Attacking): This is attempting to move the puck towards your goal. Once a team loses the puck, it immediately switches to defense.

Defensive Play: This is interfering with the opposing team's play and attempting to steal back the puck by using stick to stick contact (called stick checking).

The Poke Check is jabbing your opponent's stick with your own in order to get the puck away from them.

The Sweep Check is a more difficult maneuver where you must crouch on the ground and lay your

The Sharks and the Laceys, two Ft. Hamilton (Brooklyn) League teams, scramble for the puck (top), and position for a face-off.

Sticks slash and bodies smash in a fight for possession of the puck.

stick down flat on it. Then sweep the puck away from your attacker.

Body checking is another way to stop the opposing player who has the puck. You may only body check the player who has the puck or the one who had it last.

The Shoulder Check is pushing your shoulder into the shoulder or chest of your opponent while keeping your knees slightly bent. Be careful not to use your elbows.

The Hip Check is most effective when the puck carrier is between you and the boards so he or she can't easily change direction and throw you off balance. Keeping your knees slightly bent, push your hip into your opponent's hip or stomach area.

Goal Tending: The goal tender (or goalie) blocks shots at his cage with his body, skates, or hockey stick. A goalie may catch the puck with his glove, fall on it, hit it with his stick, kick it, or block it in any possible way. Frequently, a goalie's own defensemen may assist in blocking shots. This maneuver is called screening the goalie.

Canadien goalie Eddie Hernandez drops to his knees to block a shot.

RAY MILLER: NEW YORK CITY'S "MR. ROLLER HOCKEY"

Ray Miller, a 54-year-old native New Yorker, is a recreational director for the New York City Parks Department, and is based in Brooklyn. He founded the now famous Ft. Hamilton Parkway Roller Hockey League—acknowledged as the best example of league-style hockey in the United States. Ft. Hamilton has 21 teams and over 400 players, ranging in age from 10 to 45 years old.

Ray became involved with the game in the early '50s when the Ft. Hamilton rink was just an ordinary playground where neighborhood skaters collected every weekend morning to play hockey. They used garbage cans for hockey cages. Even in those days, the competition was fierce, so Ray wrapped the trees with blankets before every early morning game so that no one would get hurt.

Through the years, Ray, with the help of other interested hockey lovers, transformed a broken-up playground into a model hockey rink, complete with dasher boards, penalty boxes, and an electronic scoreboard—all unheard of luxuries in the rough and tough world of outdoor roller hockey. He accomplished this by salvaging all kinds of scrap lumber and other construction materials, and also by soliciting donations from the community. Today, the playground at Ft. Hamilton Parkway and 53rd Street in Brooklyn is known as the "Madison Square Garden" of roller hockey rinks.

Ray, a hard-working, even-tempered man, has his hands full running his league and still maintaining order among its super-competitive teams. He takes a lot of flak because he also referees the games and even more kidding because he does it in sneakers, instead of roller skates. But Ray, with 23 years of experience, has his reasons. "Wearing sneakers makes it easier to break up the fights," he says with a smile.

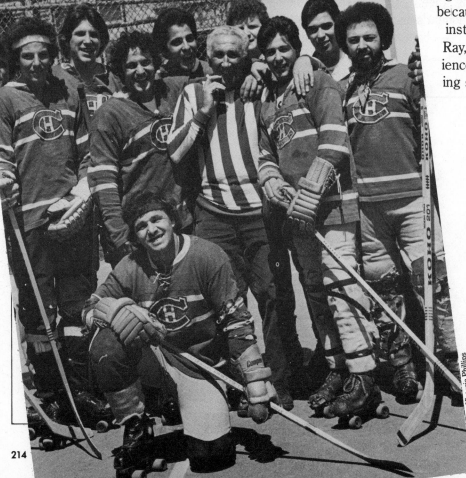

Ann-Victoria Phillips

The Canadiens, one of 21 teams in the Ft. Hamilton Roller Hockey League, proudly pose with Ray Miller, their benefactor.

TOMMY DOYLE: FT. HAMILTON ALL-STAR

Tommy Doyle, 45 years old, is the oldest player in Brooklyn's Ft. Hamilton League. He has played roller hockey every week since he was 14 years old. After 31 years, he *still* has no intention of letting up on the pace. "There are a few other players over 30 in the league, but most quit when they get to that age. Let's face it, there's an injury factor in this game. I don't fear getting hurt. If I did, I wouldn't go wild the way I do blocking shots at the goalie. Some other guys in the league also play ice hockey and they shoot the puck very, very hard."

Tommy, like many others in the league's Unlimited division, skates without a helmet and thus is very vulnerable to an attacker's shot. "Even though it's only a tape puck, you can get hit in the face. And when Ryan Boyd (from the league's Nationals team) shoots, you can feel it right through your shin guards."

Tommy, 5 feet 11 inches, 175 pounds, plays a defenseman position on the Canadiens team. That means he's responsible for body checking, attacking members of the opposing team, and also screening the goalie. This is one of the roughest jobs in the game. "I've never really gotten hurt," he says. "I've gotten scratched on the face from getting hit with the stick, but nothing bad enough to stop me from playing. Cuts heal up, and bruises go away, you know."

How long will he continue to play? "I really don't know," responds Tommy. "My wife says she wants me to quit, but she said the same thing last year and the year before! In her heart, I know she wants me to keep playing." There are some rewards. Tommy's team, the scrappy, quick-skating Canadiens, finished out the season in third place in the league standings. In addition, Tommy's teammates expressed their confidence in him when they voted him onto Ft. Hamilton's 1979 All Star Team.

Other satisfactions are on a much more personal level. "It's an exacting game. I'm not the best player on the team, but I do fairly well. I'm playing against guys younger than me and that's a big challenge."

Tommy, who works as a New York police detective sometimes switches tours in order to play on Saturday and Sunday mornings. "Roller hockey is a big outlet for me," he says. "I really get up for the game. By Thursday, I'm excited—it's something I look forward to all week. Also, I enjoy the competition and I like to win. Does that sound corny? For me, roller hockey is a terrific thrill!"

Ann-Victoria Phillips

Tommy Doyle,
a detective in the New York Police Department
has been playing roller hockey for 31 years.

SATURDAY AFTERNOON FEVER

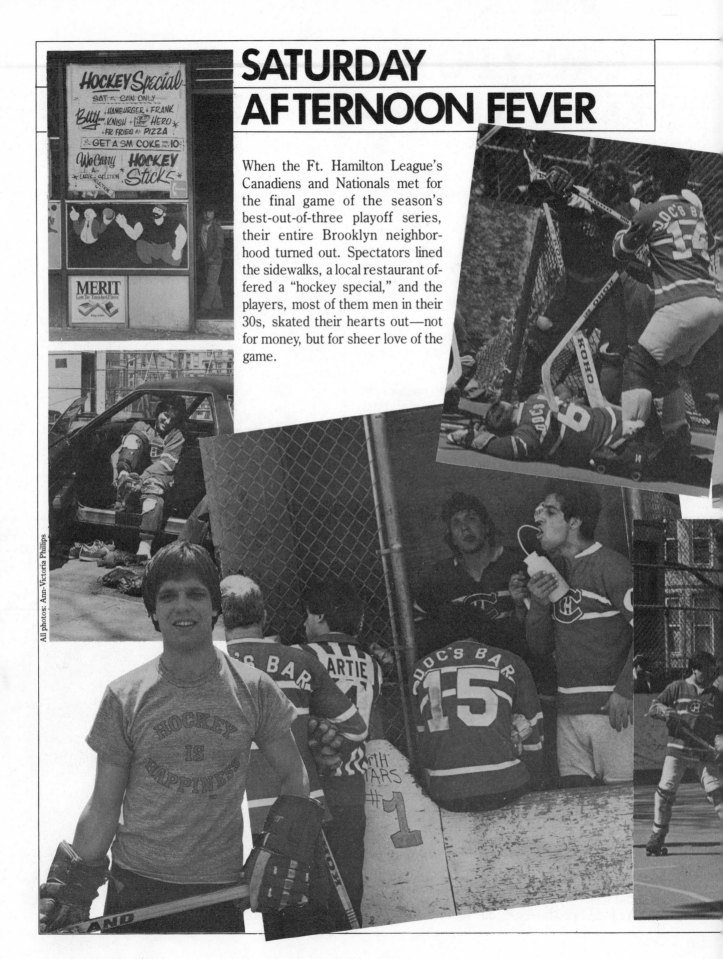

When the Ft. Hamilton League's Canadiens and Nationals met for the final game of the season's best-out-of-three playoff series, their entire Brooklyn neighborhood turned out. Spectators lined the sidewalks, a local restaurant offered a "hockey special," and the players, most of them men in their 30s, skated their hearts out—not for money, but for sheer love of the game.

All photos: Ann-Victoria Phillips

THE NORTH SHORE ROLLER HOCKEY LEAGUE

During the fall and winter months, roller hockey is one of the most popular neighborhood sports in New York City, where it is estimated that 15,000 to 20,000 skaters play in city streets and playgrounds.

There are many roller hockey leagues in the city—some are independent, others are administered by church groups or by the Police Department—but the way they are organized and scheduled is very much the same.

For those registered for official league play, the season lasts from mid-October through April. Each of the hundreds of teams will play 14 to 18 games a year—sometimes in sub-zero weather—providing there is no rain, ice, or snow.

All league games are played on neighborhood school yard playgrounds. PS 107 in Flushing, Queens, for example, is the home base of the North Shore Roller Hockey League.

North Shore is both a neighborhood league and YMCA-affiliated. Each league within the Y program has five teams, starting with the youngest—Midget (10 and under) and finishing with Junior (18 and under). In all, there are seven leagues that total 34 teams. Each has 20 to 25 players on the roster.

Running a league is expensive, so North Shore is sponsored by a local flower shop, a funeral home, and a candy store, each good for a $125 pledge. The money covers the referee's fee, hockey jerseys, an award dinner, and a trophy for every player. Each skater, however, must buy his or her own roller skates, knee pads, hockey gloves, helmet, and face mask.

All of the coaches are volunteers; most are either firemen, police officers or businessmen, and many have previous experience coaching both roller hockey and ice hockey teams. Although each league appoints their own staff, the coaches must be approved by the Y staff as well. According to Ed Moffet, one of the YMCA program administrators, "There are many, many people out there who want to coach roller hockey teams, but we have to be very careful who we select. We could have a hundred coaches but we only want adults that we know. Our coaches must understand that violence is not necessary to win a game."

The North Shore League takes anyone who

Feeling that they're a part of the team is important for Pam Kelly and Annie Quitoriano.

Ann-Victoria Phillips

wants to play, even if they can't skate. As long as their parents approve, sign a permission paper and pay the YMCA 20 dollars per season, any child can play league hockey. Skaters as young as six years old are allowed to sign up. Additionally, North Shore promises that *every* kid on the team will get to play in *every* game. While it's true that the best skaters will probably still get the most playing time, this way, the league guarantees that no one will be completely left out.

An oddity in the primitive world of playground roller hockey, North Shore has an untarnished reputation. This can be directly attributed to the dedicated work of 39-year-old Mary Schulter who along with her husband Walter, and with the cooperation of the Queens YMCA, formed the North Shore League six years ago. A local celebrity, Mary is the only woman roller hocker coach in New York City and possibly in the entire country. According to YMCA officials, she is one of the best coaches around.

But Mary is only one chapter in North Shore's unusual story—the league is also the first in the city to have girl hockey players on one of its teams.

Pam Kelly, 14 years old, and her teammate, Annie Quitoriano, 13 years old, both decked out in jeans and blue and white North Shore hockey jerseys skate down 45th Avenue on their way to play a league game. Both girls carry their helmets, gloves, and sticks in their hands. Their major piece of protective gear, plastic shin guards, are attached to their pants by five yards of black friction tape. Pam wears new, jet-black hockey skates, but Annie plays wearing rink-style Roller Derby skates that are so grey, tattered, and cut up, it's a wonder they even stay on her feet. The condition of her wheels is even more astonishing. Day-in and day-out contact with the rough, concrete surface of the playground and street has reduced her once-perfect wheels into little smooth-edged balls.

Trailing slightly behind the girls and walking on the sidewalk are Pam's mom, Martha Kelly, and her aunt, Mary Schulter. "I joined the league because of Mary," says Pam, as she dumps her gear inside the playground's chain link fence and sits down on the ground. "My aunt is the whole reason this league exists. I have always admired her."

"Pam got involved because I'm running the

League Vice-President Mary Schluter with her protegees Annie and Pam—two of the first girls to play league roller hockey in the US.

show," jokes Mary. "First, she pestered me. Then, she bugged her mother about joining the league until we had to let her play. Her mother was leery at first, but she finally signed the permission papers. Pam was lucky to have played last year with the 14-and-under team. They had a very good coach named Mike Young. He told the boys that if they gave Pam any flak, he'd throw them off the team."

Mary, who usually coaches only North Shore's youngest players, still attends every other one of her league's games and supervises all activities. As vice president of the league, she's very much in charge, and that's fortunate for Pam and Annie because without Mary's interest and support, there's no way the girls would be allowed to play roller hockey in any official league game.

As far as anyone knows, Pam was the first girl to play roller hockey on a New York City league team. "I was playing hockey in the streets with the boys when I was seven," she recalls. "We used two traffic cones for goals and the boundary lines were drawn with chalk. When I got older, the boys dared me to join the league." Was she afraid? "Yes, in the beginning," she admits, "but I'm not afraid of getting checked or hit anymore. But, I didn't want to be the only girl, so I got Annie to sign up."

Annie played in the 12-and-under division last year. This year she has joined Pam in the Ranger Division for players 13 and 14. "At first, my girlfriends laughed at me," Annie remembers. "To them, hockey is a boy's sport.

"In fact you gotta dress yourself up to look like a boy or you're dead," says Pam. "If they see you're a girl, they'll hit you twice as hard in order to teach you a lesson. Sometimes they do it even when I don't have the puck. My attitude is if they're gonna hit me I'll hit 'em back."

"A lot of the boys on our own team are nasty," continues Annie. At just 4 feet 10 inches and 85 lbs., she has a right to be concerned. "They even get mad when we steal the puck away from them during practice."

Only minutes later, during the team's pre-game warm-up, Annie's words are confirmed. The girls, who are standing in line with their 24 male teammates, wait patiently for a boy to pass them a puck. Three pucks are constantly in motion with players taking turns attacking the goalie with a puck, but the girls are ignored.

Suddenly Pam darts out from the line and scoops the puck toward her with her stick, stealing it away from one of the boys. Then, while skating forward, she dribbles the puck down court with her stick and shoots it toward the cage with a quick, wrist shot. But the goalie deflects the puck. Pam skates back up court and re-joins Annie at the back of the line to wait for her next turn. Soon they return to the sidelines.

Mary comments, "I told the boys, 'You don't like girls on the team? Then, quit! Watch your mouth or you're suspended for two games.' " It's not an idle threat. Mary as vice president of the

Annie finds herself on the other end of a body check.

league, is the only one who can back it up with action!

Annie says, "Mary always tells us, 'You girls have gotta stick up for yourselves or you'll be knocked around all your life.' Last year there was another girl who was supposed to play with us. She couldn't skate very well but she was coming around. The boys made fun of her, so she quit. She couldn't take it anymore."

All photos: Ann-Victoria Phillips

Pam shows some muscle during a practice session.

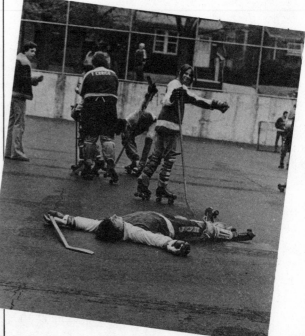

Pam joins her North Shore teammates as they do warm-up exercises before the game.

"The boys still try to discourage us," remarks Pam, "but this is our second year, and most of the players know us by now. They know we're here for real, not for kidding. Now a few of the boys treat us like hockey players. They used to call me 'dog face,' now, it's 'hey you.' "

As Pam will be the first to admit, roller hockey is one of the fastest, roughest, games in the world and with the boys out to show up the girls in particular, the sport is doubly rough for her.

"But I'm not afraid of the game," contends Pam. "I'm afraid of making mistakes: If I'm offside or I pass the puck to the wrong player or the wrong way, that's the worst because I never hear the end of it. I want to do good.

"What is my responsibility as a member of the team?" Pam asks the question. "According to the boys, it's to stay away from the puck. No, really, what I'm supposed to do is watch the other team's defense and keep the puck away from them. Also if I have the chance, I can try to score. One of my coaches, Rico, promised me a Chinese dinner when I make my first goal. I'm gonna make him stick to it."

The warm-up is over. Across the field, the Canadiens, a roller hockey team from Greenpoint, Brooklyn, sits talking with its coach. North Shore does the same. Pam and Annie take off their helmets and gloves, and sit down on the edge of the court and wait. No one smiles. Pete O'Rourke

gives a pep talk and tells his game plan. No one laughs. They all look scared to death.

"Everyone knows what line they're on, right?" Another one of the other coaches, Jerry Mele, has divided the team—forwards and defensemen—into "lines," or shifts, that will be constantly rotated throughout the game.

"Hockey is a very hard skating game," explains Mary. "It's tiring. You skate at full speed from one end of the rink to the other; it's like a 100-yard-dash every time, back and forth. You race to beat the other guy down to the other end. These skaters can't last for more than two to three minutes. They have to catch their breath. The coach changes the line to get a fresh leg."

Pam and Annie are forwards, also called "wings." Both play the same position, right wing, but are assigned to different lines. Each works with the same center and left wing when they play. Occasionally, the girls are sent out together, and in that case, Annie switches to playing left wing.

As forwards, both girls have a complex variety of responsibilities to their teammates once they're out on the field. The front line is made up of a center and two wings. The three players together patrol the rink from end to end, each staying in their own lane. The wings are specifically responsible for all hockey played toward the two outer edges of the rink. These players, often the fastest skaters and best passers on the team, are the ones who will usually attempt to score. The wings work

During pre-game warm-ups, the girls often have to fight for their turn at practice shooting.

together with the center, who plays a role similar to a football quarterback, setting up plays in order to out think the opponent's defense.

Remembering that the wings must stay in their own respective lanes and that hockey skaters, just like basketball players, many times use a one-on-one-type defense (Pam or Annie, as right wings, "play their man"—meaning the opponent's left wing), the girls will use forechecking (if North Shore loses the puck in the opponent's end of the court) or back checking (if North Shore loses it in its own part of the court). Both of these maneuvers are designed to break up the opponent's offensive play, and steal the puck away if possible.

Annie, a right wing, sprints down court and into the play.

If Pam or Annie carry the puck, the Canadiens' defense will try to stop their progress by body checks or steal the puck away with stick checks. They can get hit very hard.

Playing behind the girls are North Shore's defensemen who, like safeties in the football world, are the players who will make the last ditch effort to prevent the opposition from scoring a goal.

The moment North Shore gets the puck, it's on offense. The moment they lose it, no matter whether it's in their territory or not, they're on defense. The changeover is lightning quick and happens so unexpectedly, yet regularly, that Pam and Annie must be good at defensive play as well.

Playing defensively, the girls should use some of the checks that were previously used on them, especially the poke check. It's an effective maneuver where the girls jab their stick onehandedly at the puck carrier's stick or the puck itself to try to steal it away.

"Okay! Everyone on their feet." The coaches gather the players into a huddle. "Here we go, North Shore, here we go!" the boys chant enthusiastically. They finish cheering, all join hands and then skate across the field for the start of the game.

Pam and Annie, fully outfitted and ready to play, stand on the sidelines with Mary and watch the boys. They are still apprehensive about joining the boys in the huddle.

Out on the field, the two centers position themselves on the face-off circle. The roller skating linesman moves in gingerly and drops the puck as sticks slash. The Canadiens' center scoops the puck backwards toward his wing, who skates off down the field. The game has begun.

The sounds of outdoor roller hockey games are some of the most unique in the world. For one thing, the players' skates, all of them equipped with looseball bearings, have their own peculiar hum. Then there's the constant music of hockey skates digging into the rough concrete playground mixed with slashing sticks and sometimes the unforgettable flat, sharp, cracking sound of hockey's most flamboyant move—the slap shot. And last, but not least, there's the yelling on the sidelines.

"When is the coach gonna put the girls in?" Pam's impatient mother asks Mary. Mary responds, "O'Rourke usually puts them in when he's winning by a lot or losing by a lot. He's their coach and I'm not supposed to bother him, but when he forgets the girls are there, I have to. It's ridiculous. He doesn't think the girls are capable. But if he'd put the two girls against two good boy players, they'd do as good, or better, than most of the boys. But for now, I have to keep telling Pam and Annie to go up to him and say, 'I wanna get in.' They have to keep annoying the hell outta him."

Annie gets in first. Mary, a minute before her most sympathetic supporter, is now the girl's toughest critic. Mary expects the world from the two girls. "That guy passed the puck to Annie," says Mary, "but she had her stick up off the ground and missed it. Now she should go after that guy with the puck and take it away. Annie doesn't check—she's afraid of getting hurt. Sometimes she's just skating out there and that's not playing roller hockey.

"Annie's trying, but she's not that good a skater," explains Mary. "Most of these guys have been playing hockey since they were 6 years old. They have been in our league for a few years. Annie has only been at it for two years."

The ref blows the whistle and both teams leave the field. The game, unusually peaceful and orderly, remains scoreless at the end of the first period. All the players skate off the field for a ten-minute rest. The referee blows the whistle again and the whole team moves back into position on the line. This time both girls are sent onto the field; of course, the big problem the girls face is that once they're on the field, their own teammates won't pass them the puck. They have to go after it, but they still must play their positions. No matter how much they want to score, Pam still has to cover the right side while Annie plays the left.

North Shore takes possession of the puck. The defense man shoots it up to the center who moves it down the field and then passes it to Pam. Suddenly and unexpectedly, Pam, who is very close to the cage, slaps the puck lightly with a quick scooping shot, and drives the puck into the air and over the Canadiens' goalie's pad. The goalie tries to block the shot by dropping down on one knee and raising his glove. For a moment no one can see what has happened. Then Mary jumps straight up and screams, "She did it! Pam just scored a goal!" Even the boys are cheering as Pam skates off the field. She shakes hands down the line while the boys crowd around her, patting her on the back.

Later, Pam, smiling from ear to ear, describes her feelings. "I always wondered how it would feel to make a goal. It was great. I felt so proud. Was I dreaming?"

Tommy, nicknamed "Tuba," a player who also skated with Pam on last year's team reveals, "At first, I wondered if the girls were playing for spite or to make us look bad. This year, I don't care what their reason is, it's okay with me."

The other boys are still reluctant to give out praise. But Pam refuses to be discouraged or intimidated. "There were times last year when I felt like quitting," she says, "but the boys realize there's no way to get rid of me anymore."

The game, kept well under control by the officials, moves into the third and final period without incident. North Shore completely outskates, outpasses, and outshoots the Canadiens' defense and scores two more goals in rapid succession winning the game 3-0.

Although this match is fairly routine, it's a day Pam, Annie, and Mary will never forget.

Ann-Victoria Phillips

Pam is not intimidated by members of the opposing team.

"The game of hockey was invented by a woman!" Pam's announcement silences the rowdy group. "And I can prove it. Just go to the Hockey Hall of Fame and you'll see pictures of women playing hockey on ice using canes." Pam visited the museum in Kingston, Ontario during one summer vacation.

"The men took the game away from us," says Pam. "Now it's time to take it back."

THE SAGA OF
THE ROLLING GHOSTS

Buddy Holly was born there. Waylon Jennings grew up there. But if you ask Henry Black, a 58-year-old cotton and soybean farmer from Lubbock, Texas, what his town is *really* famous for, he's likely to answer, "Chicken Fried Steak, ball hockey, and the Rolling Ghosts!" Good Grief!

Who is Henry Black, and why are people playing roller hockey in Texas? As the story goes, Black discovered the sport of roller hockey while he was a serviceman stationed in California during World War II. A one-time high school football player, he loved the look of this new, fast-action game, and decided on the spot to bring it back to his home.

True to the legendary Texas style of doing things up big, Henry, once back in Lubbock, started his own hockey league with the help of his brother, J. P. "Preacher" Black, in 1949. The Black brothers needed a place to play so they bought the old Palace Roller Skating Rink and, according to Henry, "We proceeded to play roller hockey every day of the year." The Blacks called their team The Rolling Ghosts, and thus one of the most unusual stories in the world of roller hockey was born.

"We started out with homemade hockey equipment and played that way for the next four years," remembers Henry, who used to fashion sticks out of aluminum conduit (pipe) and then sell them for a dollar a piece. "I made all kinds of pucks—square ones, round ones—all kinds of different shapes. Some we made by nailing and gluing pieces of leather together; others were made from sawing up old bowling pins."

By 1954, the Blacks brought in regular ice hockey equipment and, with that, attracted the attention of a 16-year-old Lubbock boy named Billy Sisson, the oldest of four brothers. They, with the help of Henry's son, Rick, and Preacher's son, Jeff, would all eventually go on to form the most powerful, intimidating, and winning amateur roller hockey team in US history.

Ball hockey has taken the Ghosts team all over the world. Here Dick Sisson sets up a pass, and takes a shot on goal at the 1968 World Meet in Portugal.

Courtesy of Jackie Sisson

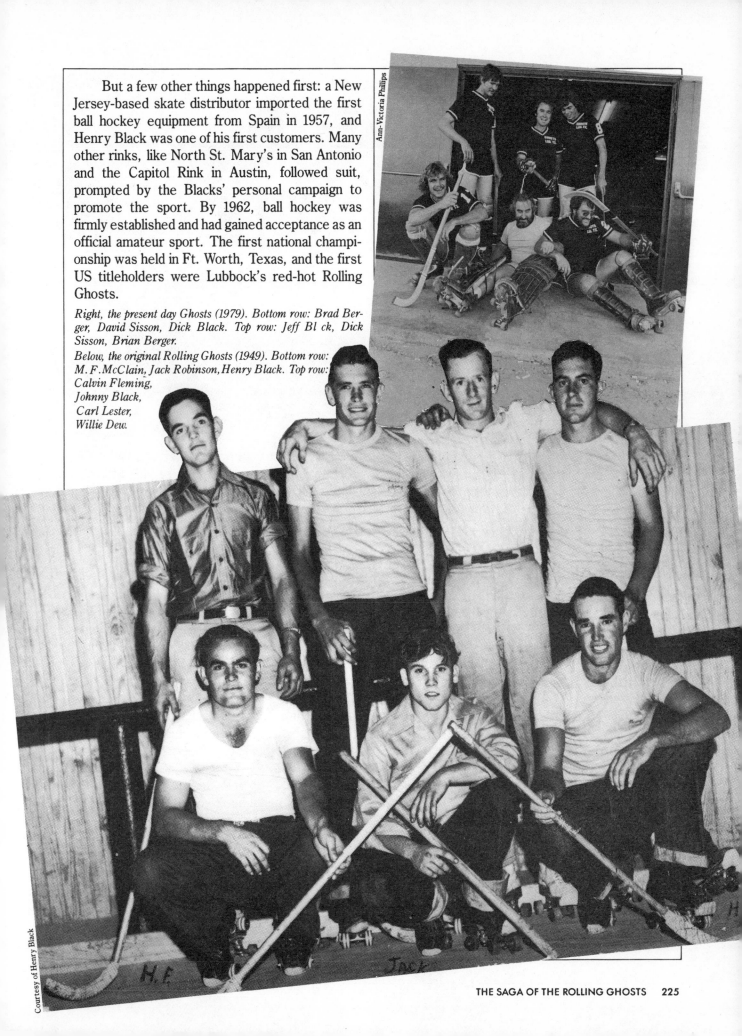

But a few other things happened first: a New Jersey-based skate distributor imported the first ball hockey equipment from Spain in 1957, and Henry Black was one of his first customers. Many other rinks, like North St. Mary's in San Antonio and the Capitol Rink in Austin, followed suit, prompted by the Blacks' personal campaign to promote the sport. By 1962, ball hockey was firmly established and had gained acceptance as an official amateur sport. The first national championship was held in Ft. Worth, Texas, and the first US titleholders were Lubbock's red-hot Rolling Ghosts.

Right, the present day Ghosts (1979). Bottom row: Brad Berger, David Sisson, Dick Black. Top row: Jeff Bl ck, Dick Sisson, Brian Berger.

Below, the original Rolling Ghosts (1949). Bottom row: M.F.McClain, Jack Robinson, Henry Black. Top row: Calvin Fleming, Johnny Black, Carl Lester, Willie Dew.

Ann-Victoria Phillips

Courtesy of Henry Black

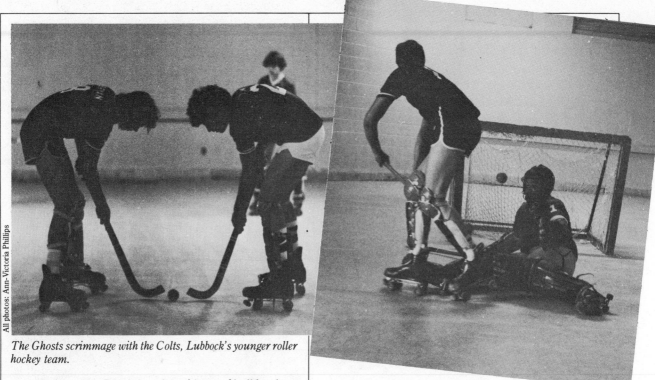

The Ghosts scrimmage with the Colts, Lubbock's younger roller hockey team.

Today, the Black brothers' love of ball hockey has been taken up by a younger group. Similar to the setup of many other amateur hockey clubs, the Rolling Ghosts Senior Men's team is still very family oriented. Two sets of brothers—three of the Sissons, and Brian and Brad Berger—plus two cousins, Rick Black and Jeff Black, make up the team. Billy Sisson, now in his forties, no longer plays. He has been appointed to coach the team which will represent the US in the Pan American Games. His brother, Dick, 35, is the Ghost's current player/coach.

The Lubbock team has totally dominated national level ball hockey competition in the US for the last 18 years. After winning 11 national championships and many second-place finishes, it was something of a surprise that the Ghosts slipped to third at the 1978 National Meet.

According to Kevin Baker, the coach of the Colts, a younger team from Lubbock, "the Ghosts didn't practice enough last year and also the age of the team is beginning to show. They're slowing down a bit, but they have experience, size, and strength on their side.

"The Ghosts are still dangerous. Both the Sissons and the Bergers are bricklayers and the Blacks are farmers. Their shoulders, arms, and wrists are incredibly strong. They are very much in contention. They could go on winning for years, if they take more time to practice."

Dick Sisson confirms this saying, "We're the most unfit team you've ever seen!" Still the Ghosts have no intention of quitting. "Once you start with ball hockey, you can't stop. It gets in your blood."

What accounts for the Ghosts' sensational success? "It's do or die for us every time we play the game," explains Dick. "No matter how bad shape we're in, we'll pull it off. We don't like to get beat. We're known as a brash and cocky team. We skate well and win because we're super-confident. We have a lot of pride. We call our style of play 'aggressive defense'. We don't hurt anyone but we do slow them down. We do use our bodies to stop players on the opposing team. We have a reputation of being a physical bunch of guys, but we're really not. We've traveled to Brazil, Portugal, Argentina, and Spain and especially at the world meets, the other teams get a lot more physical than we do. The name 'Rolling Ghosts' scares people. They might be as good as us but they get psyched out. We can play terribly and still beat the good team."

A lot of the Ghosts' energy and success can be traced back to the tremendous enthusiasm Henry Black, who played with the team until two years ago, put into the sport. "I love lots of action," he says, "and ball hockey has plenty for everyone."

11. ROLLER DERBY

THE BIRTH OF THE GAME

In 1935, Leo Seltzer, a sports entrepreneur who staged six-day bicycle races, and other dance and sports events in the Chicago Coliseum, invented a new game that would have the thrills of a race and the roughness of football. He sketched out plans on a restaurant's checkered tablecloth and named it Roller Derby.

The first version of the game was really just an endurance race held over a period of days, and it proved to be an astonishing spectacle. Between 5,000 and 10,000 people crowded nightly into the Coliseum to watch what was called Leo Seltzer's Trans-Continental Roller Derby. The object for each of the 25 teams comprised of two skaters each—a man and a woman—was to skate the equivalent of the number of miles between New York and San Francisco. So, starting at 4:30 each afternoon, five skaters at a time would step onto the huge oval track and begin their required daily laps. Meanwhile their teammates rested or slept on cots set up in the infield in full view of the spectators until they were called onto the track.

As can be imagined, spectator interest waned during the long 10-hour sessions so Seltzer staged "jams," or sprints several times during the afternoon and evening. At that time, the fans placed bets on the teams.

By 1937 it had evolved into a full team sport, each team having equal numbers of men and women skaters. Four teams were formed, Chicago, New York, Brooklyn, and Philly-Bronx, and that year they toured all over the United States highlighted by a September stint at New York's Madison Square Garden.

Although women had skated from the very beginning, two outstanding skaters, Gerry Murray and Midge "Toughie" Brasuhn, who played on opposing teams initiated the famous rivalry that firmly established the role of the Derby woman as an athlete and as a performer.

All photos: Courtesy of Gerry Murray

Roller Derby, like its predecessors the six-day bicycle race, the walk-a-thon, and the marathon dance contest, was invented to appeal to a Depression-era audience. It was an overnight success.

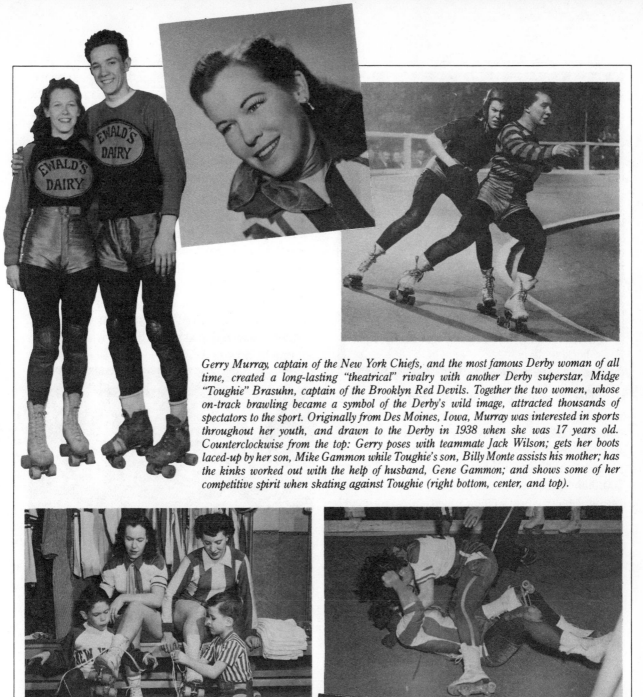

Gerry Murray, captain of the New York Chiefs, and the most famous Derby woman of all time, created a long-lasting "theatrical" rivalry with another Derby superstar, Midge "Toughie" Brasuhn, captain of the Brooklyn Red Devils. Together the two women, whose on-track brawling became a symbol of the Derby's wild image, attracted thousands of spectators to the sport. Originally from Des Moines, Iowa, Murray was interested in sports throughout her youth, and drawn to the Derby in 1938 when she was 17 years old. Counterclockwise from the top: Gerry poses with teammate Jack Wilson; gets her boots laced-up by her son, Mike Gammon while Toughie's son, Billy Monte assists his mother; has the kinks worked out with the help of husband, Gene Gammon; and shows some of her competitive spirit when skating against Toughie (right bottom, center, and top).

DERBY STARS AS ATHLETES

In spite of the fact that the Derby remains one of the most controversial subjects in sports, few people who have sat in a front row seat could dispute the extraordinary skills of the skaters. Most agree Derby men and women are some of the most versatile athletes in the world.

Roller Derby, either as a sport or a game, makes great physical demands on its athletes. Besides the fact that a player should have the quickness and endurance of a speed skater, he or she must have the reflexes of a skilled martial artist, the flexibility and acrobatic skills of a gymnast and the physical strength of a football or hockey player.

Derby skaters of the '40s and '50s had a grueling six-day-a-week, year-round schedule. They were "hot property" and the company took great care to see that they remained in super physical condition. TV brought Roller Derby into 100,000 east coast homes, and over 65 percent of the audience were women eager to see a sport where their sex got top-ranked billing.

More substantial rule changes came in the '60s. Leo's son Jerry Seltzer, a salesman for the Roller Derby Skate Company, took over the management of the Derby and brought them to the San Francisco Bay Area. Jerry syndicated the Derby through a hundred TV stations and boosted ticket sales at the live games by introducing much more theatricality to the game.

Attendance soared to new heights by the start of the '70s but late in 1972 Seltzer sold his famous team, the San Francisco Bay Bombers to settle an alimony suit. Worse yet, in 1973, a union-izing attempt by the players, and the breakdown of Seltzer's TV syndication network, caused the promoter to sell off the rest of the Derby teams. This move signaled the beginning of the end of Roller Derby in its best known form.

Bill Griffiths, a Los Angeles owner of Roller Games, (a rival derby-style group) bought Seltzer's teams and promoted the game as a carnival complete with midgets and fat ladies. Superstars Joan Weston, and Charlie O'Connell skated with Griffiths for a month and then, totally disgusted and embarrassed with the Los Angeles promoter's interpretation of the game, quit and returned to the Bay Area to re-establish themselves in new careers, as did almost all of the original Seltzer-organization skaters. There was no Derby skating in 1974 or 1975.

Courtesy of Billy Bogash

Josephine "Ma" Bogash, was a regular in the early days and stuck with Derby life until she retired at age 60.

Finally, in 1976, Charlie O'Connell, a veteran Derby skater, set up one of Seltzer's banked tracks at California State Hayward for an experimental Derby exhibition game. His tiny advertisement in a San Francisco paper brought 2,200 loyal fans running back after a two-year layoff. After the successful event David Lipschultz, a 23-year-old media entrepreneur, offered to produce the Derby for television.

Today, Lipschultz, who organized the skaters and founded a new league, stages Derby games in the Northern California area with the aim of again raising the sport to national prominence.

Derby of the '40s was a team endurance race with no theatrics. Gerry Murray, third from right, poses with the New York Chiefs.

Courtesy of Gerry Murray

230

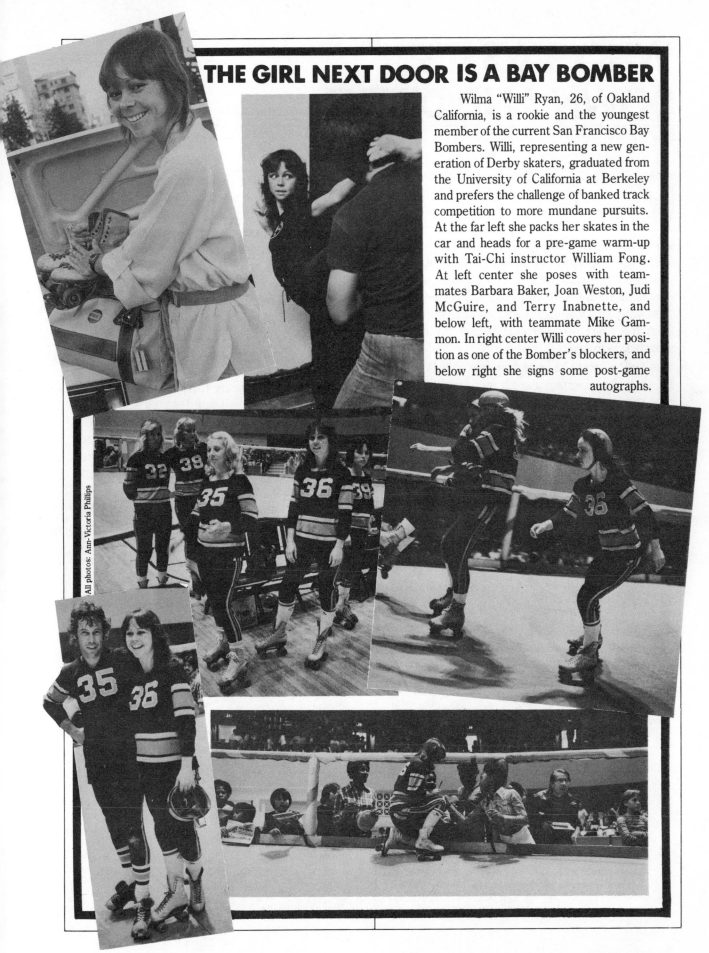

THE GIRL NEXT DOOR IS A BAY BOMBER

Wilma "Willi" Ryan, 26, of Oakland California, is a rookie and the youngest member of the current San Francisco Bay Bombers. Willi, representing a new generation of Derby skaters, graduated from the University of California at Berkeley and prefers the challenge of banked track competition to more mundane pursuits. At the far left she packs her skates in the car and heads for a pre-game warm-up with Tai-Chi instructor William Fong. At left center she poses with teammates Barbara Baker, Joan Weston, Judi McGuire, and Terry Inabnette, and below left, with teammate Mike Gammon. In right center Willi covers her position as one of the Bomber's blockers, and below right she signs some post-game autographs.

WHO SAYS IT'S DOWN AND DIRTY?

Roller Derby is a simple, direct game. It is pure entertainment—colorful, theatrical, exciting, melodramatic, and personal. But the Derby is considered the black sheep of the roller world by amateur and professional skaters, coaches, rink operators, and USAC, the group who administers amateur roller skating competitions in the United States. They perceive the Derby as a low-class game that has detracted from the sport of roller skating and given it an unfavorable image.

Other sports have evolved into social rituals. Football, for example, a much more violent game than the Derby, and one from which most players sustain some sort of life long disability, has become theater. It is helped along by pageantry, music, half-time shows, cheerleaders, electronic-score boards, instant replay, and bulky helmets which hide the features of each individual player. The athletes become shapes moving across a field.

During a Roller Derby game, on the other hand, the fans can be as close as 10 feet from the edge of the track. That close, every bone-bruising crash, every grimace, and every insulting remark is clearly visible and audible. It compels audience reaction and participation because the crowd can clearly see who performed a dirty deed and personally demand retribution for it. In fact, fans will rage until the evil is punished.

For this reason Derby games have earned the reputation as being rowdy affairs, and in contrast to other sports, fans and Derby stars exchange a lot of verbal insults during the game.

Derby skaters, situated so close to the crowd, are flesh and blood athletes who deliver real blows and get hit back. The fans empathize with the skaters, cringe when they get hurt, and sometimes cannot restrain themselves from personally avenging a wrongdoing to a favorite player. They'll even vault onto the track to do it. The closeness of the fans to the track, the speed of the game, the roughness, and the free interchange between spectators and players, repel some people but are the very elements that dedicated Derby fanatics crave.

Courtesy of David Lipschultz

Today, Ann Calvello and Joan Weston continue in the tradition of the Murray/Brasuhn rivalry (above). Charlie O'Connell (right), the famed skater #40 and now the oldest of the original Seltzer organization skaters, still rides the banked track.

12. RADICAL SKATING

DAREDEVIL SKATING

Daredevil-style roller skating is as old as the invention of the skate itself. It attracts the radical, the thrill-seeker and the skater who is turned on to speed. This style allows the skater to experience the ultimate in exhilarating sensations ranging from a sense of weightlessness and floating in space to a feeling of complete control over one's own mind and body in a challenging situation. Added to this is the excitement caused by the ever present danger and the response of the crowd. These are some of the reasons why people are attracted to the world of radical skating.

There are two types of daredevil roller skaters today: those who perform acrobatic stunts on flat ground and others who have invaded the radical skateboarder's turf—the skateboard park. Just like their more familiar counterparts who ride the vertical walls on boards, these daredevils ride them on skates. Although skateboarding and roller skating are quite different, all such activities in a skate park by either group are termed "radical" skating.

For the roller skater, this demanding style is a product of combined techniques from the sports of skateboarding, surfing, and gymnastics. In fact, the radical style looks more like skateboarding and surfing than like the more conventional artistic forms of skating that are its true ancestors.

Roller skaters have found they have certain advantages over skateboarders in the skate parks. For one thing, they get more elevation on skates than do those using a board. It's also easier to do most aerial maneuvers because the skates are attached to the foot. Skateboarders are at a disadvantage because they must hold onto the board with their hands while in the air. Skates also give

Claude Bernal, a one-legged stunt skater, clears a bar-stool pyramid during his 1930s vaudeville act.

Courtesy of Claude Bernal

more directional control than boards and skaters can take a wide stance which increases their balance while riding the walls. The one disadvantage of skates is that it's impossible to bail out of them in an emergency.

Falling is an inevitable part of learning this sport. You have to expect it and train accordingly or you'll get hurt. Wearing protective equipment is more than a requirement—it's the law of the skate park. Strength and flexibility training will minimize possible muscle strains or tears during a fall and may even prevent one in the first place.

The only way a beginner learns is by imitation and trial-and-error because there are no radical coaches to turn to. There are dangers in learning techniques this way, especially because of the age of some of the participants (as young as eight and ten years old.) Youngsters see the professionals performing high flying stunts and may be tempted themselves to try them without any knowledge of the techniques involved.

Often skate park roller skaters become professionals by the time they are 14 or 15 by accepting sponsorships from roller skate and skateboard gear manufacturers. Unfortunately, there is no formal supervision or coaching at the advanced level either. The sport is too new and, besides, skaters are not in a position to coach each other—mostly they compete with each other in order to attract sponsors. It's obvious, however, that from a safety standpoint, some type of systematic training program is desperately needed on both an amateur and professional level.

Kenny Means "getting air" on a portable ramp.

SKATE PARKS

Skateboard parks, built and first used exclusively for skateboarding, are a new resource for recreational roller skating. The earliest park is said to have been built in 1976 in Carlsbad, California,

Beth Graham drops into the oversized bowl at The Runway Skate Park in Carson, California.

although other sources name a Florida site. By early 1978, hundreds had been built all over the United States.

The skate park is a fantastically sculptured terrain, an otherworldly white concrete landscape of reservoirs, pipes, bowls, and pools. Different areas have varying degrees of difficulty. The easiest is a flat plane that is used for freestyle skating, the most demanding are the vertically walled pipes, pools, and bowls. The following is a list of the types of runs you'd find within a typical park.

Bowl: A basin with steep, graduated sides, usually with a depth of 7, 10, or 12 feet.

Freestyle Area: A flat, non-banked area used for warm-ups, practice, and competition.

Full Pipe: A very large, 360-degree pipe used by the very advanced skater only.

Half Pipe: A very large, long, 360-degree pipe that has been cut in half. A half pipe is usually 20 feet in diameter and 12 feet deep and is used by intermediate level skaters and for warm-ups.

Pool: A basin similar to a bowl except that it has a lip (coping tiles) around the top edge which skaters use while performing advanced maneuvers. For this reason, you can do more stunts in a pool than in a bowl.

Portable Ramp: A short, portable half pipe commonly used for shows and promotions. It also may be set up in the freestyle area at a park for exhibitions and competitions. A portable ramp is constructed of fiberglass; it sits above ground and is between 10 and 15 feet wide and about 15 feet high.

Reservoir: A shallow basin with graduated two- to four-foot high walls used for beginning level maneuvers.

Slalom Run: A short, steep downhill slope. It's most often used in competition when skaters, like skiers, slalom around cones.

Snake Run: A serpentine-shaped channel that may be as shallow as 4 feet or as deep as 10 feet with vertical walls.

WHAT TO EXPECT AT A SKATE PARK

First, in order to skate, you must sign a liability release, and if you are under 18, a parent must co-sign. Most skaters find it convenient to get a park membership card so they can avoid signing forms at each session.

Admission fees vary. A park may either charge by the hour (1 to 2 dollars), the session (about 3 dollars), or the day (about 5 dollars).

Most parks don't rent skates—you have to bring your own—although they do rent protective gear. Remember, wearing a helmet, gloves, knee pads, and elbow pads is mandatory. Most people buy their own safety gear because renting is too expensive and also there is no way to guarantee that rented equipment will protect you in an emergency. Frayed elastic may break or slip off

Ann-Victoria Phillips

Ticia Strickland weaves through a slalom run.

GLOSSARY OF RADICAL SKATING TERMS

Aerial: A leap into the air, done in a frontside or backside position, off the top rim of a bowl or pool.

Carving: A style of skating banked or vertical walls in a reservoir, pool, or bowl.

Competition: A roller skating contest in a skate park that includes freestyle slalom, bowl, and pool riding events.

Eating it: Taking a bad fall by crashing into a wall while skating.

Freestyle: An event seen in competition where the skater choreographs a routine and sets it to music. Freestyle events can take place in the freestyle area or in pools and bowls.

Getting air: Doing an aerial. Your skates are no longer in contact with the ground.

Getting it wired: Knowing exactly how to skate a pipe, a bowl, or a pool, based on previous experience.

Parallel stance: A normal roller skating stance where the feet are kept parallel and alongside each other

Picking your line: Knowing ahead of time the course you'll skate in a pool or a bowl.

Pumping: The style of skating using "weighting" and "unweighting" (see below) in order to skate up a vertical wall. It requires total body coordination, excellent balance, and also muscle strength to maintain sufficient momentum throughout a ride.

Radical: The most challenging or dangerous roller skating maneuvers. Radical can also refer to the degree of difficulty in a skating terrain (as in skate parks).

Road rash: Your scraped skin after falling.

Run: One ride in a pipe, pool, or a bowl.

Slalom run: A race against the clock where skaters weave between cones set up on a downhill slope. It requires agility and good balance.

Sliding out: When you lose speed and momentum while carving and slide back down the wall to the bottom of the pool or bowl.

Surfer's stance: (also called the side-surfing position) A skating stance taken from skateboarding and surfing in which the legs are completely turned out, causing the skates to be placed heel-to-heel. If you skate with your right foot forward, it's called skating "goofy-footed" and if your left foot is forward, you're said to be in a "regular" stance. This stance is most frequently seen in the skate park.

Three-sixty (360): A complete turn, either in the air or off the edge of a pool or bowl.

Weighting and unweighting: Alternately bearing down and letting up on your skates in order to get up a vertical wall.

---

under impact and worn padding will not properly cushion a fall.

In the park's beginner areas, you'll see people practicing all at the same time; it is essential for safety reasons, however, that people take turns making runs in the pipes, pools, and bowls. The advanced areas of the park may be crowded, so a degree of assertiveness is necessary for you to get your practice time in. Since no one lines up (they just crowd around) and there's very little conversation, as soon as one skater is finished and there is an opening, immediately take your turn. You must act quickly and decisively or you won't get a chance to skate.

EQUIPMENT

A complete roller skate outfit suitable for skate park riding would include: the strongest leather boots, trucks, and plates on the market, plus urethane wheels. The price will generally range between 100 and 150 dollars. Don't bother buying inexpensive skates to work out in a skate park. They will simply fall apart from stress.

A skate boot that gives maximum support and ankle protection is recommended. If you use a low-cut speed skate boot, wearing ankle guards is advisable.

Protective Gear: The essentials include helmet, leather palm-padded gloves, elbow pads, and knee pads. Optional equipment may include padded shorts (to protect the tail bone and hips), ankle guards, and wrist braces. The helmet should be well-padded, ventilated, and cover the nape of the neck and ears.

Helmets cost between 14 and 24 dollars. The estimated costs for the rest of the the equipment are: gloves, 20 dollars; wrist brace, 18 dollars; ankle guards, 15 dollars; padded shorts, 25 dollars; elbow and knee pads between 15 and 20 dollars per set.

SKATING ON ALIEN TERRAIN

Even a beginner level skateboard park is no place for a beginner, so remember, before you start skating in parks, you must first be a good flatland skater. You should be able to skate forward and backward, know how to stop, and be confident with your skills.

The next step is learning how to skate in the surfer's stance on flat ground. This is a different stance than the one commonly used by roller skaters and demands greater flexibility and strength because you propel yourself along by scissoring your skates *sideways* instead of in and out. Although a few skaters do maintain their traditional parallel stance in the skateboard park, it is seldom seen.

Next, practice skating the shallow reservoir of a skate park in a surfer's stance. You'll have to develop a "pump" so you won't lose momentum (see the glossary).

Also practice skating circles up and down the walls in the side-surfing position. This is called carving. It builds muscle strength and can improve balance as well as develop your skating skills.

You should learn to carve the walls of the reservoir in two ways: frontside (where you face the bank and edge) and backside (where your back is to the wall). Backside carves are the easiest, but still, it may take months to develop the muscle strength and coordination. In order to do it, practice at your own rate of speed.

Next, and only after you feel fully confident in your ability, move on to a shallow snake run. Prac-

All photos: Ann-Victoria Phillips

Carving the walls of a pool in a backside position.

Warming-up on the walls of a snake run using the side-surfing stance.

tice carving the walls using the same technique as in the reservoir. You'll find you need much more strength and power to accomplish the same thing than in a pool or bowl. After about a year of regular practice, you should reach an intermediate level and be able to skate all the way up the wall.

THREE ADVANCED MANEUVERS

Remember: these stunts are for advanced-level skaters only. The maneuvers can be done in a pool (as described below) or in a bowl.

Kick turn: Drop into the pool and pump straight up the opposite side. Turn at the top, keeping the back wheels of your skates on the edge. Then drop back in, while preparing to pump up the other side. The easiet kick turn is done in a backside position.

Rock walk: Drop into the pool and pump straight up the opposite wall in a frontside position. As you carve along the top edge, you'll be looking straight up at the sky. Keep your wheels near the top coping but not over the edge.

Make a half-revolution to the left as you continue to slide sideways across the tiles. Immediately rotate another half-revolution until you are looking downward into the pool. Then drop back in sideways.

Backside aerial: This is the easiest aerial to do. Drop into the pool and pump up the opposite side in a backside position. Instead of turning when your wheels are near the coping, leap into the air while remaining in the side-surf stance (legs turned out and knees bent). Drop back into the bowl, ready to pump up the opposite side. This is similar to the kick turn, except that in this case you leap into the air.

World class skater Kenny Means performs a backside aerial in a 12-foot pool at Lakewood Center Skate Park.

RADICAL SKATING AS EXERCISE

Radical skating is the most physically demanding of all skating styles. Although it develops flexibility, muscle strength (especially in the legs), muscle endurance, and balance, it still doesn't develop cardiovascular health.

To develop endurance, choose another kind of aerobic exercise to complement your skating. An exercise which develops short-term power—running wind sprints and hill climbs or playing one of the racquet sports—is recommended.

In addition, you *must* take time for warm-up flexibility exercises or risk straining or tearing your muscles because of the stressful nature of this sport. A skating session can be divided into five periods: warm-up stretching, warm-up skating, skating, cool-down skating and cool-down flexibility exercises. Begin with the warm-ups and cool-downs in Chapter 3.

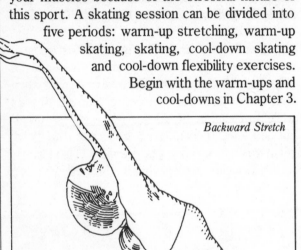

Backward Stretch

ADVANCED FLEXIBILITY AND WARM-UP EXERCISES

Flexibility exercises should be done off skates, even for the advanced level skater. The only exceptions are those exercises where you are sitting or lying down.

Again, some people are loose to begin with and improve their flexibility very quickly through exercise. Others take more time. A person's degree of flexibility is an individual thing, but no matter how stiff or loose you are when you start, stretch the muscles *slowly* and continuously until you feel a strong pull. Hold the following advanced exercises for a minimum of 60 seconds on each side. Those who are already quite flexible may find it easy to hold the postures for as long as two minutes. Remember, don't strain. Never bounce. Try stretching a bit further on each successive day.

For advanced level skaters, we recommend the following additional exercises:

Backward Stretch: An exercise to strengthen the abdomen and loosen and strengthen the lower back.

1. Stand with your legs parallel and your feet comfortably apart, about shoulder width.

2. Raise both hands straight over your head and stretch upward and over.

3. Arch backwards as far as is comfortable without straining.

4. Do this each time for a minimum of 60 seconds. Do the backward stretch twice.

The Triangle

Illustrations: Fredric Winkowski

The Triangle: A complete upper torso stretch.

1. Stand with your feet parallel and as wide as is comfortably possible beyond shoulder width. Keep your toes pointed straight ahead.

2. Bend from the waist, allowing your upper torso to sink down. Turn your upper torso toward your left ankle letting gravity pull you down. Keep your legs slightly bent at the knee. Hold this posture for a minimum of 60 seconds.

3. Rise up slowly and repeat the stretch to your other side.

4. Do the triangle two to three times on each side.

Hamstring Stretch

1. Stand with your feet parallel and as wide as is comfortably possible beyond shoulder width.

2. Shift your body to your right side, bending your right knee deeply. Allow your body to sink down toward the floor while pivoting on the heel of the left foot.

3. Hold the posture for at least one minute and then raise your body and shift to the opposite side.

4. Do this exercise two to three times on each side.

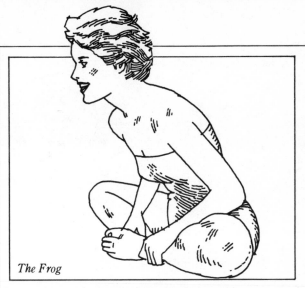

The Frog

The Frog: This thigh stretch also loosens and strengthens the lower back muscles.

1. Sit on the floor and draw the soles of your feet together in front of you, pulling them in as close to your body as you can.

2. While leaning your upper torso forward and holding onto your feet with both hands, allow your knees to sink toward the floor.

3. Then, sink your head down slowly toward your toes. Let gravity pull you down.

4. Hold the posture a minimum of one minute or as long as two, depending on your degree of flexibility. You only need to do this exercise once.

Hamstring Stretch #2

Twisting Exercise

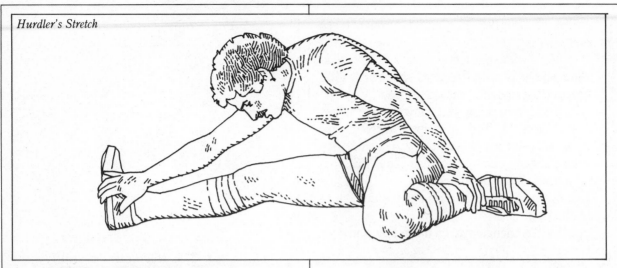

Twisting Exercise: This loosens and strengthens the major muscles of the back.

1. Sit on the floor with your legs spread as widely as is comfortable.

2. Place your left hand on the outside of your right knee and your right hand on the floor about 10 to 12 inches behind your back.

3. Rotate your head, upper torso, and lower back slowly and as far as is comfortable.

4. Hold the posture a minimum of one minute and then rotate to your other side.

5. Do this exercise two to three times on each side.

Hurdler's Stretch: This loosens and strengthens the thigh muscles.

1. Sit on the ground with your right leg extended forward and your left leg bent back and to the side of your body.

2. Sink your head and body forward, letting gravity pull you down over your right knee. Your right hand should be forward, reaching toward your ankle, while your left hand is backward grasping your left knee.

3. Hold the posture a minimum of one minute, and then reverse positions, left leg forward and right leg back.

4. Do this two to three times on each side, each time holding the posture for a minimum of one minute.

The Plow: stretches the back muscles and also is an exercise to help you relax.

1. Lie down on the floor, raising your legs and torso toward the sky (as in a shoulder stand). Allow your knees to hang down beside your ears. Hold this position a minimum of two minutes.

2. While in this hanging position, straighten your knees and allow your toes to touch the ground in back of you. Hold this position an additional two minutes.

The Plow

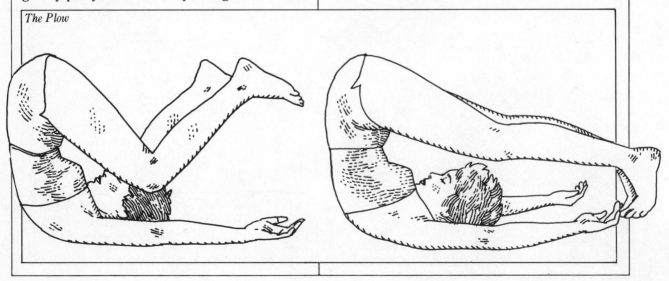

CURTIS HESSELGRAVE: TEACHING THE FUNDAMENTALS

Skaters call him "Dr. Wig Out" but that doesn't bother 32-year-old Curtis Hesselgrave, skater, skateboarder, surfer, skier, and Aikido instructor from Cardiff-By-The-Sea, California. But some people do think Curtis has unusual ideas. The phenomenon of the roller skater in the skateboard park is still so new, Hesselgrave stands out as the only "voice of reason" in what is basically a self-taught sport. According to Hesselgrave, skaters come into this sport and "want to take a giant step up to working the bowl and pools right away, yet they have no understanding of the fundamentals. And that's dangerous."

What Hesselgrave is attempting to do is to design a systematic teaching and training program for both kinds of radical skaters, the skateboarder as well as the roller skater. "I'm certainly not a

Hesselgrave works with Bobby Means, brother of Kenny, and a well-known radical skater in his own right.

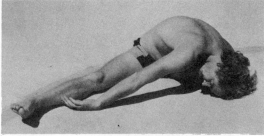

All photos: Ann-Victoria Phillips

Hesselgrave demonstrates the extended form that flexibility exercising can produce.

medical doctor," he explains. "But, because of my experience with the martial arts, I am able to work with some of the skaters on basic training principles such as the importance of warming up the muscles gradually before a workout, a more coordinated and total mind and body approach, and injury prevention, as well as treatment of injuries."

Curtis writes a monthly "Skate Safe" column in *Skateboarder* magazine, so many of his needed and well thought-out concepts reach the right audience. Hesselgrave also aids skaters by collaborating with Mike Rector, an excellent safety gear designer/manufacturer who produces a line of equipment well-suited to skater's health and safety needs.

Curtis Hesselgrave, an innovative thinker and a concerned athlete, is the best friend the radical skater has.

FRED BLOOD:
SKATING AT THE RUNWAY

Fred Blood, a 16-year-old high school student from Hermosa Beach, California, is one of the highest paid and commercially successful radical roller skaters in the United States.

He boasts that he can do as many as 50 different tricks and maneuvers on the vertical walls of a skate park's half-pipes, full-pipes, bowls, or pools. Some of his items are variations of the crowd-pleasing, show-stopping backside aerial while others have funny names like roll-ins, lip stalls, toe spins, spider taps, three-sixties, and pirouettes.

Fred is one of an exclusive group of skaters and skateboarders who gets paid top dollar to represent and promote skate equipment and protective gear to the public.

Since the sport of skating in skate parks is so new, much of the roller skater's equipment is borrowed from the sport of skateboarding. So, there's a good deal of closeness between these two groups: they skate the same surface, they use the same gear, and even do some of the same stunts. It's not unusual for a roller skater to represent a skateboard equipment manufacturer.

*Fred Blood, fearless
daredevil innovator, in mid-aerial.*

As a professional roller skater, Fred's set-up is typical. He's sponsored by Lazer, a skate truck manufacturer, and also Belair, a company where wheels are made. Both pay him to wear their products and skate for them at trade shows and new skate park openings, as well as do demonstrations at shopping centers, hotels, and other public places around the Los Angeles area. Fred also models his sponsors' gear and is photographed for advertising and publicity purposes.

Fred at 16 has already established his skill and is now more interested in the commercial aspect of skating. Recreational skating is out for him. "The stuff they do on the Strand (roller acrobatics at Hermosa Beach) is rinky-dink," he says. "The stuff in the parks is what I get paid for."

Fred earns hundreds of dollars a week by applying stickers and patches featuring the logos of his major, as well as minor, sponsors to his clothes, skates, helmet, and even his kneepads. Although he looks like a human billboard, Fred claims it's worth the trouble because his sponsors pay extra every time they see their company logo in a magazine layout or in a book. This, according to Fred, is another way professional roller skaters make their living.

Fred also spends an enormous amount of time perfecting his skating skills. He practices religiously. Because Fred is too young to get a license, one of his buddies will pick him up and drive him to a nearby skate park, usually The Runway in Carson. Tuesdays are specially reserved for roller skaters, but a professional of Fred's status can practice there anytime.

First, he'll stretch out and then warm up by carving every terrain in the park and then the huge 18-foot concrete bowl. This is all done in synch with the driving, pounding beat of hard rock music that continuously blasts from the park's loud speakers.

If it rains, Fred goes to a disco rink or to an underground parking lot where he practices riding ramps. If he worries about the dangers, he doesn't show it. "The hardcore radical skaters are people like me who skate with fluid style and don't worry about getting hurt," reports Fred.

Blood, surprisingly sensitive and introspective despite his mad drive for success, says, "My weak point is that I tend to make skating more competitive than it needs to be because of my goal—I want to be the best in the world on vertical terrain. I'm competitive with people all the time, even my friends. We're always trying to outdo one another."

A flatland skater until two years ago, Fred got turned on to the radical style when he saw skater Kenny Means ("the first roller skater in the world to go vertical on skateboarders' turf"), demonstrate his skill in a little-known movie called *Freewheelin'*, mostly about the world of the skateboarder. Means was the only one on roller skates. "I just decided that I would be as good as Kenny," remembers Fred. "Before that I just skated on the Strand with my friends. Back then, I never expected to be as good as I am.

"I'll never forget the first time I accelerated up a vertical wall," Fred continues. "That feeling you get in the air is incredible. It's total weightlessness. It is probably the most thrilling thing I've done in my whole life. It's like taking off in a plane. Every time I do it, I get butterflies. It's always a rush."

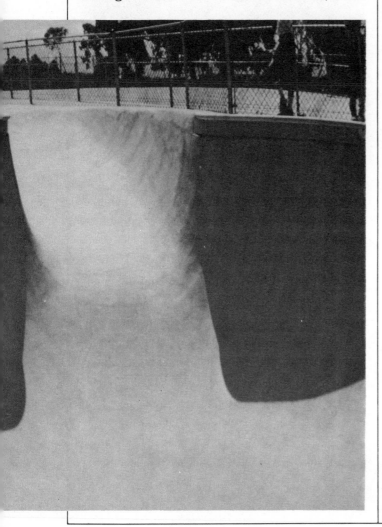

JOE RICE: STUNT SKATER

Joe Rice, 28 years old, living in Hawthorne, California, specializes in a kind of radical roller skating some people call stunt skating. His style includes many varieties of acrobatics: jumping over barrels, cars, motorcycles, and people.

This style is nothing new. Acrobatics on skates date back a hundred years when they were commonly performed by exhibition and Vaudeville skaters on stage, in rinks, and outdoors. Rice, roller skatings' answer to Evel Knievel, practices at Hermosa Beach, the birthplace of the most recent acrobatic revival. There he regularly astonishes residents and sightseers alike. On a weekend afternoon, a casual passerby can expect to see Rice, or other members of the group, soar over motorcycles or, perhaps, a Cadillac left unattended in a beachfront parking lot. "Sometimes I'll come down here just to try to jump or stunt," says

Joe, a wiry, but hard-muscled man. "If I don't do something physical, I go crazy."

In addition, Joe also loves to try new stunts, adding more risks to the already present danger in his life.

An unusual degree of flexibility and muscle strength is necessary to pull off these jumps, leaps, and high-riding skate park maneuvers without injury. "I practice a form of martial arts called Shorin-Ryu (a kind of Chinese boxing) every day," says Joe. "This keeps me loose. I also play handball and do gymnastics." To build endurance, Joe regularly races other skaters down the Strand, all of them flying along in the characteristic side-surfing position that immediately identifies the radical-style roller skater.

All photos: Ann-Victoria Phillips

He also skates alone and may travel from Redondo Beach to as far north as the Santa Monica Pier, a 20-mile trip along the ocean.

Involved in a high-risk sport that has no coaches, Joe stands alone among his fellow skaters. Many of them, though sport-oriented all their lives, still lack a systematic training program to condition their bodies to withstand the rigors of this dangerous sport. But, Rice, unlike the rest, is covered because of his involvement with martial arts. It automatically provides a high-level training program suitable for almost *any* sport.

What are the rewards? According to Joe, it's "the expressions on people's faces when I do my crazy stunts. Sometimes, I jump motorcycles. Other days I'll shoot up out of the bowl and see faces, about two feet away, with their mouths hanging open. To me, that's the best part."

Stunts unlimited: On Hermosa Beach, Joe leaps a barrel, high kicks, limbers up, jumps off and skates on a board.

TICIA STRICKLAND AND BETH GRAHAM: RADICAL WOMEN

It's a thrill. I have the chance of being the first woman to do aerials," says 18-year-old Ticia Strickland of Los Angeles. Ticia, a small, dark-haired roller skater who is covered head-to-foot in plastic and leather-padded protective gear, stands at the top of a 42-foot wide, 18-foot deep bowl, ready to start her run. Tired of waiting for a turn, she abruptly skates on to the entrance ramp and drops down into the bowl. For a moment, she completely disappears from sight. Then, a small figure, almost lost in the vastness of the super-sized bowl, pumps up the 18-foot vertical wall, brushes the top edge, turns, and drops straight back down toward the bottom, lost to sight again. Ticia carves the bowl two more times and then

Ticia and Beth kid around in front of The Runway's big bowl.

skates up and onto the ramp, her run over. As soon as Ticia is out of the bowl, Beth Graham, her friend and also 18, drops in for her ride. Beth is tall but looks small and compressed as she rips across the bottom of the bowl and gathers momentum for the trip up the opposite side.

Both skaters have years of flatland skating experience behind them, yet have been practicing in the parks for only a few weeks. They have progressed at a frighteningly fast rate, starting with reservoirs, snake runs, and half-pipes, then graduating to the big bowls—all without injury and in spite of the guys telling them that, "we don't have the ability and that we're gonna get hurt." Reports Ticia, "The men all push the other guys to work harder, but they tell us to be patient." Beth adds, "Yet it took most of them two months to do what we did in two weeks, and now we're even better than them."

Ticia and Beth can both do bowl-to-bowl aerial jumps and Ticia, as far as anyone knows, is the first woman to do a backside aerial while on roller skates. According to Ticia, "It was exciting. My heart was beating fast. I was floating. Some guys thought it was great. Others said I did good, for a *girl.*"

Ticia and Beth work together part-time at Venice Precision Roller Works, a skate rental shop in Venice, California. They are great friends and provide mutual support for each other's goals. Ticia, a senior at Los Angeles High School, is interested in a commercial art career but first, "I want to be the best woman radical skater in the world. I want to go pro and do tours. After that, I'll go to college," she says.

Beth also wants to turn pro, but for her, school comes first. She attends Santa Monica City College, aiming for a bachelor's degree in speech pathology, and later, a master's degree in education.

Both women consider themselves daredevils but Ticia breathlessly claims to have "the most guts. I'm always ready to try something new, but

Beth performing a bowl-to-bowl aerial jump.

Ticia does a backside aerial in a parallel stance.

Beth is always right there with me."

"We want the thrills," adds Beth, still flushed from her ride. "But we're not masochists. We don't want to get hurt."

"The injuries we get the most are burns from scraping against the wall," says Ticia. "Three weeks ago, I lost about four inches of skin. But

everything's alright now.

"The next thing I want to learn is called a 'Heel Stall' up on the edge of the bowl. When you come around, you hesitate up there for a minute and look straight down 18 feet," says Ticia, her face glowing with excitement and anticipation.

Two carving styles: Beth is side-surfing, Ticia is behind her in the parallel stance.

KENNY MEANS:
TOPS IN HIS SPORT

Kenny Means is the man who invented the newest variety daredevil-style roller skating. Being the first to skate on vertical walls (in 1974), he has more years of experience than anyone else. Besides, Means is acknowledged as the best in the world by other skaters (both amateur and professional), equipment manufacturers, and by members of the press.

Although Kenny Means is a professional athlete—he gets paid to roller skate—he appears to have little interest in the flamboyant life-style characteristic of many in the business. Unlike most of his highly paid skating colleagues, Kenny is modest and soft-spoken. He never brags; in fact, he rarely talks about his skating at all. Though he practices every day, it is never in the

Kenny Means cooling out between runs.

All photos: Ann-Victoria Phillips

same skate park two days in a row. Because of this, he's rarely seen skating. A mysterious figure in a very media-conscious sport, Kenny doesn't hang out with any other roller skaters, even though he's idolized by most of them.

Kenny is known to be an independent thinker and doer who skates without fear or anxiety, mostly for the pure love of the sport. While other skaters of his class sharpen their skills because skating is big business and they want the rewards, Means appears to be only casually interested in making money through the sport—that was not his goal when he started skating and still isn't. He skates today, as he always has, simply because he enjoys how it makes him feel.

Kenny is 23 years old and comes from a family of roller skaters. Although his mother and father don't skate, his five brothers and sisters all do; most of them were, or now are, competitive speed skaters. His brother, Bobby, 22 years old, is another radical skater, also considered to be one of the very best.

Kenny started skating at age 11, and eventually moved to speed training and local competition. Very involved as a high school athlete, he ran track and cross country for four years. The marathon was his specialty—he practiced in the hills near his hometown, San Pedro, California, a suburb of Los Angeles. Kenny also became an accomplished surfer and skateboarder.

By the time he was 17, Kenny was looking for new challenges. The thrill-seeking group of guys he hung out with were mostly skateboarders, all of them bored with working out on sidewalks and roads. As bizarre as it may seem, the group, like many others in the mid-'70s, went on daily reconnaissance trips all over Los Angeles searching out secret, private, and more challenging terrain— empty swimming pools in people's backyards and industrial drainage ditches provided new thrills. "We would jump over fences to get to the spots." Then, Kenny and his friends would ride the banked walls until someone kicked them out. "A lot of times people called the cops, but we never got caught," he said.

Kenny didn't like the feel of the skateboard so he tried going vertical in his roller skates. "At first, everyone thought he was crazy," remembers his brother, Bobby. "Then he started getting in movies and the magazines and people started thinking about it more seriously, but for years, Kenny was the only one."

Even though radical skating has shifted locations from backyard pools to the ultra-modern skate park, the Means training schedule has remained much the same. Kenny gets up at about 6 o'clock to go surfing (the biggest waves are in the morning). Then he comes home, rests for about two hours, then goes skating, most likely with a long-time friend, Mike Weed, a world-class skateboard champion. In addition, Kenny works as a consultant for Bad Co., a skateboard equipment manufacturer who's interested in breaking into the roller skating field. He's designing a new roller skate for this company and also advises them about every aspect of the new thriving market.

"Kenny is my hero," says 16-year-old Fred Blood, another well-known skating pro. "He's 23,

Kenny was the first athlete to roller skate into skateboard territory—tackling the sculptural terrain of their specially designed parks.

and still goes for everything. Kenny's the best until he quits."

In the world of the skate park, Kenny is, at his age, over the hill—really, an old man. The

Kenny carves the top edge of a half pipe the first time around and then "gets air" on his second run.

hottest skaters are in the 15- to 18-year-old range. In fact, even what Kenny does best, specializing in aerial maneuvers, is not unusual today. The younger skaters are ambitious, very competitive, and are quickly catching up to Kenny in terms of the number and variety of tricks they can do. But there are certain *qualities* which Kenny has as a skater that are so unusual, it's doubtful whether anyone will ever really surpass him.

Just like everyone else in this advanced skating sub-culture, Kenny pulls off spectacular and dangerous maneuvers, but, unlike the rest, he makes it look effortless. He has an unusually high level of control. No other skater today can make split-second decisions, changing course in the middle of a run, the way Kenny does, and survive it injury-free. Other skaters, once they drop in the pool or bowl, are committed. They have to skate out the run or chicken out and try again. Kenny can instantly change his line during the run without incurring disaster. He can put his wheels in contact with any square inch of concrete, whether or not he's planned it beforehand.

He appears to play with the surfaces and arcs of the pools and bowls almost as if they had human-like qualities and were capable of communicating with him. He seems happiest when the ride provides him with unexpected thrills. If it doesn't come naturally, he'll tempt fate and thrill himself. To other professionals, a bowl or pool is an inanimate concrete object, an obstacle to overcome or to conquer. But Kenny appears to have a connection with and a deep respect for the concrete surface.

Kenny has the most refined pool or bowl-riding style of any skater in the world. Radical skating expert Curtis Hesselgrave, who knows Means and has seen him work, says, "Kenny generates a tremendous amount of power from the compression and extension of his body, most of it coming from his legs. Unlike most other skaters, Kenny doesn't use his arms to help his pump. There are

All photos: Ann-Victoria Phillips

Kenny on the verge of a backside aerial in Lakewood Center's 12-foot pool.

Kenny demonstrates his control and superior technique as he carves the walls of the full pipe at Superbowl I, Torrance, California.

no wasted motions." Kenny is as graceful as a gazelle when climbing the vertical walls. Other skaters, including top professionals, look more like birds who have to flap their wings to get up the power and go.

His attitude toward what he does in unusual. He approaches this dangerous sport with a serenity difficult to understand. Like many world-class athletes, Kenny appears to be free of internal fear and anxieties about his career. His work, what he does with his skates, seems to calm him, if anything.

To Kenny, skating is a joyful, painless experience. He doesn't fall; he only occasionally loses his balance. Having so little control doesn't bother him. He merely adjusts and laughs it off as if it's just one more secret thrill. In fact, the more frequently the unexpected happens, the better he seems to like it. Where another skater might lose control, smash into the wall, roll up into a little ball, and tumble, head-over-heels, down the sides to the bottom, Kenny turns the slight miscalculation into a new trick.

All photos: Ann-Victoria Phillips

Kenny's considerable experience contributes to his casual attitude toward the risky sport of radical skating.

Kenny doesn't seem to psych himself up to do any maneuver. Other skaters pause at the entrance ramp to the pool and plan their run. Kenny never uses the graduated entrance ramps; he just drops in, his skates rolling over the edge of the pool, and then, 12 feet straight down.

Although they don't talk much about it, it's easy to see why the younger skaters idolize him. They watch Kenny skate and his casual, effortless style stuns them. He's carefree—skating as though every stroke is a celebration. He appears to feel totally at ease with himself and his body. It looks like he *allows* his skates to take him for a ride, his wheels doodling lines on a vertical drawing board.

Other skaters are far more purposeful about their skating. They spend an enormous amount of time accumulating a variety of showy tricks. It's a business to them and that means pressure. Their sponsors want them to both invent new maneuvers and make sure they keep up with the competition. The trade magazines devote more space to those skaters who innovate and take the greatest risks.

Since Kenny's on top, he doesn't seem to need to compete with anyone. Anyway, he's always skated to the beat of his own drum. While other skaters work up routines to show off to an audience, Kenny skates to please himself. Even though the nature of the business is unusually cut-throat and competitive, Kenny works to achieve his own personal goals an hour or a day at a time.

Kenny Means is a living legend in southern California. Other skaters are constantly on the lookout for him. Since there are no coaches in the sport, they learn by imitating the stars and then incorporate the new items into their personal repertoire. Although Kenny has five favorite parks (there must be 50 or more within driving distance of his house), no one knows where Kenny will pop up next. Everyone wonders what new stunts he's working on and once they have spotted him at a park, what he's holding back from them.

Curtis Hesselgrave says of the roller skating superstar, "Kenny is a very clear-thinking person and he's very bright. He intuitively understands principles of ballistics—the arcs and trajectories involved in skating a pool or a bowl. Kenny would be skating even if no one were there watching. He enjoys the sensations. It's a way of channeling the great energies he finds inside himself."

Carving a snake run in a frontside position.

13. LIFESTYLES

SUZI SKATES: SPECIAL DELIVERIES

I offer entertainment. I brighten up the office. Whenever I come in, it's a special day. I sing 'Happy Birthday,' give people flowers or messages that say 'I love you'. It's a shock but most are flattered. My whistle makes everyone drop what they're doing. Restaurants are funny but offices are best. People wonder, 'Is it a fire or the police?' They drop everything and look up. It's a perfect way to announce myself," says Suzi Skates of San Francisco.

Suzi Skates (born Susan Ann Johnson) is 21 years old, six feet tall and one of San Francisco's most colorful residents. As creator and president of her own roller skating messenger service, she glides through city streets and makes deliveries dressed in a red leotard, polka dot mini-skirt, and roller skates with pink pompoms.

"I'll try anything," says Suzi, "especially at the airport. There are all kinds of people who tell me roller skating is not allowed there," but Suzi has learned to handle any emergencies. "If security guards try to stop me, I just skate on by, fast!" she says emphatically.

"If I'm hired to wish someone a happy birthday, I try to get their description beforehand. But even if I don't, when I skate into a restaurant and blow my whistle and say I have a message for so-and-so, I always know who it's for. I just look for the one who is laughing or trying to hide under the table.

"I'm most out of place in office elevators. People look at how funny I'm dressed and don't even see the skates. The funniest thing is when they do see the skates but still don't say a word. When I zoom out of the elevator they're even more surprised."

Suzi, daughter of a rocket engineer and teacher/librarian, grew up in Encinitas, California. She has been skating outdoors since she was six years old but, unlike everyone else, she never gave it up. On a trip to England, she astonished propriety-conscious Londoners and stopped downtown traffic. "They had never seen anyone

Ms. Skates in her official roller delivery outfit.

like me before," recalls Suzi. She skated into pubs, Hyde Park, Kensington Gardens, Westminster Abbey, across the grounds near Parliament, over London Bridge, and through the Chelsea Flower Show. The police stopped Suzi a few times and tried to get her off the sidewalks and streets, but they were unsuccessful. Ms. Skates continued undaunted. Next, she skated in France and the Parisians adored her. "It was so American," remembers Suzi.

In 1977, when she was 19, Suzi moved to San Francisco to be close to a new boyfriend and together they roller skated in Golden Gate Park. She needed money and tried to get a job but she had problems because she looked too eccentric. One day she went into Lolly's Yogurt Farm on Greenwich Street to apply for a counter job, but all they wanted was someone to hand out flyers. Suddenly everything clicked. She needed a job and loved roller skating, so she decided to combine the two.

Wearing satin shorts, matching blouse, a Dodger's baseball cap, colored and striped knee socks, and white roller skates, Suzi patroled the sidewalk in front of the store and handed out advertisements. She caused a sensation. People gaped. Whenever she worked, passersby lined up and crowded into the tiny yogurt shop.

She was so successful that she asked for a raise. When the manager refused to increase her two dollars per-hour salary, Suzi quit. The next day, she skated off to the annual Union Street Fair.

Union Street, with its fancy boutiques and shops housed in elegant, Victorian mansions and hotel dining rooms, is a meeting place for San Francisco's street musicians and mimes. Even there, Suzi attracted attention because of her looks—her height coupled with her skating outfit: a red and white polka dot skirt, black leotard, hair tied back in a ponytail with a red chiffon scarf. She announced to one and all that she would deliver messages on skates for five dollars but she really had just decided to make the offer for fun. However, lots of people told her she had a unique business idea, and she soon realized she'd found her niche.

Everyone asked for her name and phone number, and Suzi was put on the spot. She didn't have a phone and was a little embarrassed to give people her real name—her roller skating messenger service idea seemed a little kooky to her, too—so she made up the name, "Suzi Skates" on the spot. It stuck and attracted even more attention.

A reporter wrote a story about her and it was published in the *San Francisco Bay Guardian*. Suddenly, everyone wanted to hire Suzi Skates. She was overwhelmed with her unexpected notoriety and decided she needed a manager. Michael Christopher, a publicity agent that she met at the Palm Restaurant, advertised the business, took care of scheduling her jobs and billing her clients, and also got her an answering service.

"The first time I saw my story in print, it blew my mind," remembers Suzi. "I didn't work for it. The idea just came to me. To the press, I was brilliant. To me, it just happened and everything fell into place. I couldn't believe it when I had my first radio interview and then I was on a local TV station. When the *New York Times* called, I was really nervous—it seemed like such a big deal. Then, when *Penthouse* called, I flipped." Suzi has also been featured in magazines such as *Time* and *Oui*, Associated Press and United Press International wire service stories, and has also been interviewed for network news presentations.

Suzi on the way back from making a delivery competes with one of San Francisco's famed cable cars.

Suzi Skates was such a solid business venture that Christopher wanted to organize a fleet of roller skaters to work under her name. But Suzi wouldn't go for it. She wanted to be the only one. Says Christopher, "Suzi felt that no one else could do it as well." She wears a special kind of indelible lipstick so that her kissprint stays on someone's cheek forever—that's her trademark."

So she alone skates through offices, private homes, stores, restaurants, airports, and fashion shows. Funny, unexpected things happen on almost every job. A secretary hired Suzi to come in one morning to make coffee for her boss. It was the last thing the secretary did before she quit.

The brother of a bride hired Suzi to skate into City Hall and present her with flowers just as the wedding ended. The cops and City Hall security guards thought the whole incident was very funny and didn't interfere. Suzi made a delivery at the Marin County Civic Center when she escorted a public defender to court on his birthday. "The Civic Center is a very conservative place, and the looks on the people's faces were great," she reports.

Michael says that it is mostly women who hire Suzi to deliver gifts to their girlfriends, boyfriends, and sometimes co-workers. She gets lots of business from reporters and from people who have watched her in the process of making deliveries to others. When people call, Michael asks them what kind of floor Suzi will skate on to make the delivery (tile is okay, marble is fantastic, and shag carpet—forget it), how many steps she must climb, if any, and then gives them the rates (20 dollars for deliveries in the Bay area, 25 dollars for out-of-town, plus all traveling expenses).

Suzi has a passion for hot pink clothes and also shoes. "I'd buy shoes with my last hundred

From time to time, high-spirited Suzi tries roller shopping.

bucks," she says, "especially '50s-style spike heels." Her fantasy is to own a shocking pink Harley Sportster motorcycle. "I gawk at them in the shop. They're powerful and dangerous and I'd like to drive one with confidence."

Susan Ann Johnson not only thinks of Suzi Skates as a cartoon character she created, but as someone who represents a part of her own personality. "Suzi Skates is as all-American as apple pie but not quite as smart as me. Suzi is more like a dizzy blond. Ms. Skates doesn't smoke or drink in public, doesn't say bad words, and has nothing to do with politics. Suzi Skates is the girl next door, just taller. She always keeps things very light, doesn't talk for long, and sticks to business. She never hangs out to have a drink or a piece of cake after delivery. But if it's a real good delivery, I'll ham it up," she says. "If they're drunk, so much the better.

"Nobody is ever rude to me. How could they be? Suzi is so sweet. I don't offend anybody and I'm always smiling and happy. Even if I have a fight with my boyfriend, I can still get happy for a few minutes and make a delivery. It's not alway fun though. Once in a while my mind goes blank and I forget some small detail. If it's a birthday or anniversary, I can usually cover it up. I panic on out-of-town deliveries if the car breaks down. I have problems downtown with cable cars. I am aware of other people when I skate but they're not always aware of me, so I have to skate defensively. Children like me, the skateboarder guys trust me, street freaks adore me, but little old ladies think I'm going to knock them over.

"The fun part is that everyone would like to have my job. When I skate downtown during the lunch hour, I feel sorry for all the poor secretaries. People say to me 'I would love to have your job. You look like you're having so much fun!'

"I hate to hear people talk about their boring jobs. I have no sympathy for them continuing to do what they hate. I'm my own boss. I'm supporting myself—not luxuriously but I get by. Respect and fame are more important to me than money.

"One push and I'm flying. I get to a corner and I'll do a few little turns, both forward and backward instead of just standing there waiting for the light to change. I love it when the light is red. It won't stop me in my tracks. I'll twirl around and keep moving. Just because everyone else has stopped, I won't freeze at the curb."

LEE ANDERSON: WHEELS AT WARD'S

Lee Anderson wheeling a hand truck through Montgomery Ward's Chicago warehouse.

Roller skating clerks are a tradition at the Montgomery Ward Catalogue Sales Department warehouse where they have had a team regularly employed since 1920. Getting around the Chicago-based warehouse, an eight-story building with two and one-half million square feet of storage bins, makes speedy transportation a necessity. What is an enormously time-consuming job for the walker becomes easy for the skater.

In days gone by, Ward's had a whole warehouse full of skaters. Today, there are seven men and women who work eight to four, five days a week.

"What's fun," confides Lee Anderson, one of the rolling clerks, "is that during lunch hour, we disco on skates. The warehouse floor is smoother than the one at the rink."

KEVIN COUNTRYMAN: ROLLER SKATING ENGINEER

"'m very self-disciplined, very ambitious, and very devoted to engineering," states 26-year-old Kevin Countryman. Although he's reluctant to talk about his accomplishments, when questioned Kevin will reveal that he's a straight-A student at the University of California in Berkeley, president of the Engineering Society, a consulting civil engineer, and the resident manager of his apartment building.

Like most Cal students, Kevin wears his hair long, even though he considers himself fairly conservative. He was just as surprised as everyone else to find himself putting on roller skates instead of shoes to get to class each morning.

It started one Sunday afternoon. Kevin and his friends decided to rent roller skates in Golden Gate Park for kicks. By the end of the day, Kevin

For Kevin, an engineering student, wearing skates is as natural as reading a computer printout.

All photos: Ann-Victoria Phillips

was hooked. Usually one who thinks out every move thoroughly, Kevin impulsively withdrew 150 dollars from his bank, went to a sporting goods store, and bought his own roller skates the very next day. His life has never been the same since.

Today, Kevin has given up wearing shoes—he literally skates *everywhere*. "I cut my commuting time to class by 80 percent; the best part is that I can sleep a lot later in the morning," he says. Kevin can usually be seen gliding around the Engineering Building and other parts of the campus in a herringbone suit. As a young engineer, he'd like to wear the matching vest as well, but can't because it's too hot for skating. A pair of leather gloves completes his on campus-uniform.

Kevin comes from a diverse background and has a wide variety of interests. Originally from Tacoma, Washington, his father is a research technologist and his mother is a chemist. He "grew up in the shadow of Mt. Rainier," and that explains many of his other interests. He's an experienced mountain climber, cross-country skier, and classical dancer. He used to run five to ten miles a day, but now he skates the same distance instead. Kevin has found that both skating and dance use the same muscles. Further, he feels that skating is less of a strain on the body. As a dancer, Kevin was plagued by injuries. Since he changed to skating, perfect health has been his reward.

Kevin's fantasy is to skate on an open freeway with no cars, only skaters. "Car drivers are the bad guys," says the skating devotee. "Bicycles and pedestrians are also in the way. Roller skaters don't like to slow down or stop, you know."

Sunday is the high point of the week: that's when he, and a group of friends go roller skating in Golden Gate Park. "When I dance on skates, I get into the music. I don't want to be a show-off, but I get to the point where I just don't care. I feel so uninhibited. I'd like to be able to skate and dance around all day. I become the music. I'm gone: my feet don't touch the ground."

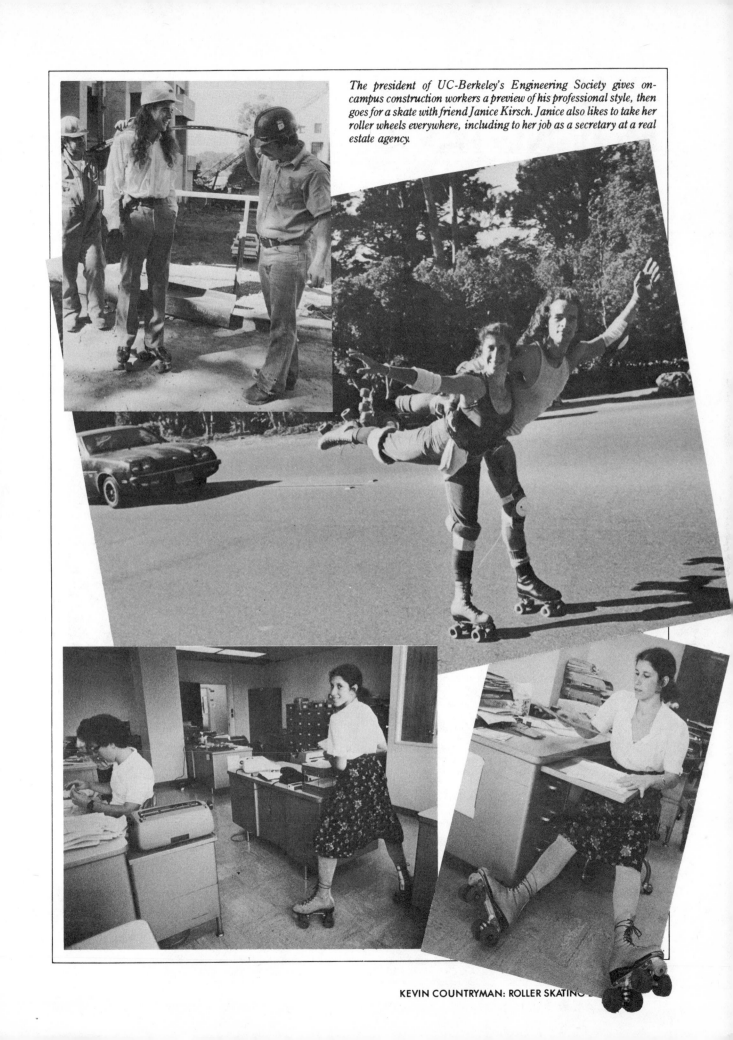

The president of UC-Berkeley's Engineering Society gives on-campus construction workers a preview of his professional style, then goes for a skate with friend Janice Kirsch. Janice also likes to take her roller wheels everywhere, including to her job as a secretary at a real estate agency.

KEVIN COUNTRYMAN: ROLLER SKATING

JIMMY SNOOK: MOVING PARTS

We get a lot of funny looks from customers when we skate into the showroom or the body shop," reports 50-year-old Jimmie Snook, who is an assistant manager of the Parts Department at Modern Chevrolet in Lubbock, Texas. Jimmie has worked there for twelve years. "I never gave roller skating a thought until we moved into our new building two years ago. This new shop is a huge place—75 employees work here, including 12 line mechanics. The eight of us who work in the back room supply parts to both walk-in customers and our own mechanics."

Modern Chevrolet is one of the largest dealerships in the Southwest. The stockroom area alone, where Jimmie and seven other roller skating employees work, consists of more than 10,000 square feet of shelves, storage bins, and lofts—all crammed full of body or engine component parts.

"We run after the small items, such as one nut or one bolt, as well as large parts, such as fenders, quarter panels, hoods, and also large cases of antifreeze. Since we started wearing skates on the job nine months ago, we've figured we save time and do 20 percent more work," says Jimmie. "Even though I've been athletic all my life, my legs are much stronger and tighter since I've been skating. That helps my bowling score. The best part of the job is that we all have so much fun—I look forward to coming to work these days."

Jimmy Snook fills an order for auto parts with rolling ease.

ON THE ROLL . . .

From the '30s, when United Airlines (below right), American Telephone and Telegraph (top left), and Western Union (bottom left) hoped to speed up service with employees on wheels, to the '70s, when a Virginia couple (center) asked Navy chaplain Cmd. Edward Hughes to officiate at their skating wedding—on skates—there have been people who've found themselves on the job *and* on the roll.

Courtesy of American Telephone & Telegraph

David Hollingsworth

Courtesy of American Telephone & Telegraph

Courtesy of Chicago Roller Skate Company

... ON THE JOB

Below, from left to right: Fenyoaee McKinney, a Carmel, California mime; Gene Sloane, a Chicago businessman; Cassie Hill, an Asheboro, North Carolina waitress; Ray DiTomaso, a San Diego mailman; Kathy Glascock, a Los Angeles handbag designer; Ray Martucci, a New York City police officer.

Top, from left to right: Cimarron, "the skating horse" from Hindsville, Arkansas; Gary "the Breeze" Feathergill, professional traveler, on a Washington to California skate; Kathleen Gaskin and Joan Durkee, clothing buyers at New York's Capezio in the Village.

Mary Anne Yarbrough

Ann-Victoria Phillips

Ann-Victoria Phillips

Richard Malec/Suburban Sun Times

Gary Hinshaw/The Courier Tribune

Ron Ramey/Bremerton Sun Photo

Ann-Victoria Phillips

Ann-Victoria Phillips

Ann-Victoria Phillips

Ann-Victoria Phillips

ON THE ROLL ... ON THE

TOMMY TUNES: SKATING MUSICIAN

Every day, Union Square's population of chess players, shoeshine boys, sailors, weary shoppers, tourists, sun worshipers, and lunching office workers rise to attention, laughing and applauding, as Tommy Tunes glides into the scene playing "I Left My Heart in San Francisco" on his accordion.

Tommy, a young, bearded, bespectacled figure who performs in the park wearing lederhosen, plaid vest, colorful shirt, and green beret, earns his living, in San Francisco, as an outdoor entertainer. He can play hundreds of om-pah-pah, mer-

ry-go-round tunes. When he's tired of his Swiss look, Tommy changes over to his "Going West" costume: jeans, shirt, vest, leather chaps, ten-gallon hat, and cowboy boots mounted on roller skate trucks. Then he swaggers to the tune of "Red River Valley" and other folksy western numbers.

"I'm an entertainer," Tommy says, "the bigger the crowd, the better I like it. I like the energy, the color, the costumes and, more than

Tommy serenades the noonday crowd in San Francisco's Union Square.

All photos: Ann-Victoria Phillips

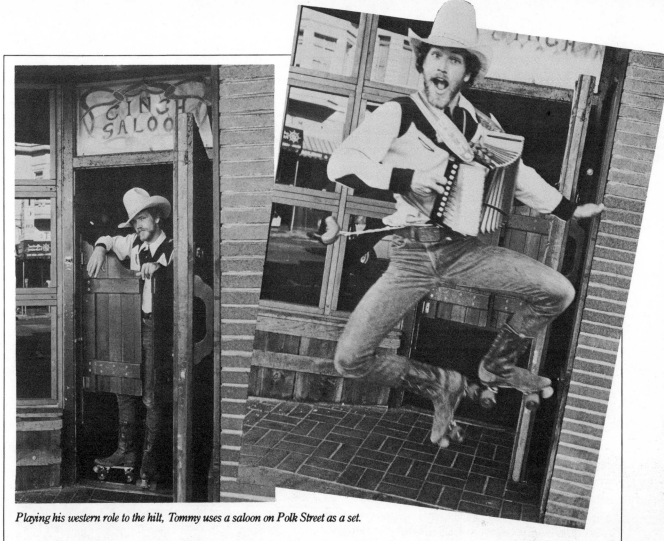

Playing his western role to the hilt, Tommy uses a saloon on Polk Street as a set.

anything else, I love the applause. It makes me feel great for the rest of the day."

Tommy, who is 25 years old, has joined the ranks of hundreds of street troubadours who regularly perform outdoors all over the city of San Francisco. But his background is so refined that his chosen career comes as a bit of a surprise. He has a BFA from the University of Michigan and has studied classical music for years.

Tommy, the son of a doctor, grew up in Ohio and only started skating recently. Skating in the sunshine became a passion for him so he drew from his background in classical and popular music, combining his talents with his love of wheels, speed, and motion to become a skating street musician. Says Tommy, "Accordion playing and roller skating are so corny, they're a perfect match." He also delivers "Tune-O-Grams," birthday greetings that he sings and sets to music. His reputation has grown so that now he plays the clarinet in the local civic orchestra during the winter.

Like most outdoor roller skaters from San Francisco and Los Angeles, Tommy adds skiing to his list of skills. He used to run until he discovered that skating was just as good for developing strength and endurance, and also gave him the sensations he felt while skiing—the pleasure of speed or, as he calls it, "free thrills on the hills." Explains Tommy, "You can really scare yourself on these hills. After you skate down hills in San Francisco, the flatlands just don't make it anymore. Without my accordion, I'm a crazy man on skates. Some people think what I do is bizarre, but most admire my athletic abilities and my skill."

Tommy's only reservation about his career is that local publicity has cast him as a star. "I even have girl groupies, but they're after Mr. Tunes, not me," says Tommy. Although "Mr. Tunes" is starting to pay his rent, Tommy is undecided as to whether to make his act more commercial or keep it the way it is today. He wants to make money but doesn't want the financial aspect of his work to consume him. "I do this for a living but I don't pass the hat. This performance of mine brings people so much joy. It's the skating and music together that does it. Their faces light right up."

CATHY LIPINSKI: SKATING WAITRESS

During the summer, Cathy Lipinski, a waitress at Cafe Un Deux Trois in New York, served salade Nicoise to actor Al Pacino, while wearing roller skates.

Cathy, an outgoing, vivacious, free spirit was given a pair of European clamp skates by the restaurant's two French owners. It was her idea to start waiting tables and serving drinks on skates. "I found I covered ground quicker and it made the work easier," reports Cathy, a former English Literature and Theater major from Penn State University.

Cafe Un Deux Trois, a theater district restaurant, has an Art Deco-styled interior with blue clouds painted on the walls and ceiling. Another wall is painted to look like old, patterned wallpaper. The funky mood and French food appeal to a wide variety of people. It's a gathering place for theater people as well as models and Seventh Avenue designers, all of whom enthusiastically applaud Cathy's style and skating. The most frequently asked question is a simple one, "Do you ever drop anything?" In spite of skating over a tiled floor and around a frantic lunch hour staff, Cathy is happy to answer that she has had no problems.

Today, either because of her skill as a waitress or skater, maybe both, Cathy is skating as the restaurant's hostess, greeting people at the door and escorting them to a table. Her informal work outfit consists of black, baggy Kenzo pants held up by suspenders, pink floral shirt or aqua bowling shirt that once belonged to her father, a pair of blue, striped knee socks, and blue and yellow sneakers. Cathy clamps on her French skates over her shoes.

On more formal occasions, she wears black satin pants, and a black vest with a white tuxedo shirt and black string tie.

"So now I skate to greet people at the door. They all laugh. It brings a smile. The restaurant is very informal," says Cathy. "My skating started as a kind of a lark or a joke, but now people expect it."

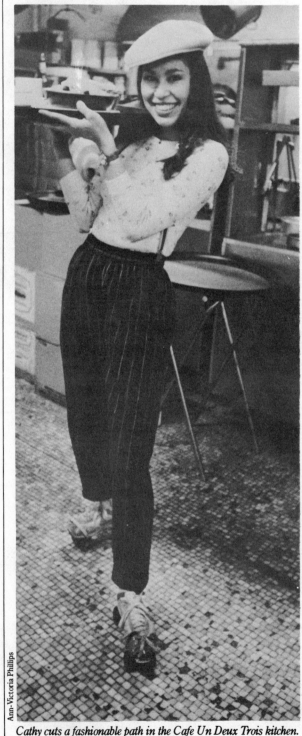

Ann-Victoria Phillips

Cathy cuts a fashionable path in the Cafe Un Deux Trois kitchen.

14. SKATING EQUIPMENT

BEFORE YOU BUY

If you're considering buying your own skates you're likely to be confronted with a bewildering variety of decisions regarding the selection of equipment. Let's simplify the process by first understanding the basics.

Since the days of thinking of the roller skate as a toy are long gone (typically a skater will spend between 100 and 150 dollars for a complete outfit), it's best to decide what kind of skating you want to do before you arrive at the skate shop door.

An outfit designed for outdoor skating is usually set up quite differently from one used in the rink. Although there are ways you can set up your equipment so you can do both (this will be discussed later), most skates today are either road skates or rink skates. Once you've decided between the two, your salesperson will be able to suggest the proper set-up. Already the skate buying process becomes much easier.

The next decision is where to buy your skates. Because of the skating craze, new shops are opening up all the time and this makes roller

Courtesy of Chicago Roller Skate Company

Choosing the right kind of skate equipment was a lot easier in the '30s when all clamp skates came pre-assembled. Today, even beginners assemble their own outfits.

skate equipment more widely available than ever before. However, the disadvantage to you, the consumer, is that the new places may not have a trained staff. So consider buying your skates from a local rink; it's a safe choice. Next best is to buy from a rental shop. The salespeople are likely to be skaters themselves who have tested many of the products they sell.

No matter where you decide to go, try to find a place that is in the business of setting up complete outfits rather than stores which present an equipment smorgasbord, then leave you on your own. As long as you are clear about the style of skating you want to do, an experienced person will be able to build you a skate that will both satisfy your needs and conform to your budget.

THE BOOT
SELECTING YOUR BOOTS

Although every component of your skate is important, the boot—the part closest to your tender feet—should be given the most consideration.

First, we recommend that you consult an expert fitter when making your selection.

Next, since skates are expensive and represent a big investment, it's best to buy medium-priced, quality leather boots rather than those constructed from synthetic materials. Your boot should have a good, firm counter built into the inside of the heel, one that will continue to give you foot support after the boot has been broken in.

PARTS OF A ROLLER SKATE

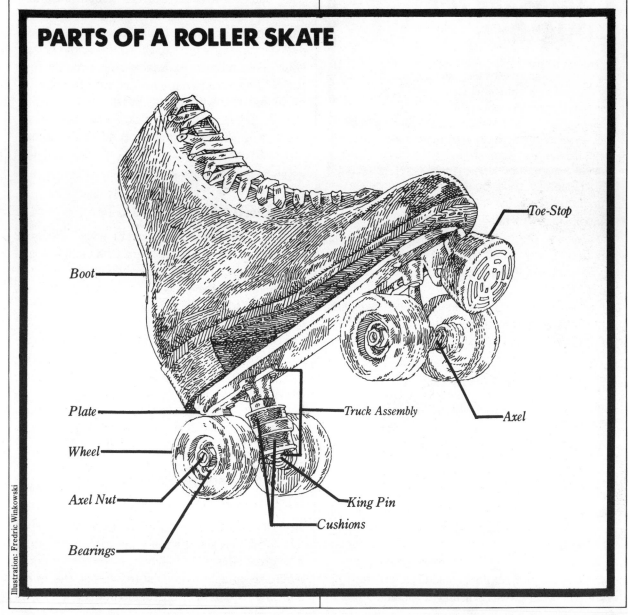

Illustration: Fredric Winkowski

Boot

Plate

Wheel

Axel Nut

Bearings

Truck Assembly

Cushions

King Pin

Toe-Stop

Axel

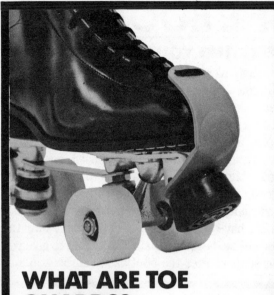

WHAT ARE TOE GUARDS?

Toe guards are protective strips of leather or heavy-duty plastic that can be attached to the front of your outdoor skates to save your boots from excessive wear and tear.

They can be purchased at roller rinks or any skate rental store. They range in price from 3 to 10 dollars per pair.

Generally, roller boots are fitted more snugly than shoes. This is done to increase your control—it's hard to hold your edges if your foot is loose inside the boot. Remember, when you go out to buy your boots, wear the same style socks you plan to use when skating. This will insure the best fit.

Finally, as you try on different sizes and styles, make sure your heel sits firmly in the heel of the boot and doesn't slide up and down as you move around.

BREAKING IN YOUR BOOTS

Once you've gone out and bought yourself a new pair of roller skates, what happens next? First, you're going to have to break in your boots.

Skate short periods of time for the first few sessions. Stop, unlace the boots, then relace them. If sore spots or blisters form, insert a small sponge pad over the tender area or stop skating until it heals. If the sore spot continues to occur, the boot may need to be adjusted. For adjustments it is best to return to where you bought the skate. If the heel support (called the "counter") is too tight, your pro shop manager should be able to

relax it by pushing in on the back of the boot with the heel of his or her hand and then pushing it back out again. If you attempt to do this yourself, do it carefully so as not to damage the boot.

KEEPING YOUR BOOTS DRY

Tender loving care must be given to your boots or the leather will deteriorate from perspiration. If you want your boots to enjoy a long and happy life, follow these directions:

1. If you skate a lot and hard, your boot will become wet from perspiration. Using a damp cloth (not wet) wipe off any perspiration stains on the inside and outside of your boots.

2. Unlace your boots, pull the tongues forward and let them dry at room temperature in a well-ventilated area. Do not store them in a skate bag, locker, or closet until they are completely dry. That may take 24 to 36 hours. Avoid drying your boots next to excessive heat such as fireplaces, radiators, ovens, or electric heaters. Remove any mud with a small brush.

3. If you're an outdoor skater and get caught in the rain, follow the same procedure, also wiping the plate and truck assembly, wheels and the outsides of the bearings dry.

CLEANING, TREATING AND POLISHING YOUR BOOTS

1. If the boots are dirty or have a build up of old polish on them, clean them with saddle soap.

2. Next, use Lexol or another good grade of light boot oil on the outside. Apply with a soft cloth or sponge. Ideally, the inside of the boot should be treated each time before skating with a product like Silicone Shoe Saver. This will prevent damage from perspiration.

3. For white boots use a good white professional buff type liquid or cream polish. For black boots use a black liquid or high-quality cream polish like Meltonian. Don't use cheap, paste-type polishes. They dry out leather and may encourage cracking.

WHAT IF YOUR BOOTS NEED TO BE REPAIRED?

It's not unusual for properly-cared-for boots to last for years. But sometimes problems can develop. The great advantage in buying good leather boots from a reputable manufacturer is that the *workmanship* is guaranteed. If something major is wrong with your boots through no fault of your own, you can return them directly to the factory, or to the rink or store where you bought them. They will be repaired at no charge. If you've abused your boots to a point where they're falling apart at the seams, the factory will repair them, but you will have to pay.

Minor problems requiring small, routine repairs don't require a return trip to the factory. If you bought your boots from a skate shop, they may do repairs right there. If not, you can take the boots to a local shoe repair shop. Your skating instructor or rink owner may have suggestions on who is qualified to handle this kind of specialized repair.

THE SKATE

The "skate" is a unit that includes a "plate," a flat piece of heavyweight aluminum that the boot is mounted on, and two "trucks," one in the front of your skate and the other in back, which contain the movable parts that allow you to turn corners. They will be attached to the plate.

If you're a recreational skater it's best to get a "sand cast" aluminum plate and either a $^9/_{32}$ inch diameter precision axle (suitable for the smaller 2- to 2½-inch rink wheels but too short to hold the wider 60mm or 65mm outdoor wheels) or a $^5/_{16}$-inch diameter axle which is long enough to hold both indoor and outdoor wheels.

WHEELS

Walk into any skate shop today and you'll see over fifty skate wheels on display. They come in every imaginable color, size and material and are available at every price range. Even though there seem to be so many styles to choose from, once you decide what kind of skating you want to do, your choice will be narrowed considerably.

Indoor: Rink wheels are smaller in diameter and harder in composition than outdoor wheels and are classified into two types. One is the composition wheel (so called because it's made up of a combination of rubber and clay) and the other is the polyurethane (plastic) wheel. The composition wheel is known for having good grip and a fast front roll while the urethane type is popular because it provides the skater with a comfortable ride. However, the urethane wheel, because it's softer, has a slower roll. There are about six major brands of rink wheels and they range in price from 12 to 40 dollars. Bearings always cost extra.

Indoor wheels are too small and hard to give a comfortable ride outdoors, so don't bother trying. Not only will you get a rough ride, you'll feel every individual crack and pebble you roll over. If you want to skate both outdoors and indoors, do one of two things: set up your skates with outdoor wheels and take them everywhere or buy two different sets of wheels and switch them back and forth.

Outdoor: Getting a smooth and fast ride is the top priority for outdoor skaters. They choose larger 60mm, 65mm or 70mm wheels that have good front roll, are soft, yet have a high degree of resiliency or "rebound." "Rebound" means that the wheels will automatically bounce back into shape even after rolling over sticks and stones.

How do you test a wheel's degree of resiliency? Take two wheels and bounce them off the floor. The wheel that bounces the highest has the most rebound and it's this quality that is important to the outdoor recreational skater.

Artistic: Artistic skaters use different equipment entirely. They want a harder wheel—one that will give them a very fast front roll—yet one that will also hold the floor. The most popular general-use wheel is Rannalli's No. 300 but other

models are also available. Wheels used by artistic skaters range in price from 25 to 100 dollars a set.

Using outdoor skate wheels on a wooden rink floor is okay for recreational and disco skaters but if you intend to learn any kind of artistic skating (figures, freestyle or dance), forget it. The outdoor wheels will prove to be a handicap because, although they provide tremendous traction, you will have to push off twice as hard to get yourself rolling and you won't go as fast once you do start to move.

Speed: After wooden wheels were banned from indoor competition during the 1977-1978

THE HISTORY OF THE OUTDOOR WHEEL

The urethane wheel was first developed for use in the roller rink as far back as 1965 and it gradually gained in popularity. Toward the mid-70's, skateboard equipment manufacturers designed their own updated version of the plastic rink wheel with the hopes of revitalizing their faltering sport; this time the results were revolutionary. Because the new models were bigger, softer and more resilient than anything that had ever come before, they provided skateboarders with a smoother, more comfortable ride for the first time. The outcome was a nation-wide boost in popularity for the skateboarder craze.

Then, around 1976, someone in southern California got the idea of putting these same skateboard wheels on roller skates. At the same time, Jeff Rosenberg of Venice, California, opened Cheapskates, the first outdoor rental operation in America. He was one of the very first to popularize the big wheels by putting them on his rental skates. Because the wheel's performance on the rough sidewalk pavement was so superior—outdoor skaters got a smooth, comfortable ride for the first time in history—people noticed, tried them out and a whole new roller craze was born.

Over a period of the next two years, a multitude of companies produced the oversized urethane wheels yet only one brand stood out. Kryptonics, a small manufacturer from Boulder, Colorado, was as surprised as everyone else by the immense popularity of their bright red, blue and green wheels. One of their styles, the blue 65mm model, became a part of every outdoor skater's uniform.

Later, another excellent wheel was manufac-

tured by Dan Hendrickson and Buzz Besozzi of Fairfax, California, but this time the wheel, called City Rollers, was designed just for roller skaters. It proved to be fast and highly resilient yet it's main attraction to skaters was that because of its much narrower shape, it looked and felt more like a traditional rink wheel. Skaters went out and bought City Rollers by the thousands.

Today, City Rollers and Kryptos (Kryptonics also designed a thinner outdoor wheel, so this new style has replaced the earlier skateboarder style) dominate the outdoor skating market—they're the most popular general-use wheels in America.

Ann-Victoria Phillips

competitive year, US speed skaters all changed over to some kind of a plastic compound. Since the sport of speed skating is an all-out race to the finish line, members of this group switch brands as quickly as a manufacturer can dream up a new formula and pour it into a mold. So, today's hot set-up may be outdated three months after it's introduced on the market as speed coaches search for the wheel that produces the fastest front roll and a super grip on the plastic-coated floor. Although the evolution in speed equipment is very rapid, Rannalli's, Labeda's and Cook's remain popular choices. They range in price from 25 to 100 dollars a set.

Hockey: Roller hockey players are less concerned with using "proper" equipment than any other group of skaters and, in fact, have been known to play with *any* wheel, regardless of quality. So generally they use inexpensive wheels. Just like most recreational skaters, their choice depends on the type of surface they play on.

Radical: Radical skaters, those who skate in the skateboard parks, choose the same kind of wheel as most outdoor skaters. Though the poured concrete surface of half-pipes, pools and bowls is smoother than most others, it's still concrete, so park skaters, just like everyone else, look for a comfortable ride.

Rotating your wheels: Your skate wheels will eventually wear down around the edges. To slow this process, rotate your wheels as you would the tires on a car. Switch your inside front wheel to the outside back and so on.

BEARINGS

If you are a beginner, the kind of bearings you put in your wheels is a small matter. In reality, you can learn to skate on any wheel and use any of the three types of bearings with equal ease.

If you use wheels with looseball bearings, the bearings should be oiled very frequently with one drop of oil in each wheel. Wheels using semi-precision or precision bearings need less maintenance but still occasionally need to be oiled.

Skate mechanics at roller rinks prefer using ordinary engine oil while competitive skaters use lighter weight oil like sewing machine oil to get a faster roll. Your skating instructor or pro shop manager will show you how to clean and lubricate your bearings.

Sometimes the whole bearing needs to be replaced because of excessive dirt or rust. Looseball bearings wear out more quickly than the precision type.

Looseball Bearings: The main advantage in using looseball bearings is their low cost. If you buy a pair of sidewalk skates or lower-priced rink skates, these bearings are included as part of the complete outfit. If you spin a wheel, you can easily see the steel balls that move freely inside of what is called a "bearing race."

Besides being noisy, a second disadvantage of using this type of bearing is that the steel balls are exposed to dust and moisture. Although they can rust easily, if properly maintained, skates having looseball bearings can last quite a while.

Precision Bearings: These are the most popular kind of bearings in use today. If you look at a skate wheel that is set up with precision bearings, you won't see the steel balls at all because they're packed in grease and "sealed" inside the bearing race.

There are two kinds of precision bearings: *semi-sealed* bearings are sealed on the outside but not on the inside and require regular lubication just like the looseball type. But unlike looseball bearings, semi-sealed precision bearings are quiet. The price of semi-sealed bearings is about 10 dollars for a set of 16.

Sealed bearings are sealed on both the outside and the inside of the bearing race. They require very little maintenance—all the necessary lubrication is sealed inside and should last the lifetime of the skates. These bearings are the most expensive type and cost about 25 dollars for a set of 16.

TOE STOPS

Toe stops were originally designed for freestyle skaters who use them to perform single and multiple revolution jumps in competition, but to a beginner, toe stops—rubber, ball-shaped parts that screw into the front-end of the skate plate— are "brakes," a means of stopping. Especially common are skaters who stop by extending one leg out in back and bumping or dragging the toe stop against the pavement until they come to a halt. While it's okay to do this in a rink, it's hazardous outdoors. Not only can you lose your balance stopping this way on rough pavement, but your toe stops will

HOW TO CHANGE YOUR WHEELS

As a beginner the idea of changing your own wheels may seem risky, but as long as you're using precision bearings, it's a very simple procedure.

First, unscrew the axle nut with your socket wrench and slip the wheel off the axle (right). You'll see that each of your wheels contain two bearings and a spacer that rests in between. Now, push the bearings out of the wheel with your finger or tap them out with your wrench.

After taking the bearings out, press one into your new wheel (a drop of oil on the bearing will help ease it in). Next, insert the spacer through the other side and press in the second bearing on top of it. Slip the wheel onto the skate axle and screw on the axle nut.

If you do decide to change your own wheels, remember to tighten up the axle nut that holds the wheel on the axle until you feel a slight resistance. Then, spin the wheel. Is it rolling freely? If not, loosen the axle nut *slightly*, or just enough to give you a free roll. But don't loosen it too much or you'll run the risk of having your wheel fall off!

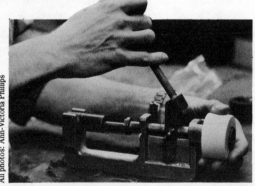

All photos: Ann-Victoria Phillips

If your wheels are new or if they have aluminum hubs, you may need to use a bearing press to remove the bearings or push them back in for the first few times (left). The skate mechanic at your rink or the manager of your pro shop will help you with this.

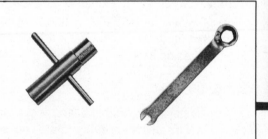

Chicago/Sure-Grip socket wrench (left) and Snyder socket wrench (right).

rapidly wear down to the metal. Toe stops are not expensive (3 to 10 dollars a pair) but why abuse your equipment? Learn the simple T-stop (Chapter 4) and keep your toe stops in good condition.

Whenever you buy a complete skate outfit—boots, plates, trucks, wheels and bearings—the toe stops will be included. Usually, they match the wheels. If you want to mix-and-match, other stops are available in a wide variety of shapes and colors.

SKATE ADJUSTMENT

Truck action is adjustable. The amount of looseness or tightness you need depends on the type of skating you do. Generally, the truck action should be loose enough to respond to your every move yet not so free as to cause rattles or let the wheels touch the skate plate.

Most skate trucks have two axles and two rubber cushions that can be tightened or loosened. By adjusting the king pin (the bolt that holds the truck onto the plate) you can make the action of the skate stiffer or looser.

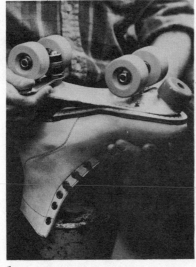

1 **2** **3**

How to adjust the action of most Chicago, Roller Derby and Sure-Grip Skates:

1. Using your open end wrench, loosen the hex nut on each truck one-eighth to one-quarter of a turn in a counterclockwise direction.

2. Next, using the flat screwdriver end of your wrench, either loosen the action of each truck (by turning the kingpin in a counterclockwise direction) or tighten it (by turning the kingpin in a clockwise direction).

3. To test that you've adjusted the action of all four trucks the same way, Mike Schneider, skate mechanic at Levittown Arena suggests you grasp the wheels and flex the front and rear trucks of each skate by hand. Ideally, you should feel a small amount of flex in each truck.

4. Skate around to test your adjustment. If you are comfortable, tighten the hex nut by turning it in a clockwise direction. This locks your adjustment in place and prevents your truck from falling off the plate.

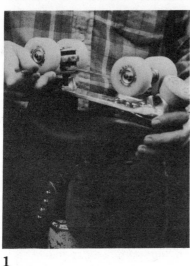

1 **2**

How to adjust the action of your Snyder Skates:
These adjustments are made much the same way as the others, except that the tools are different.

1. Using the large end of your open end wrench, loosen the hex nut on each truck one-eighth to one-quarter of a turn in a counterclockwise direction.

2. Next, insert your Allen wrench into the kingpin and either loosen the action of each truck (by turning the kingpin in a countercockwise direction) or tighten it (by turning the kingpin in a clockwise direction).

Follow steps 3 and 4 (above) to complete your adjustment.

Allen wrench (top), Snyder open-end wrench (center), and Chicago/Sure-Grip open-end wrench (bottom). You can adjust your skates without having to remove them from your feet. If you're an outdoor skater, carry your wrenches with you at all times for adjustments and emergency repairs.

Truck action should be adjusted when you first try out your new skates and also if you feel something is wrong. If you're skating straight ahead and one of your skates keeps trying to make a radical right or left turn inward or outward, your action is probably too tight. If your wheels are wobbling back and forth, your action is too loose.

If you take lessons from a skating instructor, he or she will always show you how to adjust your skates but you should still learn how to do it on your own.

SNEAKER SKATES

A "sneaker" skate is a roller skate that features a tennis or jogging shoe mounted on a skate truck. The idea is not new, but no one is really sure who thought the first one up. It could be Chicago Roller Skate Company—in 1968 they bolted a grey tennis sneaker to a regular skate truck to be used as an advertising tie-in with *Funny Girl*, a movie in which Barbra Streisand dances on skates to the tune of "Roller Skate Rag." But America, in 1968, was not yet ready for the sneaker skate.

Today, after the successful introduction of Sure-Grip's "Jogger" (a bright blue and yellow sneaker skate with yellow wheels) in 1977, every roller skate manufacturer in the United States is making some kind of updated version of the old Chicago style. The new sneaker-type skates are becoming enormously popular.

SUGGESTIONS FOR SNEAKER SKATE LOVERS

• Most tennis sneakers and jogging shoes cannot compare with firm leather boots in terms of support for your feet. So, if you buy sneaker skates, look for a style with the firmest construction, the thickest sole and the best arch.

• Sneaker skates are meant to be used for regular forward and backward skating—they should not be used to perform spins, jumps, or acrobatic stunts.

• Sneaker skates are "fun skates," but they still are roller skates. Keep them away from water and check all parts regularly for signs of wear and tear.

• If you love sneaker-style skates, consider designing your own. First select a running/jogging

All photos: Ann-Victoria Phillips

*Victor Burgos
of New York City, tests out
his new sneaker skates with characteristic style.*

shoe with a very firm sole. Then talk to the skate mechanic at a roller rink or skate rental shop. He or she will tell you whether your shoes are strong enough to be mounted on skates.

• It's possible to improve the fit of your sneaker skates by adding jogger-type orthopedic inserts to the shoes. These inserts can be purchased wherever running gear is sold.

SKATES FOR CHILDREN

SIDEWALK SKATES

Adjustable clamp skates; the skates that most of us grew up with, are still around and holding their own in spite of the deluge of more expensive and sophisticated equipment. Properly maintained, kept away from water, and oiled regularly, these skates will last for years.

It's advisable to buy clamp skates (or the similar slip-on style) when a child is just starting out in skating. First decide whether you want the traditional clamp-on style (these work best over

AMERICA'S CHEAPEST ROLLER SKATE

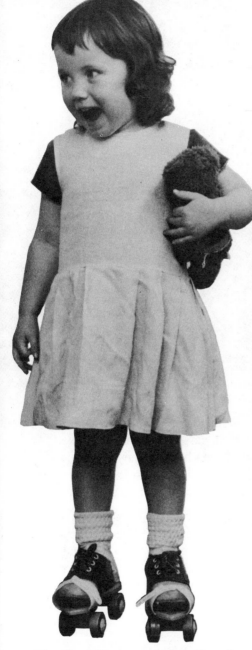

The winner is an orange and white, slip-on style with blue plastic wheels. The "Zooomer Skate" is manufactured by Kingsway and is priced at $1.99. The skate can be adjusted to fit a child two to eight years old.

Inexpensive skates, such as this, are widely available in toy shops and discount department stores.

In brand new clamp skates, Sarah Lynas, Andy Barrett, and Ellen Macnow navigate Central Park's sticks and stones.

leather, firm-soled shoes) or slip-ons (they stay on best when the child is wearing sneakers). Most styles have steel wheels, but because of the outdoor skating craze, a few manufacturers have introduced models with the softer urethane wheels (they give a smoother ride over rough pavement). Clamp-ons and slip-ons range in price from 2 to 12 dollars.

Inexpensive vinyl boot skates are also a very popular choice for sidewalk skating. Available everywhere, they're priced from 8 to 14 dollars.

LEATHER BOOT SKATES

Parents who buy boots several sizes too large for their young skating son or daughter are not doing themselves or their children a favor. You may think you're saving money, but it's really a short-lived gain if your child can barely stand up in the boots due to lack of support.

There are alternatives. Good leather boot skates last for years so if you have several children, they can be passed down from child to child. In a community where many children roller skate, skates can also be traded from family to family. In addition, many roller rinks have their own skate exchange program. The color or style of the new or used boot is a trivial matter. What is important is that it fit the child and provide the proper support whenever he or she is skating.

Quality leather boot skates for children are available in a variety of brands and styles. They range in price from 20 to 100 dollars.

SKATING SAFE

Safety equipment, which includes helmets, knee and elbow pads, wrist braces, gloves, ankle guards and padded shorts, was originally designed to give skateboarders protection—should they accidently fall on the sidewalk, road or in the skate park—while still providing freedom of movement. Since roller skaters are now invading the skate parks by the thousands, they need the same protection as their skateboarding cousins. So, for radical skaters, a complete outfit of safety equipment is mandatory. If you're an outdoor flatland skater, protective gear is optional, but still recommended.

Even though there are many manufacturers of safety equipment, most of it is still inadequately designed. Although wearing any kind of gear is better than wearing nothing at all, it is recommended that you outfit yourself with the most firmly-constructed protective equipment on the market. It may be expensive, but the heavy-duty leather, vinyl and elastic will spare you unnecessary cuts and bruises and it may even save you from serious injury.

A COMPLETE OUTFIT FOR THE RADICAL SKATER

The helmet: It should fit snugly, covering your entire head, and, ideally, the nape of your neck and ears. The helmet should be well-ventilated and equipped with a heavy chin strap.

Knee and elbow pads: For the most complete protection, buy those with high impact plastic caps riveted to the pad. Choose styles with heavy-duty elastic, so the pads won't tear or slide off under impact.

Wrist brace: These braces are designed to prevent the wrist from breaking should you fall. Most styles are either too rigid in construction or too flimsy to be of any real help to a skater in an emergency. Choose wrist braces that are well-padded on the palm side and that fit snugly yet are still slightly flexible.

Gloves: They are usually worn over the wrist braces in order to provide the hand with complete protection. Choose heavy, leather, palm-padded gloves.

Ankle guards: For those who wear low-top

All photos: Ann-Victoria Phillips

Designer Mike Rector, an experienced skateboarder, models the safety equipment he manufactures.

skate boots, these are recommended to protect ankles from cuts and scrapes.

Padded shorts: They provide a skater protection to the hips and lower back should he or she fall while skating in a skate park.

If you're an outdoor flatland skater, the only piece of safety gear you need is a heavy pair of leather gloves but if you skate up and down steep hills (a common sight in San Francisco), knee and elbow pads and wrist braces are also recommended.

EQUIPMENT YOU CAN COUNT ON

The following equipment is a sampling of the many styles offered by our recommended manufacturers. The prices are approximations based on the "suggested retail price." As with any kind of sporting goods, the price of roller skate equipment will vary slightly depending on where in the US you live and also where you purchase your skates. Those given for wheels are for a set of eight.

FIGURE BOOTS

The vast majority of skaters buy figure boots regardless of whether they plan to skate indoors or out.

Hyde figure boot model nos. 364 for women (left) and 365 for men (right): $42.50.

Riedell Figure Boot, no. 220: $64.

Riedell "Silver Star," no. 355: $118.

WHEELS

Recreational rink wheels: Metaflex "Easy Rider," $16; Chicago urethane wheel, $30; Chicago composition wheel, $8; Classic "All American Plus", $22; Sure-Grip urethane wheel, $14; Sure-Grip composition wheel, $14; Rannalli no. 50XX, $16.

Outdoor wheels: City Roller, $38; Kryptos, $30.

Wheels for figure, freestyle and dance: Rannalli no. 300, $40; Weber 55mm yellow wheel, $100; Mercury, $20.

INDOOR/OUTDOOR OUTFITS

Manufacturers are designing new, more fashionable indoor/outdoor skate outfits to go along with the latest skating craze.

Chicago "Pro Roadster" includes a Riedell suede leather boot mounted on a Chicago "Medalist" plate, with red 65mm urethane wheels, stops, and precision bearings: $90.

Oak Street's complete outfit includes a Bauer boot mounted on an Oak Street skate with 65mm wheels and precision bearings: $135.

SNEAKER SKATES

Sneaker skates are soft shoe styles which are gaining in popularity.

Sure-Grip "Jogger" includes a blue and yellow Hyde sport shoe mounted on a Sure-Grip "Jogger" plate, with 65mm urethane wheels, matching stops, and precision bearings: $75.

ASC's "off the Wall" skate, includes a Van Doren high-top skateboard shoe mounted on an ACS 430 truck with "Super Pro" wheels and precision sealed bearings: $85.

Two Mattel models: no. 800 (left), $42; no. 1600-SX (right) $44.

Chicago "Sports Roadster II" includes a blue and white sneaker shoe mounted on a Chicago "standard" plate with red 65mm urethane wheels, stops and precision bearings: $60.

OUTFITS FOR THE RINK

Members of the Workman Wizards Skating Club model complete outfits (left to right): from Chicago Skate, a Riedell leather boot mounted on a Chicago "GM-II" plate, with urethane wheels, stops, and precision bearings—under $100; also from Chicago, a Hyde leather boot mounted on a Chicago "Super Patriot" plate, with composition wheels, stops, and looseball bearings—under $60; from Sure-Grip, a Hyde leather boot mounted on a Sure-Grip "Super-X" plate, with urethane wheels, stops, and precision bearings—under $60; and also from Sure-Grip, a Riedell leather boot mounted on a Sure-Grip "Century" plate, with "White Velvet" wheels, matching stops, and precision bearings—under $100.

SPEED EQUIPMENT

Speed boots are recommended for competition only, not for recreation.

Oberhamer Speed Boot, no. 41: $50.

Riedell Speed Boot, no. 595: $87.

Riedell Speed Boot, no. 295: $95.

SPEED OUTFIT

Speed skaters purchase their outfits by choosing each component separately.

Butch Ford models a complete Sure-Grip speed skate outfit including a leather Riedell speed boot, no. 295 mounted on a Sure-Grip "XK-4" racing plate with Rannalli no. 100L speed wheels, stops and precision bearings: $200.

HOCKEY OUTFIT

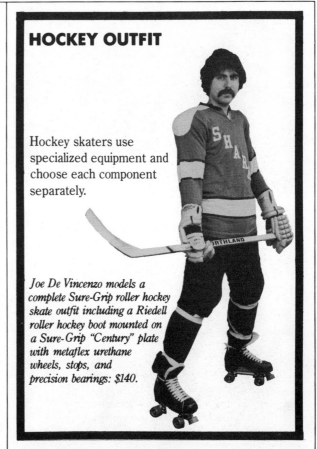

Hockey skaters use specialized equipment and choose each component separately.

Joe De Vincenzo models a complete Sure-Grip roller hockey skate outfit including a Riedell roller hockey boot mounted on a Sure-Grip "Century" plate with metaflex urethane wheels, stops, and precision bearings: $140.

CHILDREN'S SKATES

Steven/Union "The Trainer," no. 1411: $5.

Globe Beginner's Skate, no. 36: $6.

Chicago Glide Skates: $19.

Three Roller Derby models: "Street King" (left girl's, right boy's), $9; "Fireball" (center): $15.

SAFETY EQUIPMENT

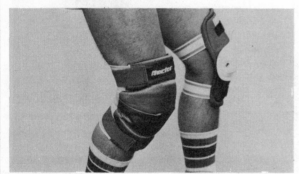

Knee Pads: Rector Flexline (left leg), $20; Norcon (right leg), $16.

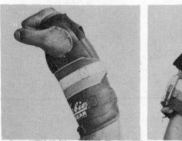 

Wrist braces: Hobie (left), $25; Rector (right), $27.

Norcon helmet: $13.

All photos: Ann-Victoria Phillips

PROTECTIVE GEAR

Bill Jenks models a radical skater's outfit: Rector Palm Pad gloves, $18; Rector Protector Elbow Guards, $21; Rector Protector Knee Guards, $24; Van's ankle guard, $8; Powell Helmet, $23.

EQUIPMENT SUPPLIERS

It should be noted that most suppliers do not sell directly to individuals.

Although the list of roller skate equipment manufacturers grows by the day, those mentioned in the following pages are recommended because:

- They maintain high standards of quality.
- They guarantee all workmanship.
- Many are or were involved in amateur or professional skating and thus tend to manufacture products designed to meet the skater's needs.
- Their products have been fully tested.

ACS Roller Skates
PO Box 1439, Covina, CA 91722

ACS features a complete skating outfit which includes Van's excellent high-top skateboard shoe bonded to a fiberglass base plate. The ACS "430" trucks are mounted onto the base plate.

Chicago Roller Skate Company
4458 West Lake Street, Chicago, IL 60624

The Chicago Roller Skate Company, founded by Elisha Ware in 1905, is the oldest surviving skate

Chicago Roller Skate Company's Bob Ware (left) and Joe Shevelson have created a new line of "Roadster" boot skates as well as an updated version of their famous clamp skate.

manufacturer in America. It is the one company to flourish while other early manufacturers have fallen by the wayside, done in by alternating periods of boom and bust in roller skating popularity.

Elisha Ware and his sons Walter, Ralph, and Robert, were originally in real estate. Walter was the first of the family to invest in the already existing Chicago Roller Skate Company. Later the brothers gradually purchased the entire business. Gordon Ware, Walter's son, is now president, Robert Ware, Jr., is vice president, and Joseph Shevelson, a friend of the Ware family, is also a vice president.

Chicago represents a tradition of quality products and good customer service. Today the offices of Chicago Skate are filled with hundreds of photos dating from the '20s, '30s, and '40s, all inscribed with handwritten thank you notes from professional and amateur skaters.

Chicago products include complete outfits for the recreational skater.

Classic Sales Company
11665 East 21 Street, PO Box 35246, Tulsa, OK 74135

John Matejec, owner of Classic Sales and a former competitive roller skater, develops and sells a line of Vanguard wheels that are popular with both beginners and competitive skaters alike. One wheel is recommended for recreational use—"American Plus"—while others are for specialized skating—"American Dream (dance), and the "Red Devil" and the "Blue Spruce" (both for speed skating).

James H. Cook
PO Box S, Cedar Knolls, NJ 07927

Competitive speed skaters wear "Cook's," a line of urethane wheels popular because of their "roll" and "gripping" qualities on slippery indoor tracks. These wheels are not for the beginner rink skater.

Globe Skate Corporation
N. 92 W158 Megal Drive, Menomonee Falls, WI 53051

Globe is a sidewalk skate manufacturer of both clamp-on and slip-on styles. Unlike skates from days gone by, none of these skates require keys. All feature steel wheels with looseball bearings, and all are adjustable. The slip-on styles work especially well over sneakers.

Harlick and Co., Inc.
893 American Street, San Carlos, CA 94070

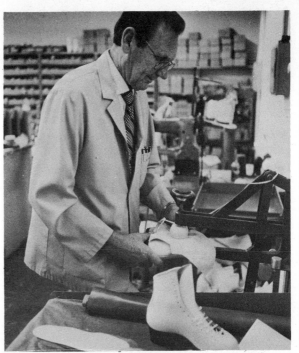

Bob Henderson, President of Harlick, personally supervises every stage of production.

Harlick is a small ice and roller skate boot manufacturer, located about 15 miles south of San Francisco. Company president Bob Henderson is known to be one of the finest boot makers in the world. He runs a highly specialized operation—the production of quality stock and custom boots for top competitive skaters, their coaches, and other professionals. They are not boots for beginners.

Hobie
PO Box 812, Dana Point, CA 92629

Hobie is a well-known manufacturer of surfboards, skateboards, and protective gear. They have designed a particularly good wrist brace that gives a roller skater superior protection, especially in a skateboard park.

Hyde Shoe Company
324 Columbia Avenue, Cambridge, MA 02141

Hyde manufactures three styles of stock boots. While they are not as well-known as other boot manufacturers, they deliver top quality products just the same. They sell stock sizes and widths only and do no custom work.

Krytonics, Inc.
5660 Central Avenue, Boulder, CO 80301

Although many different skateboard wheels have aided the growth of outdoor roller skating, the Krytonics 65mm wheel called Kryptos, is by far the most popular.

Lazer Speed Skate Co.
5141 West 23 Street, Cicero, IL 60650

Lazer, a small company located near Chicago, is best known for making a popular lightweight, nylon plate that is used exclusively by competitive speed skaters. Lazer offers the plate alone or as part of a complete skate outfit—you can order it mounted on either a Hyde baseball boot or an Oberhamer speed boot.

Mattel, Inc.
5150 Rosecrans Avenue, Hawthorne, CA 90250

The Mattel Athletics Group, a division of the well-known toy manufacturer, has produced a new line of indoor/outdoor roller skates called "Sunrunners." These roller skates feature brightly colored sneaker shoes mounted on a steel "chassis." All models can be purchased fully assembled and include urethane wheels with precision bearings.

Mercury Wheel Company
15 Hillcrest Road, Norwood, MA 02062

Mercury wheels have been around for years and are known to offer the competitive dance skater good "roll" and "grip."

Metaflex, Inc.
17957 Kennedy Road, Pitt Meadows, BC, Canada

Metaflex makes a bright red, blue, or yellow urethane wheel suitable for the rink skater. Matching toestops are also available.

Norcon Manufacturing
PO Box 247, Forest Lake, MN

Norcon makes protective gear for skateboarders but these products are also widely used by roller skaters.

Oak Street Skates
23854 Via Fabricante, G-4, Mission Viejo, CA

Oak Street is a small surfboard, skateboard, and roller skate manufacturer. Ed Gottschlich, the president of the company is generally acknowledged to have created an excellent outdoor roller skate by combining a high quality Bauer hockey boot with an Oak Street plate and truck.

Oak Street skates are offered with a choice of either 65mm Oak Street wheels or 65mm Kryptonic wheels. If you buy this skate, you can choose one of three different kinds of bearings—semiprecision, precision, or German precision.

Oberhamer Shoe Company
689 North Dale Street, St. Paul, MN 55103

Roy Oberhamer, the president of Oberhamer, has had years of experience making many kinds of roller boots. The company carries artistic skating styles but is perhaps best known among competitive speed skaters because they make the most popular racing boots in the United States.

Powell Corporation
725 Union Avenue, Santa Barbara, CA 93103

Powell manufactures one of the highest quality protective helmets on the market, Pro-Tec. It's commonly used in skateboard parks.

Precision Sports
2340 Arcdale, Rowland Heights, CA 91745

Bob Labeda, a southern California based manufacturer, is making one of the most popular wheels used in competitive speed skating—the Labeda Mark I. He also offers speed wheels of other "compounds" (with differing degrees of hardness), and two types of wheels for artistic skaters.

Rannalli Wheels
G&F Products, 1420 East 20 Street, Santa Ana, CA 92701

Rannalli makes a top line of urethane wheels for the competitive and professional skater. Their No. 300 wheel is the most popular among artistic skaters while their No. 100L wheel is the choice of over 50 percent of all speed skaters in the United States.

Importantly, Rannalli also offers a colorful, good quality urethane wheel for the recreational rink skater called the No. 50XX.

Riedell Shoes, Inc.
PO Box 21, Red Wing, MN 55066

Riedell's busy staff is working overtime to keep up with the recent demand for quality leather skate boots.

Riedell is a large, well-established manufacturer of ice and roller skate boots that are popular with the recreational skater as well as the competitor. The factory produces one thousand pairs of artistic, speed, and hockey boots every day. They offer an extraordinary number of stock styles in almost every size and width. All Riedell boots feature leather uppers and linings, and firm counters—all styles have leather outsoles.

Riedell will do custom boot fittings in their factory by appointment and also have a network of expert fitters at skating rinks and skate shops all across the country.

Roller Derby Skate Corporation
311 Edwards Street, Litchfield, IL 90262

Roller Derby sells more skates than any other manufacturer in the United States. Their sidewalk shoe skates are widely available, colorful, and inexpensive—three reasons why these roller skates are so popular with children.

Roller Derby skates are bought as a complete outfit and include a vinyl boot, steel chassis and base plate, and either steel or urethane wheels (depending on the model), plus looseball bearings.

The Skyborn Corporation
4 Main Street, PO Box 2368, Zanesville, OH 43701

Skyborn imports Weber wheels, a top-of-the-line product from Switzerland for competitive artistic skaters. "Webers" are available in a variety of different sizes and durometers (degrees of hardness). Colors (pale yellow, green, and blue) identify the degree of firmness. Most popular are the 60mm green, used for figure skating.

Smoothill Skates
1595-F Francisco Boulevard, San Rafael, CA 94901

Dan Henrickson, co-owner of Smoothill Skates, claims that he's manufacturing "the only true outdoor roller skate wheel." Since almost all of the other wheels currently being used on outdoor skates were originally developed for use on skateboards, he just may be right! His "City Rollers," a very smooth and fast-rolling indoor/outdoor wheel, is available in the 65mm size.

Snyder Skate Co., Inc.
2552 Titus Avenue, Dayton, OH 45414

Snyder plates and trucks are used by almost all figure, freestyle, and dance skaters, but because this equipment is so expensive, it's not recommended for the beginner unless he or she intends to take lessons or enter amateur competition.

A Snyder assembly includes plates, hangers, trucks, toe-stops, wheels, and bearings. The roller boot is extra. If you prefer wheels other than those offered, they too, will be extra.

SP-Teri
2490 South Bruno Avenue, San Francisco, CA

SP-Teri is primarily known as a maker of ice skating boots but roller skaters also like their styles. The company was founded by Joseph Spiteri who got most of his boot making experience at Harlick and Company before going out on his own in 1962. Today SP-Teri manufactures both stock and custom boots.

Stanzione
30 West 56 Street, New York, NY 10019

Stanzione (left) and Hohner at work in their shop.

Stanzione, an ice and roller skate bootmaker for 74 years, does custom work only. Gustav Stanzione and Bela Hohner construct every part of the boot entirely by hand.

The staff is small and the number of boots produced each year is limited, but Stanzione represents the finest quality in the United States.

Steven Manufacturing
224 East 4 Street, Herman, MO 65041

Steven, a well-known toy and skate manufacturer bought out Union Hardware, one of the oldest skate companies in the United States and now offers a combined Steven/Union line of outdoor skates.

Some of the skates are classically styled clamp-ons, and there are also slip-ons. All are meant to be worn over shoes.

Sure-Grip International
11223 Peach Street, Lynwood, CA 90262

Sure-Grip, the third-largest skate company in the United States, sells a large variety of skate products. Some, like the famous "XK-4" racing plate, they themselves manufacture. They also act as a distributor for other manufacturers.

STX-Rector Sports
PO Box 2041, Santa Rosa, CA 95405

STX now manufactures top-of-the-line protective gear for skateboarders and roller skaters such as gloves, wrist braces, elbow and knee pads and padded shorts.

Michael Rector, the designer, has personally tested every one of his products under a variety of different skating conditions. All the gear, made from the highest quality materials, is constructed to withstand extreme abuse.

Van Doren Rubber Company
1240 South Carolina, Anaheim, CA 92805

Protection is important to the roller skater, especially someone who rides in skateboard parks or one who does acrobatic stunts. The Van's ankle guard is recommended for those who wear low-top boots, in order to protect the delicate ankle area.

Western Skate Sales
189 Constitution Drive, PO Box 2766, Menlo Park, CA 94025

Western imports Waldeck wheels from West Germany. These wheels have a small following in this country and are mainly used by the International style figure skating community.